AN AUTOBIOGRAPHY FROM THE
JESUIT UNDERGROUND

Also translated by Philip Caraman

THE AUTOBIOGRAPHY OF A HUNTED PRIEST
The Story of John Gerard

El venerable P.ᵉ Guilliehmo Weston, n̄ral de Durham, tube singular d̄minio sobre los demonios, y despues de ... de carçel y prisiones
por la fe desterrado, murió Rector de este Colē de edad de 63 a̅ a 9 de abril de...

WILLIAM WESTON

An Autobiography from the
JESUIT UNDERGROUND

by William Weston

Translated from the Latin by
PHILIP CARAMAN

With a Foreword by
EVELYN WAUGH

FARRAR, STRAUS AND CUDAHY
NEW YORK

TO
SIR JOHN AND LADY McEWEN
OF MARCHMONT

FOREWORD

There is no Independence Day in the English calendar. The determining events of our history are, two of them, conquests and one betrayal. It may seem to us now that for the fullest development of our national genius we required a third conquest, by Philip of Spain. Instead of him we got, just a hundred years later, William of Orange. The Elizabethans could not have foreseen that and it is plain that, except for a few *emigrés*, they were all of them, Catholic and Protestant alike, infected with the spirit of nationalism which had been gnawing at the vitals of Europe for three generations. Thus we have the strange complex of plots, so modern in character, and the astute confusion, by its instigators, of the conspiracy to extirpate the Catholic faith with the cause of insular independence.

These plots and that confusion cast a shadow over many noble lives, William Weston's among them. We can understand the temper of the Elizabethan age better than our grandparents could. Its modernity is partly of Germany— there are many Goerings strutting about the Court and the glimpse of more than one Himmler. But there was no Hitler. Where did power reside ? It is in Russia and her dependencies that one finds the closer analogy. Hitler's bloody acts were irrational dooms. Whoever ruled in Elizabeth's time had a philosophy and a policy. There were efforts to persuade and to extort confessions. There were plots in which it is even now impossible to extricate the genuine from the fabricated. How much of the indictments did the judges and prosecutors believe ? How much did they care ?

One by one the lives of the Catholics are being disinterred from scholarly and sectarian works and presented to the general public. Father Caraman who has already served John Gerard so well, now gives us a very different character in William Weston. Here the work of editing is of even greater importance for the gentle, self-effacing little narrative that forms the core of this book, tells us little of the hero. With Gerard we were reading Buchan. Here it is Bernanos; one the unambiguous man of action; the other the mystic beset with the mystic's devils, drawn to the desperate; contemporaries of the same Society, pursuing the same ends and the same dangers, but distinct from one another by all the breadth of catholicity. If any is tempted to suppose that the discipline of Ignatius produces a uniform type, he will find assurance in the careers of these two holy and heroic men.

EVELYN WAUGH

CONTENTS

ILLUSTRATIONS

INTRODUCTION

Father William Weston was born at Maidstone, Kent, in 1550. Nothing is known of his family or of his early years. In 1564, at the age of fourteen, he entered Christ Church, Oxford. Edmund Campion was then a fellow of St. John's College in the same University, and it is not improbable that the two future Jesuits met there for the first time. Weston graduated B.A. in 1569. In the following year both he and Campion left the University. Then for some months Weston studied law at Lincoln's Inn, London. Although his name does not appear on the registers, he and Henry Hubert, the companion of his first days as a missionary priest, are listed among the Catholic students who refused to attend Protestant church service, and were consequently summoned before the Bishop of London and deprived of their fellowship of the Inn.[1] 'His desire openly to profess the Catholic faith', says Fr. de Peralta, his Spanish friend and first biographer, led him to Paris. While there he was invited to Douai by Cardinal Allen, the founder of the English seminary in the town. In 1575, the year of jubilee, he made a pilgrimage on foot to Rome, where he met four remarkable Englishmen, who before the end of the year had entered the Jesuit noviciate with him at Sant' Andrea: Robert Persons, the leader of the Jesuit 'invasion' of England in 1580; William Holt, the founder of the Scottish Jesuit Mission; Thomas Stephens, an outstanding successor of Francis Xavier in India; and, lastly, Henry Garnet—the only one of the group who had not come from Oxford—who was to succeed Weston as Jesuit

[1] *C. R. S.*, vol. 22, p. 102.

Superior in England. 'God, as though he had a new war to
be taken in hand, began to muster his men upon the sudden.'[1]
But there was no question of an immediate return to England.
His final studies and his first years as a priest—he was ordained
in 1579—were passed in Cordova, Seville, San Lucar and
Cadiz, partly teaching, partly working among his exiled
fellow-countrymen. The summons to England reached him
in Seville two days before Christmas 1583, but he was unable
to set out before the end of Easter Week the following year.
Selling the horse that had been given to him for the journey
and distributing the money to the poor, he travelled on foot,
begging his way to Paris. It was his spiritual preparation for
his mission. On 11 June he wrote from Paris to Fr. Aquaviva,
the General of the Jesuits, saying that he was in sound health
and high spirits. 'I am both glad and fearful to go to
England.'[2] Three months later he landed in East Anglia.
It is at this point that his *Autobiography* opens. It concludes
with his return to the Continent twenty years later. He was
then apparently a broken man, still only fifty-four years of
age. He rallied, however, and after visiting Rome was
welcomed back by his old friends in Spain. The warm sun
of Seville, which he reached in 1605, restored his health so
that he was able to do a full day's work at the English College,
again giving classes in Greek and Hebrew and acting as
spiritual director to the young English students, the townspeople and the Canons of the Cathedrals. He was extremely
happy here. In June 1614 he was called away to meet a
crisis at the seminary at Valladolid, where he was now
appointed Rector. As he left he told his friend, Fr. de Peralta,
that he was going there to die. His last illness was brief and

[1] *Memoirs of Fr. Persons*, C. R. S., vol. 2, p. 191.
[2] Arch S. J. Rome, *Gall.*, Ep. XIV, f. 43.

sudden. He caught fever a few months after his arrival and died on 9 April 1615, about two o'clock in the morning. He was in his sixty-fifth year.

The *Autobiography* was written at Seville in 1611, eight years after he had been exiled from England. The simple and unstudied narrative reveals a man eminently honest and anxious to recall faithfully the smallest detail of his experiences. A hasty reader might get the impression that the author was merely a pious priest, perhaps also an obstinate man, and credulous to a point that impairs the value of his word for the historian. This was the judgment passed on him by the *Dictionary of National Biography* and the *Catholic Encyclopedia*. However, the recent development of the science of psychological medicine makes it necessary to revise this verdict. So far from impugning his truthfulness, many of the strange stories told in this book, which led earlier writers to dismiss Weston as a credulous dupe, can now be shown to exemplify common forms of hysteria; in fact, they offer a fascinating case-history of Elizabethan melancholic disorders and reveal in an intimate manner the mental agony endured by men and women who accepted the change of religion against their conscience. Nor are they haphazardly pulled out of a jumble of experience. There is an order and an economy in their selection, perhaps not apparent at first reading. ' I have not thought it necessary ', he writes, ' to recount every detail, but what seemed to me better established or of greater significance and historical moment.' This is a large claim, but being familiar as I am with the book, I can see that it is a just one. The story, for instance, of Francis Wodehouse attempting to quench the fire raging in his bowels with eight gallons of ale, or of Evan Floyd flogged by brutal tutors almost to the point of death, or of the two Wisbech lads fastened in the stocks in the market-place—told in that sequence—are intended to show the effect of conscientious refusal to attend Protestant services on different groups of the Catholic community. Moreover, each story can be confirmed by the current records of the Council or other official papers.

It is only with the help of these papers that we can measure the importance of Fr. Weston's missionary work—he is tantalizingly modest when writing of himself and too appreciative of the heroism of his fellow-priests from Douai to reckon anything of his own achievement: 'I can never admire too much the affection they show one another and their contempt for danger in their effort to win souls.'[1] Fortunately there is evidence enough to show that he himself held a special place in the esteem of his hard-pressed fellow-Catholics. 'If I spoke with the tongue of Father Campion', ran the current saying, 'and wrote with the pen of Father Persons and led the austere life of Father Weston, and yet had not charity, it would avail me nothing.'[2] Although in such aphorisms exaggeration is natural, still they enshrine a popular verdict, in the same way as the stories of 'extraordinary and miraculous things' told of him after his death 'such as are related in the Ancients and holy Fathers of the desert'.[3] The writer of the Diary at Douai College, who is ordinarily laconic in his entries, described him as a 'very learned and devout man' on the day he left College in 1575 to complete his studies for the priesthood in Rome. At Cordova and Seville, where he taught as a young priest before his return to England, his words were taken as those of 'a prophet and coming from a

[1] Stonyhurst MSS., *Anglia I*, No. 28.
[2] Valladolid Archives, *Seville* 17 B, 686.
[3] de Peralta, f. 221.

man who had a special light from heaven '—a remarkable
tribute to an Englishman by the fellow-countrymen of St.
Teresa and St. John of the Cross. It is a judgment shared by
his fellow-priests in England. ' This very high opinion of
his saintliness is indeed his due ', wrote Fr. Robert Southwell.
' God grant that we may follow in his steps.' [1] As the notes
to this book will show, there are other witnesses also to the
almost universal veneration in which he was held. The
crowds that stood in the London streets on 21 January 1588
as Fr. Weston and his eleven companions set out for Wisbech,
were there—Weston does not say this—to get a glimpse of a
famed priest and perhaps to receive his blessing. Equally
large crowds watched the last stage of his journey; and they
were there again, pressing coins and gifts into his hands, when
he embarked at the Tower Wharf on his way into final exile.
Similarly, while Fr. Weston speaks of the continuous throng
of Catholics from all over the country who came to seek the
advice of the priests imprisoned at Wisbech, it is another
writer who points out that Fr. Weston was at that time ' the
most esteemed and consulted man in England '. There is no
doubt that Fr. Weston was writing sincerely and was unaware
of the attraction of his name. There is no self-conscious
attempt to suppress references to himself, yet as far as truthfulness allowed, his extreme modesty compelled him to play
down his own work.

Landing in the late summer of 1584, Fr. Weston was soon
confronted with a persecution that was designed finally to
crush the Catholic resistance. ' Let us admit that they [the
Papists] convict us of being in the wrong both as to religion
and government ', a member of the Council was reported to
have said that year, ' [but] they ought to consider that now

[1] See p. 147.

we have gone so far we cannot draw back with safety and honour, and that so powerful a queen cannot give way before any proofs or clamours of these poor men '.[1]   The crisis is described in the early chapters of this book, and it is apparent that within a few weeks of his arrival Fr. Weston became one of the acknowledged leaders among the priests.   But again, if we remain content with his self-portrait, we may fail to see the extent to which he possessed the qualities for the part. He draws a picture of himself, for example, in the cellar of a friend's house while a search was on, standing cloaked in cobwebs on the top rung of a ladder, finishing his Office for the day with one ear cocked to catch the footfall of the pursuivants—a picture that hardly suggests an intrepid or inspired leader.   Yet there can be no question that he was.

First of all, Fr. Weston possessed remarkable courage.   For example, he is the only Elizabethan priest, so far as I can find out, who ventured in disguise into the Tower for a full day's conference with a fellow-priest.   Fr. Weston merely records the fact and the sense of awe he felt when the Tower gates closed behind him.   ' For no hour are we certain to survive ', he wrote of his fellow-priests some months later, ' but as we make no account of living, the expectation of death only puts an edge on our zeal '.[2]   While his courage and zeal are apparent, his wisdom is often concealed; yet when he gives the reasons for his decisions, they are full of significance.   He advised Philip, Earl of Arundel, not to fly the country after his conversion.   The advice, which was unquestionably wise, was rejected in favour of what can now be proved a spurious message from Cardinal Allen.   As it turned out, Arundel was walking straight into a trap elaborately prepared by the

---

[1] Nicolas Sander, *Anglican Schism* (ed. 1877), p. 335.
[2] See p. 55.

Government, though, even at the time of writing his *Auto-biography*, Weston was unaware of this. In his dealings with Babington and his gullible but distinguished associates, he stepped so warily that the Government could not engineer a case against him. Thanks again to his discreet and prompt action, Fr. Henry Garnet and Fr. Robert Southwell, encircled by spies in their very first days in London, were preserved for an apostolate of inestimable importance to the mission. His only ill-judged action, it would seem, was his practice of exorcism; but it must be realized that this was considered a universal remedy for all cases that would now be classified as hysteria, mental derangement, obsession and the like. When Fr. Weston says that ' something had to be attempted, as much for the sake of those who suffered the affliction, as from compassion towards the persons who had them in their houses ',[1] he had in mind the cruel fate of the victims at the hands of the witch-hunters, for possession and witchcraft were closely allied both in the current Protestant theology and in legal procedure; and, indeed, in the eighteen months during which Weston and his fellow-priests exorcised the prosecutions for sorcery, especially in the southern counties, were increasing alarmingly.[2] With the capture of the principal priests associated with Fr. Weston at the time of the Babington Plot, little more is heard of exorcisms. Fr. Garnet would appear to have discouraged the practice, except in extra-ordinary cases committed to priests acting with special faculties from Rome. And it is possible that Fr. Garnet's advice to the Catholic clergy inspired the Anglican canon of 1604 which forbade the use of exorcism without express

[1] See p. 24.
[2] C. L'Estrange Ewen, *Witch Hunting and Witch Trials* (1929), pp. 110, 148–57.

consent of the bishop. Not improbably Fr. Weston was at
fault in associating missionary priests with a practice that
had been taken up with such enthusiasm by Anglican and
Puritan clergy and was watched with unhealthy interest by
the Queen and a number of the Councillors. Unfortunately
this section of Fr. Weston's narrative is difficult to check.
The depositions of the so-called possessed that were taken
later by the Ecclesiastical Commissioners and incorporated in
Samuel Harsnet's *Egregious Popish Impostures* (1603) are
worthless as historical evidence.[1] The purpose of this enquiry,
made nearly twenty years later, was to discredit the priests
who had taken part, and the book contains charges of such
gross immortality both against Weston and the other partici-
pant priests that it must be rejected as Protestant propaganda
on the most unscrupulous level. The book is of interest only
in that it provided Shakespeare with the names of his demons
in *King Lear*.

Courageous certainly, Fr. Weston possessed also a talent
for organisation which, like all his great gifts that made him
a leader, is concealed in his story. During the crisis of the
spring, 1585, Fr. Weston presided at the meeting at Hoxton,
on the outskirts of London, where plans were made for the
support of priests driven from their refuges in country and
town houses. It was a bitter emergency. In England more
than a hundred priests from Douai were left shelterless.
Abroad, the leadership of Allen was being undermined by
some factious priests in the Roman Curia in collusion with
the Council at home.[2] The new foundation of the College
in Rome had been nearly wrecked. It was perhaps the only

---

[1] Wallace Notestein, *A History of Witchcraft in England* (1911), p. 87.
[2] Leo Hicks, ' An Elizabethan Propagandist. The Career of Solomon
Aldred ', in *The Month*, May–June, 1945.

occasion in their long years of intimate co-operation on which Fr. Persons seized the initiative and had his friend Allen created a Cardinal in order to enhance his position. When Fr. Weston explains: ' I thought it would be well to retire by myself to some place where I could judge from my own observation the way things were likely to go ', he was acting, no doubt, as did all the English priests, who knew they had no moral right to demand or even counsel defiance of the law against harbouring at the price of a traitor's death. While Allen temporarily held up the supply of priests, Weston waited the unsolicited assurance of Catholic layfolk that they were prepared to shelter priests at the risk of their possessions and lives. It was their heroic response that saved English Catholicism. No wonder Fr. Garnet wrote three years later, ' The resolute patience of the Catholics is a model to us. . . . We receive from them more than we give '.[1] Fr. Weston describes the meeting at Hoxton, where it was decided that priests should fend for themselves in lodging houses and inns, and the subsequent raid three months later on the lodgings where they had taken refuge. It was then that Catholics came forward to offer their homes to priests, and with such enthusiasm that a year later, in the only conference that Fr. Weston had with his fellow-Jesuits, plans were laid for the systematic organisation of the Catholic resistance, house by house, county by county; though, after Weston's capture, it was to fall to Fr. Garnet in the south and to Fr. Richard Holtby in the north to carry it through. Fr. Persons, indeed, had reason to watch Weston's work with satisfaction—' Fr. Weston is doing wonders and giving great edification to everyone '.[2]

[1] Fr. Garnet to Aquaviva, 11 July 1588, Arch. S. J. Rome, *Fondo Gesuitico*, 651.
[2] See p. 9.

Even in prison at Wisbech he held a position in the esteem of
his fellow-Catholics that came close to that occupied by
Cardinal Allen; and he paid the price of it with four final
years of confinement in such utter solitude in the Tower
that for a period he would seem to have lost his mental
balance.

Hope never failed him. In the midst of all his setbacks he
went about his priestly work with unshakable faith in victory.
'Peter's ship is as safe as ever. She may be tossed by the
waves but never can she become a wreck. Buffeted and
beaten by the surge, she is never broken. Hell can open wide
its jaws, belch forth fire, shroud her in clouds of black smoke,
but God's promise stands unaltered. . . . From the day the
storm first struck her the Church has gathered great increase.
Wherever she is brought to the test, she conquers. When
persecution strikes her, she is there all the firmer for it. Violently oppressed, she reigns in glory. . . . Prisons are full of
priests, but God's word is not in chains. In the midst of
tribulation, sorrow and weariness our mother Jerusalem is not
sterile, and ceases not to bear her children. One day she shall
see peace '.[1] Not the words of a disheartened man! Weston
urged that more priests should be sent over at once. It was
bold advice for the summer of 1585 and happily for the country
it was acted upon. At the very end of his *Autobiography*, in
his last recorded conversation, he strikes a note of hope—the
hostess who served him at the inn in Canterbury is typical of
the great mass of his fellow-countrymen, ready to receive the
Faith if only it could be freely preached to them. In his
reckoning England, even then, had found no substitute for
Catholicism. ' Religion is in almost total neglect. The only
god the people worship is their belly and the prince of this

[1] Arch S. J. Rome, *Fondo Gesuitico*, 651.

world. And now they have had enough of both. Unreckon-able numbers groan and sigh to bring forth. . . . It has reached this point now that if we were given freedom to preach and teach publicly, I believe we would hardly see a thousand heretics left within a year'. This was written in 1585. Within the next forty years the opportunity was slowly to pass as a new generation of Englishmen were catechised in the Anglican belief and found satisfaction in the services it provided. But Weston saw the opportunity there, though all appearances belied it. 'Pray send men to help us and someone to take charge. Then we shall gather in sheaves on sheaves with laden arms'. And he adds the words of caution, 'I beg you examine the men inside out, for there is great need of prudence'.[1]

Fr. Weston was indeed that rare type of priest, a man of highest contemplation and assured action. If he was in the habit of passing seven or eight hours of his day in prayer, he was always present in an emergency to take or give the lead. The two years of his freedom were perhaps the most crucial of English Catholicism. In a passage of remarkable accuracy and vividness he describes the straits to which Catholics were reduced. It is not surprising that on the arrival of Fr. Garnet and Fr. Southwell he retired for a period of rest. For two years he had borne an almost intolerable strain. Lonely, physically exhausted, harassed by technical problems of marriage, disquieted by the behaviour of Babington and his young friends, he had been a rock of fidelity and discretion. Even in prison he was a force to be reckoned with. The deliberate attempt to smear his name was so vicious that it can be compared only with the slanders against Fr. Persons. In both cases the campaign against them is a measure of the

[1] Stonyhurst MSS., *Anglia I*, No. 28.

influence they exercised. Consequently Fr. Weston, who was an exemplary priest, was of all things accused of ambition, avarice, even looseness of morals. While he never lost his place in the affections of contemporary Catholics, it is not surprising that historians who have defended the Appellant cause have dealt harshly with him. Not one of the accusations brought against his conduct at Wisbech had any substance outside the imagination of his accusers. His behaviour was unimpeachable. In editing this text I have only touched on the controversy. To go deeper would upset the balance of the book. However, I trust I have given the reader sufficient material to form his own judgment. In my opinion Fr. Weston stands in no need of defence. The two long letters [1] on the subject of the factious priests at Wisbech belong more to a book on that subject than to his *Autobiography*. Historians who judged Weston at fault in these disputes appear to have read neither of these letters nor the testimony of the secular priests who wished to maintain the peaceful collegiate life which had been inaugurated by universal agreement. In his references to the Wisbech stirs Fr. Weston is both temperate and courteous. Here as elsewhere in his *Autobiography* he shows his charm of manner, his quick appreciation of goodness in others, his delicate humour, his meekness joined with strength of purpose. These were natural gifts, made more attractive in the setting of his own saintliness. Indeed in a Catholic century Fr. Weston might well have had a place in the calendar of his country's saints.

The original manuscript of his *Autobiography*, written, I think, in the hand of a secretary, is at Stonyhurst. This was the text used by Fr. John Morris for his edition of the *Auto-*

---

[1] See Appendix E.

biography.[1] It is in very bad condition, particularly towards
the end, and missing what corresponds to the last three and a
half chapters in this book. In piecing the text together, Fr.
Morris relied on a transcript of this manuscript which was
made by a careless hand at the end of the eighteenth century,
when the manuscript was already beginning to decay. The
text I have followed is the only entire and well-preserved
transcript which, as far as I know, exists. It was made early
in the seventeenth century from the original Stonyhurst
manuscript, which was then complete and in good condition.
This transcript is now preserved at Rome, and I am indebted
to Fr. E. Burrus, S.J., for the photographs of it from which I
have worked. I have to thank Fr. Burrus also for finding in
the archives of the Jesuit Curia the misplaced manuscript of
Fr. de Peralta's brief Life of Fr. Weston after I had searched
for it without success. This is a primary source and a brief
first-hand account by the most intimate of Weston's Spanish
friends. Here also I would like to thank all others who have
in one way or another assisted me: the Irish Nuns at Seville,
who translated Fr. de Peralta's work for me; Mgr. Edwin
Henson, Rector of the English College at Valladolid, who
was my guide to the archives there; Fr. Anthony Kenny, who
found and transcribed for me very important documents in
the archives of the English College at Rome ; the Librarian
of Blairs College, who had microfilmed at my request a very
imperfect copy of the *Autobiography* preserved there; Fr.
Christopher Devlin, for guiding me through the intricacies of
the Babington Plot; Lady Dormer, Fr. Hugh Bowler, O.S.B.,
Fr. Aelred Watkin, O.S.B., the Rev. Francis Edwards, the
Librarian of Norwich, and the Vicar of Wisbech; Dr. E. B.

---

[1] ' The Life of Father William Weston ', edited by Fr. John Morris,
S.J., in *Two Missionaries under Elizabeth* (1875).

Strauss, for some interesting notes which bear his initials; Fr. Hubert Chadwick, Fr. Leo Hicks and Fr. Basil FitzGibbon, for their constant help, and finally, Mr. Evelyn Waugh, for his Foreword and for much valuable advice.

P. C.

NOTE TO THE READER

I must ask the reader's pardon for the number and arrangement of the notes. For the most part the notes contain material which a biographer of William Weston would have included in his narrative, and they are therefore essential to the understanding of the man and his place in the history of the Catholic community of his day. It was my first intention to divide the notes into two groups: those that directly illustrated Weston's story and contained matter of human interest, and the remainder which would concern merely the specialist historian. The first group I proposed to place at the foot of the page, the second at the back of the book. For reasons which will become clear to the reader, such a dichotomy proved unworkable. Rather than place all the notes at the foot of the page and give the book an appearance of learning which it does not claim for itself, I arranged them in groups at the close of the chapter to which they refer. This system at least makes reference easy and stresses the importance that I attach to them. It is an imperfect solution but the least unsatisfactory that I was able to reach.

P. C.

ABBREVIATIONS USED IN NOTES

C.R.S.	Catholic Record Society.
C.S.P., Dom. Eliz.	Calendar of State Papers, Domestic Series, Elizabeth.
C.Sc.P.	Calendar of Scottish Papers.
Complete Peerage	*Complete Peerage of England, Scotland, Ireland, Great Britain and the United Kingdom.* The references are to the edition in progress unless otherwise noted.
de Peralta	*Puntos que el P̃ ̣ de Peralta de la Comp̃ ̣ de Jesus, junto de personas fidedinas de la Comp̃ ̣ y seglares, cerca de la s.ᵗᵃ vida del P. Guillermo Weston, etc.*
Foley	*Records of the English Province of the Society of Jesus,* by Henry Foley, S.J.
Hat. Cal.	Calendar of Manuscripts of the Marquess of Salisbury preserved at Hatfield House.
Hist. Prov. Angl.	*Historia Provinciae Anglicanae Societatis Jesu* (1660) by Henry More, S.J.
Humble Supplication	*An Humble Supplication to Her Majestie* by Robert Southwell, S.J. (edited by R. C. Bald).
John Gerard	*John Gerard, The Autobiography of an Elizabethan,* translated by Philip Caraman, S.J.
Life	*The Life and Death of the Renowned Confessor Philip Howard, Earl of Arundel, etc.* (ed. 1857).
S.P.D.	State Papers, Domestic.
Two Missionaries	*Two Missionaries under Elizabeth,* edited by John Morris, S.J., in *The Troubles of our Catholic Forefathers,* Second Series (1875).

1

INITIAL MISHAPS

On receiving instructions from our Father General to go to England and work there for the salvation of souls, I left Seville and made my way to Paris. There I stayed some days and spoke to Father Persons: then, with Ralph Emerson, who had been appointed my companion, I went on to Rouen; and thence to the port of Dieppe where I embarked.[1]

We had a favourable wind for the voyage, and it was the middle of the day when we caught sight of the English coast; and on a stretch of open beach, between two ports,[2] we were set ashore—myself, that is, and Henry Hubert.[3] (This gentleman's house had been ransacked by the heretics a short time before and he had fled to France, where he remained until the storm had abated.) The two of us then, taking his servant with us, went by the shortest route to the house of a friend whom Henry knew very well. In the meantime Ralph stayed in the boat with our baggage—it was our plan to send him a horse secretly, under cover of night, and collect our possessions, together with our books, for we had brought over a large number of them to distribute in England. This was done very quickly.

So far all had gone well, and he joined us with his valuable burden safe and entire.

The next day, after we had made arrangements for their conveyance by river, Ralph put the cases of books aboard a light boat and sailed with them to Norwich—the starting-place for the freight-waggons and carriers that take the merchandise of the district to London.[4] Meanwhile we got on our horses, and making our way by comfortable stages, arrived in London ahead of him.

Hardly had we entered the city along the very busy main thoroughfare,[5] when a man came up to us. Publicly, in the open street, he hailed Henry by name. This indeed alarmed us, for Henry had taken every precaution to keep his return from France a secret. However we went into an inn and had dinner. Then, without wasting any time, we left for a distant part of the city and there anxiously awaited Ralph's arrival.

The fact that I was entirely unknown gave me courage, and several times I went out to the place where the freight-waggons from Norwich assembled and waited there looking round for Ralph.[6] In the end, to my great relief, I ran into him in the middle of the road. I asked him what had happened. Everything, he said, had gone well. But he added that the cases had been detained at an inn, and we could not get them away until the searcher[7] gave his consent.

We were in a dilemma now and hard put to it to know what to do. It would be distressing and cowardly to abandon the books, yet we would be incurring a great risk if we tried to recover them. Whatever we did, we were in trouble.

Ralph, nevertheless, thought that bold action was called for, and he was against abandoning lightly any responsibility that had been entrusted to him. Also he felt certain that, if it came to the point, he could bribe his way through with cash. The first thing he did, therefore, was to commend his undertaking to God: then unfalteringly he made his way back to the inn. There he was instantly arrested and brought before the magistrates. Already they had examined the packages. Now they cross-examined Ralph about the books, then imprisoned him in a very dark and cramped cell.[8] For a year or more he lay completely concealed so that, in spite of all our enquiries, we were unable to discover what had become of him or where he was confined. We began, therefore, to think that he must have been transferred to the Tower of London: actually they held him in the prison called the Poultry.

Such was Ralph's misadventure on our first coming to England.[9]

Meanwhile we stayed at the inn, praying that God would prosper him. But when his return became overdue—there was no sign of him that day nor the next—it was not difficult to guess what in fact had been his fate. So we gave up hope of his return, and once again began to discuss our own position. Indeed we were in a great difficulty, for Ralph was to have been our escort, instructing us in our work and introducing us to Catholics, and it was hard to decide the best thing to do. Father Persons, however, had given me an introduction to a gentlewoman named Bellamy, of whom I shall have occasion to say more later, as well as some small articles, tokens of friendship, which she would recognise. She had been Father Persons's hostess, and had a large house and was wealthy. Like a stalwart Catholic, she was full of good-will towards the Father who, as I heard, had done much of his work and writing under her roof.[10]

This lady's house was nine miles or more from London, and there we went and asked to speak with her. When we met I handed over the tokens, but secretly, as had to be done on such an occasion. She protested that she did not understand a word I said; that she had never set eyes on Father Persons: she had never even heard of him, and it was inconceivable that messages such as this should pass between them.

There was nothing to be gained by dallying; and as it would be useless, I thought, to press further, I decided to leave at once. Besides, I suspected I might be treading on unsafe ground, and feared that we might have made a mistake either about the house or about the lady, or that the situation might have altered, as it so often does in the present troubled state of the country. So giving the rein to our horses, Henry and I rode off, taking a different road from that by which we had come. We thought that if, by some mischance, we had been at an unfriendly house, they might send men after us to search or arrest us as public enemies.

Actually our anxiety was not altogether unfounded. As we learned later, the lady had given shelter to three or four Catholic priests who were hiding in her house, and also to another person, a layman and impostor, who acted as if he were a Catholic and made a wicked pretence of being a devout man. No sooner had we left than this man pursued us in order to discover our identity. But while we were following another road, he took the public highway and so failed to find us. A short time afterwards this man turned out to be an undoubted spy and notorious persecutor. Indeed, he brought suffering to many people and confusion to many homes. But retribution was not long delayed, for he was run through by the sword of a personal enemy with whom he had quarrelled, and so paid the just penalty for his crimes and died a wretched death.

We returned therefore to London, our starting-point, and tried to devise some new plan.[11]

Now, while Henry was still in France he had received news that his wife, whom he had left pregnant, had gone from home to live secretly in the house of a Catholic gentleman until the child was born; she was anxious that it should not fall into the hands of heretics and be baptised according to their rites.[12] Though we were not certain she was hiding there, we thought it worth trying. But as Henry himself was frightened to be seen in public—every house and building appeared suspect and unsafe to him—I went alone, and enquired whether his wife was living there.

Suspecting that I had come on some evil errand or was a spy, the people of the house said she was not there, and never had been. I was rebuffed a second time, and a third; but still, from one or two indications, I felt fairly certain that this was her retreat, and became rather more daring. I said that there could be no doubt about it, that she must be there, and I added a few words which made it plain how distressed I was at being so repeatedly contradicted. All the same, they sent me away. But as I was going off, a girl followed me and enquired whether I had ever known or seen the lady I was looking for. No, I replied, but I had irrefutable tokens from her husband and she would be glad to see and check them. At this she asked me to return, and as she led me into the house, she pointed the woman out to me. I immediately showed her the jewelled ornament belonging to her husband. As evidence it was beyond question, and its recognition put me in high favour both with her and the whole family. In their joy they lavished on me every courtesy and attention their kind-ness could suggest. They asked me many questions about Henry, and I gave them all the information I had and told them where he was staying. Then I went away again and turned bringing him with me. That was a very happy day.

The following morning a priest arrived, and I talked to him about our present situation: then, after offering Mass, we both said good-bye. Henry stayed behind to be with his wife, while the priest took me to the house of the lady who, earlier, had protested she knew nothing about Father Persons. Now she received me with great kindness and explained the reason for her mistrust, namely, that she had presumed we belonged to that company of rascals commonly called pursuivants.

Here I stayed a few days. Several Catholic priests visited us. And it was here that I made a start with the work that was our appointed task; and before long my presence became known to many people.[13]

NOTES

Page 1

[1] W. W. left Paris on 26 August 1584 and embarked on 8 September. Before sailing he sent a letter to Fr. Persons and was in such good spirits that he 'burst into poetry and wrote a number of Greek verses in Homeric and other metres'. *C.R.S.*, vol. 39, p. 252.

[2] Between Yarmouth and Lowestoft on the East Anglian coast.

[3] Henry Hubert or Hubbard, son and heir of James Hubbard of Hales Hall in Norfolk (*Two Missionaries*, p. 365). The recusant Exchequer Roll (1592–3) shows that Hubbard or Hubert owned considerable property immediately south of Lowestoft at Kitley, Kessingland and Pakefield which had been seized by the Crown on account of his recusancy (*C.R.S.*, vol. 18, p. 312). It is interesting to note that all this land either bordered the sea or stretched towards it, thus giving protection for the landing of priests.

Page 2

[4] The books were probably carried on pack-horses to Yarmouth and taken up the river Yare by boat to Norwich.

[5] W. W. would have entered the city through Bishopsgate which stood opposite the present entrance to Liverpool Street Station. Bishopsgate Street was the 'main thoroughfare' into London from the eastern counties, and was then a wide, irregular road with low and scattered houses.

[6] This was probably the *Dolphin*, outside Bishopsgate and opposite the famous *White Hart*. As carriers often arrived after the gates had closed, it was convenient for them to make their terminus a short distance outside the city boundaries. John Taylor, *The Carriers Cosmographie* (1637).

[7] The Latin word is *publicanus*. In the context it is more likely to mean customs officer or searcher than innkeeper.

Page 3

[8] Ralph was committed to the Poultry on 26 September 1584 'for bringing over certain books touching some of the Council'. Most of these books were Catholic works recently published on the Continent —the Rheims *New Testament*, Persons's *Christian Directory*, Allen's *Apology* and *Defence of English Catholics*. This last directly 'touched the Council' for it was a reply to Burghley's *Execution of Justice in England*. Only from a later examination taken before the Ecclesiastical Commissioners in 1593 does it appear that copies of 'My Lord of Leicester's

7

book ' were found in the packages. This is, of course, the slanderous pamphlet later known as *Leicester's Commonwealth*, written by Charles Arundell (Arch. Vat., *Nunc. Div.* 264, f. 239). Probably Arundell persuaded Ralph that it was a harmless tract and asked him to take over copies for distribution in England (*S.P.D.*, *Eliz.*, vol. cxc, no. 32; *Harleian MSS.* 6998, f. 65; Strype, *Annals* vol. 4, p. 256). Ralph would certainly have been executed had he not been able to prove that he had been deceived by Arundell.

⁹ From the Poultry Ralph Emerson was moved to the Clink, where he met Fr. John Gerard in 1594, then to Wisbech, after W. W.'s transfer to the Tower, and finally to Framlingham Castle. Like W. W., he was exiled on the accession of James I. Altogether he had spent nearly twenty years in prison. He died at St. Omer about ten months after his release on 12 March 1604 at the age of fifty-three. ' It was his greatest consolation, spent as he was by so many sufferings and labours endured for his beloved England, that the feast of the great St. Gregory, the Apostle of England, was to him the closing day of his life.' W. W. was particularly devoted to Ralph, because he had also been the companion of Edmund Campion, W. W.'s ideal of a missionary priest. *John Gerard*, pp. 78–9, 102–3; Foley, iii, pp. 17–37.

¹⁰ This was Uxenden, the house of Catherine Bellamy, the daughter of Richard Page, one of the founders of Harrow School. It was situated on a tributary of the river Brent, about two miles east of Harrow. A farm house, probably part of the original mansion, survived until 1933 when the Bakerloo Line was extended to Stanmore. The exact site is the present junction of this line with the Metropolitan. In the sixteenth century Uxenden House was hidden in thick wooded country, traversed by very rough and difficult roads, and, being close to London, it provided an excellent hiding-place for priests in an emergency. It was here that Fr. Persons wrote the greater part of his classic spiritual treatise, *The Book of Resolution*, later known as *The Christian Directory*.

Page 4

¹¹ Fr. Persons meanwhile was waiting in Paris for the news of their safe arrival. On 4 October he wrote to Rome, ' We have no news yet of the arrival of Fr. Weston and Ralph, but the very fact that we have received no bad news of them is sufficiently satisfactory and a sign that all is well '. (*C.R.S.*, vol. 39, p. 252.)

Page 5

¹² This is typical of the plight of Catholic mothers at this period.

Many other similar instances are recorded of women, like Hubert's wife, who left their homes in order to conceal their pregnancy from the local ecclesiastical authorities. If it became known that they were expecting a child, they were watched and incurred suspicion as Catholics if they did not in due course present the child for baptism by the parson. On the other hand, if they left home, they could always claim on their return that the child had been baptised elsewhere.

Page 6

[13] W. W. soon gained a reputation as a remarkable priest. ' Everybody writes most favourably of Fr. Weston ', Fr. Persons reported as early as 26 November, two months after W. W. had reached London. On 2 July the following year Persons again wrote, ' Fr. Weston is doing wonders and is giving great edification to all'. *C.R.S.*, vol. 39, pp. 265, 271.

2

A PEER OF TWO REALMS

This was the time that Father Heywood was held a prisoner in the Tower of London.[1] There, in addition to the ordinary discomforts of prison life, he was suffering from a very severe illness and was in great pain. In consideration of his age and poor health he was allowed to receive visits from his sister,[2] who in some measure was able to attend to his needs and nurse him. She was a Catholic, and it was through her that I got in touch with him by letter and received letters from him in reply.[3]

It was now near the opening of Parliament—the Parliament which passed the most severe and fearful laws against Catholics and against priests in particular,[4] and at this time such priests as were still in prison were ordered into exile. One of them was Father Heywood, and I was most anxious to see and speak to him before he left. I discussed the matter, therefore, with his sister, and I understood from her that it could be arranged without grave risk, for in view of his imminent exile he was granted greater liberty to deal with his friends. So I accompanied her to the Tower, but with a feeling of great trepidation as I saw the vast battlements, and was led by the warder past the gates with their iron fastenings, which were closed behind me. So I came to the cell where the Father was confined. We greeted one another and then, as was natural, exchanged the information we each had about the affairs that concerned us.

Among other things, he told me that in spite of all the steps I had taken to keep my arrival in England secret, the news of it had reached him. He had learnt of it, and of my companion Ralph, from the Earl of Northumberland, and there could be no doubt that the Queen's Council had been informed. (The Earl at that time was held a close prisoner in the Tower. Shortly afterwards he was foully murdered in his cell in the middle of the night by some villains who discharged into his heart a musket loaded with two bullets.[5] Such at least was the report abroad.[6])

At last, when I had finished talking to Father Heywood —we spent almost the whole day together—I embraced him and said goodbye.[7] Then I returned the same way that I had come; and the moment I reached safety outside the walls I felt as if I had been restored to the light of day.

Some weeks later he was put in a boat together with a large number of other priests and sent off into exile. Apart from ourselves he left behind him his country, his relatives and his friends.[8] Then I was alone in England, deprived of my Superior and of Ralph, my brother.[9]

Several Catholics, however, invited me to their homes and I had many opportunities of preaching and hearing confessions. As for Mass, I was never forced to omit it. But while I was busy in this way and mixed more freely and openly in Catholic society, the following incident occurred. Whether, as commonly happens, it was the work of some shameful impostor who passed himself off as a Catholic, or whether it was due to the carelessness of some ceaseless prattler who could keep nothing secret, I cannot say. But it became known that on a certain day I was to visit the house of a Catholic gentleman to preach there. This I did. And considering the distracted times, the congregation was quite large. All went according to plan, but as I stepped out through the door I noticed a man walking up and down in front of the entrance. He appeared to be waiting for something, and I passed him by. Later, when I was safely away, a Catholic gentleman told me that the following night his own house had been searched by heretics who had pressed him very closely for information concerning me. And he added that when on the previous day I had been present at the house I mentioned, I had been observed by a man who had been sent there to arrest me, but somehow or other—nobody could say how—I had suddenly vanished from his sight. Thus, thanks to the goodness of God, I escaped danger on that occasion.

About the same time I came to know intimately a fervent Catholic who was in the service of the Earl of Arundel.[10] He was most remarkable for his steadfast devotion to the Earl, and in addition he showed great prudence and ability in managing all the business placed in his hands.[11] In fact, this nobleman confided in him matters of his private concern; and now he explained that he was very anxious to alter the manner of his life—he was wearied by heresy and wished to become a Catholic. The Earl asked him, therefore, to search for a priest who, in his judgment, would best assist him to carry out his resolution. All this the good man passed on to me. A convenient meeting place and time were arranged for it, but at night after dark so that no one should see me coming in and going out or having a long conversation in private with the Earl in a room apart, for some of his household were watching his behaviour closely and already suspected that he was contemplating this very step. A day or two later I was sent for again. And in a private place, in the

presence of himself and one or two of his very near relatives
—not more—I said Mass and gave him Holy Communion.[12]

But the Parliament which I mentioned had already been
summoned and had started its sessions in London. This was,
I think, at the beginning of the year 1585.[13] The Earl had to
attend, for he held a high place in the government and had,
besides, ceremonial duties to perform in attendance on the
Queen's person—he was in fact one of the principal noblemen
of the kingdom. The difficulty of his position perplexed him
greatly. He knew that if he absented himself from the
heretical services conducted at the inauguration of Parliament,
he would be immediately marked out as a Catholic, not just be
suspected of being one. So he turned over in his mind every
imaginable scheme and pretext for evasion. Could he feign
sickness, or be engrossed in other business, or hide or fly?
There was no practicable plan, none, that is, which did not
involve some considerable and immediate risk. The day
arrived. The peers of the realm assembled. Everything was
prepared and everyone in readiness for the pomp of the
royal procession. Among the rest came the Earl of Arundel
to carry out his assigned tasks in attendance on the Queen.
But he was trembling with anxiety over the plan which God
had suggested to his mind. Would it succeed?

The procession moved to Parliament House, each man
intent on his precedence and duty. The Earl's position was
close to the Queen's person as one of her trainbearers. They
entered the Parliament building. All, Queen and peers, took
their appointed places, and the signal was given for the heretical
service to begin. Then the Earl, pretending to be overcome
by the crowd and suffocated by the heat, hurried off from the
ceremony. With a flushed look on his face, he unbuttoned
his dress, and walked up and down outside, ostensibly taking

the fresh air while the service was going on inside. And he acted the part so well that for some time the secret was kept.[14]

However his religion could not be hidden for long.[15] I learnt all this from his own lips and at the same time he told me that he was constantly preoccupied with plans of escape into France. When I heard of this, I did my best to dissuade him, for I thought it would endanger both his life and estate. I doubted also whether his enemies would go to the extreme of imprisonment and execution, so long as his religion was the only crime they could charge him with. This indeed was borne out by the actual cases of other noblemen.[16] Besides, his mere presence in the country and his open profession of the faith would be an encouragement to the whole Catholic body and brace them to follow resolutely his fine and noble lead. All the same, he replied that his plan had been commended by Doctor Allen, who was then President of the seminary at Rheims; he had asked his advice by letter and had decided to follow it.[17]

As I had no wish to oppose such a wise and experienced person, I left the Earl to pursue his own course.[18] And he did all he could to execute his plan immediately, for delay would increase the danger. By sheer chance he fell in with a man who undertook to arrange the details of the escape and see it through faithfully.[19] The date was fixed, the harbour determined, the boat fitted out. Everything required for the voyage was laid on board—all was ready. They weighed anchor and with the breeze in their favour they made for the open sea. They were safe away—or so they thought—and beyond the reach of danger, when a hostile ship headed them off. It had been keeping a distance all the time, for it had been decided to seize the Earl in actual flight, and not in harbour.[20]

PHILIP HOWARD, EARL OF ARUNDEL

P. GUILLELMUS WESTONUS CANTUARIENSIS INGRESSUS
HOC TYROCINIUM 5 Nov. 1575.—17 ANNORUM CARCERE PRO FIDE.
ILLUSTRIS. OBIIT VALLISOLETI 19 APP. 1615. ÆT. 65.

WILLIAM WESTON

So the Earl was brought back a prisoner. How his plan of escape became known to the heretics, he was never able to discover, though suspicion fell on one of the men who was with him in the boat.

Under strict guard he was returned to London and placed in the Tower. A short time afterwards sentence was pronounced against him.[21] His estates were confiscated, and for many years he suffered with fortitude the hardships of a most painful imprisonment.[22] Cut off from the sight and companionship of those he loved most dearly, he comforted his spirit by daily meditation and devout reading, until, full of the faith which he so bravely professed, he gave up his soul to its Creator.[23]

There were some who thought he was carried off by poison. I, however, made careful enquiries of a certain Catholic who had served him as a page at that time in the Tower, but I was never able to get any confirmation of this. As he lay dying he bequeathed me the breviary which he used: but Father Garnet decided to keep it himself for posterity like some religious object. He did not dare to entrust it to me, for everything I had was liable to be seized any moment, and he did not think it right to expose to such manifest risk a possession which, he declared, was more precious than any gold.[24]

This also I should have mentioned in my tribute to the soldier of Christ. While he was enduring these cruel sufferings an offer of liberation was made him in the Queen's name, but on condition that he held a disputation with the so-called Archbishop of Canterbury. This he refused to do. He preferred to be afflicted in the company of God's people than to possess the passing pleasures of temporal freedom.[25] Indeed he reckoned persecution a greater happiness than the frail and shallow satisfaction of worldly well-being.

NOTES

1 Fr. Jasper Heywood, the son of the famous epigrammatist and grandnephew of St. Thomas More.

2 Fr. Heywood's sister was Elizabeth, the mother of the poet, John Donne.

3 Heywood, who had been a page of honour to the young Princess Elizabeth, had many friends at court, and through their favour seems to have been given full freedom to correspond with his friends. Once when the Earl of Warwick asked him whether he had any needs in prison, he replied with a letter in verse, which concluded:

> Thanks to that Lord that wills me good;
> For I want all things saving Hay and Wood.

A. Wood, *Athenae Oxonienses*, vol. i, pp. 663–6.

4 The Act (27 Eliz. c. 2) which made it high treason for any Jesuit or seminary priest to be within the Queen's dominions and felony for any lay person to receive or relieve them. In the remaining eighteen years of Elizabeth's reign a hundred priests and fifty-three layfolk (including two women) were executed under this statute. Fr. Southwell's *Humble Supplication*, to which W. W. refers later in the narrative, was in part an appeal against the severity of the law. Southwell writes: 'Heaven and earth shall witness with us in the dreadful day of doom that our breast never harboured such horrible treasons and that the end of our coming is the salvation of souls, not the murdering of bodies; we being rather willing to die than contribute the least hair of our heads to the latter, and not so willing to live as to shed the best blood of our bodies for the first.' *Humble Supplication*, pp. 13–14.

Page 11

5 Henry Percy, eighth Earl of Northumberland, was imprisoned in the Tower for alleged plotting in favour of Mary, Queen of Scots. He was found shot on 21 June 1585. Suspicion of murder was increased by the fact that the day before his death the Lieutenant of the Tower, Sir Owen Hopton, had been ordered by the Vice-Chamberlain, Sir Christopher Hatton, to place his prisoner under a new warder. In a remarkable letter written to Robert Cecil in 1600, Walter Raleigh assumes that it is knowledge common to them both that Northumberland was murdered by Hatton, and argues that if Cecil does away with his rival Essex he need fear no 'after-revenges' from Essex's son, 'for Northumberland that now is thinks not of Hatton's issue' (E. Edwards, *Sir Walter Raleigh*, vol. 2, p. 222). Certainly the Government had to

take great trouble to clear itself in the Star Chamber enquiry. The report of the proceedings is in the Hatfield Calendar, and it is clear that much of the evidence used by the Government was obtained by torture. Robert Cecil completed the ruin of the family by involving Henry's brother, the ninth Earl, in the Gunpowder Plot.

[6] A letter from Bernardino de Mendoza, the former Spanish Ambassador to England, reporting the news to Philip II (16 July 1585) shows that little credence was given to the report of suicide. ' The Earl of Northumberland ', writes Mendoza, ' has killed himself, according to the account written by secretary Walsingham, who says that he asked the guard for a pistol loaded with three bullets. This is very hard to believe, for those who know how strictly prisoners are kept there, and that the guards are not allowed even to give them food without the intervention of the constable, in the case of so important a person as the Earl, to whom they certainly would not have dared to give arms. It is therefore concluded, from the fact that he was found with three bullet wounds, that the thing had been managed by the councillors, and it is to be feared that they may do the same thing to the Earl of Arundel and other Catholic prisoners, who are now very numerous.' C.S.P., Spanish (1580–6), p. 542, no. 400.

[7] Although Heywood was an amiable eccentric and very zealous priest—it was said that during a few months in Staffordshire he had received 280 persons back into the Church in that county alone—he had caused much anxiety to Cardinal Allen and Fr. Persons by his self-opinionated teaching and high-handed treatment of both seminary priests and layfolk. He had been sent to England in 1581, and was obeying an order to return for consultations with Fr. Persons at Rouen when he was captured at sea and imprisoned in December 1583. On account of his tactless behaviour, Fr. Persons advised Aquaviva, the General of the Jesuits, to have particular care in future in his selection of men for the English mission. Since W. W. was the first Jesuit to land in England after Heywood's failure, Fr. Persons followed reports of his work with special interest and satisfaction. C.R.S., vol. 39, passim.

[8] See Appendix A, p. 233: Fr. Heywood's Journey into Exile.

[9] W. W.'s visit to Heywood took place at the end of 1584, since Heywood started his journey into exile on 21 January 1585. With Heywood went two other Jesuits, Fr. Thomas Bosgrave and Fr. John Hart, who like him had been held prisoners in the Tower. Apart from Emerson, who was in the Poultry prison, W. W. remained the only Jesuit in England until the arrival of Fr. Southwell and Fr. Garnet in July 1586.

Page 12

[10] Philip Howard, Earl of Arundel, the son of Thomas, fourth Duke of Norfolk, Earl of Surrey, who had been attainted on 16 January 1572, and beheaded on 2 June following. Philip was born on 28 June 1557, and was so christened to honour his godfather King Philip, consort of Mary Tudor.

[11] This servant has not been identified; he may have been Mr. John Momford, who did other confidential business for the Earl. *C.R.S.*, vol. 21, pp. 41, 96.

Page 13

[12] The indictment of the Earl gives the date of the reconciliation as 30 September. Like all the dates in the document, it cannot be trusted. For example, it speaks of W. W. plotting with the Earl on 23 June, at least two months before the men met. All that is certain is that the Earl was reconciled before Parliament opened. 'By this good man [W. W.] was the Earl reconciled in the year 1584', writes the author of the *Life* (p. 27), 'and by this means received such comfort to his soul as he never had felt before in all his life, and such good directions for amending and ordering of his life, as afterwards did greatly help and farther him therein.' Before his reception by W. W. the Earl was well known for his extravagance and love of pleasure, taking special delight in tiltings and tourneys, in entertaining ambassadors and the Queen herself, and was so much in debt that he had been forced to sell much of his own and his wife's lands (*Complete Peerage*, vol. 1, p. 254). Henceforth, as the *Life* reports, ' he lived in such manner, as he seemed to be changed into another man, having great care and vigilance over all his actions and addicting himself to piety and devotions ', keeping always a priest in his London house ' by whom he might frequently receive the Holy Sacraments and daily have the comfort to be present at . . . the Holy Sacrifice, whereto with great humility and reverence he himself in person would many times serve '. *Life*, p. 28.

[13] ' The first day of this Parliament was 23 November 1584.' *Journals of the House of Lords*, vol. 2, p. 61.

Page 14

[14] After his arrest, the Earl himself referred to this incident in a letter to the Queen (14 April 1585): 'The first day of this Parliament, when your Majesty with all your nobility was hearing of a sermon in the Collegiate Church of Westminster above in the chancel, I was driven to walk by myself in one of the aisles.' *C.R.S.*, vol. 21, p. 105.

[15] In his letter to the Queen he makes the same point. ' The true cause of my refusal to attend service could no longer be hidden, though for a while it was not generally noted and observed.' Apart from the occasion described by W. W., the Earl mentions others: ' And one day this last Lent 1585, when your Majesty was hearing another sermon in the chapel at Greenwich, I was forced to stay all the while in the Presence Chamber. To be short, when your Majesty went upon a Sunday or Holiday to your great closet, I was enforced to stay either in the Privy Chamber and not to wait upon you at all, or presently to depart as soon as I had brought you to the chapel.' C.R.S., vol. 21, p. 105.

[16] The case history of the Catholic peers made the decision very perplexing. W. W. must have known the fate of the Earl of Southampton, Lord Vaux and Lord Morley, who had been imprisoned. On the other hand, there were others like Lord Montagu who enjoyed special protection. Arundel's case was made more difficult because his father and grandfather had been executed, and the new nobility were likely to be jealous of the Howards, as they were of the Percys and later the Stanleys.

[17] The Earl himself describes the reasons for his decision. ' For when I considered in what continual danger I did remain here in England both by laws heretofore established and by a new act lately made, I did think it my safest way to depart the realm and abide in some other place where I might live without danger to my conscience, without offence to your Majesty, without the servile subjection to mine enemies, and without this peril to my life. . . . For on the one side my native country, friends, wife and kinsfolk did invite me to stay; on the other side the misfortune of my house, the power of mine adversaries, the remembrance of my former troubles, and the knowledge of my present danger, did hasten me to go.'

The ' new act ' to which the Earl refers was the Act of 27 Elizabeth making it high treason to entertain a priest. The Earl, as his biographer points out, was determined to keep a priest in his house. C.R.S., vol. 21, p. 106.

[18] There was no letter from Allen, but only a counterfeit message brought by Edward Grately, a renegade priest acting in collusion with the Government, which was anxious to induce the Earl to fly and arrest him in the act of flight. Allen's advice, had he given it, would no doubt have endorsed W. W.'s. But W. W. withdrew his counsel in deference to the acknowledged leader of the Catholic body. W. W.'s respect for Allen was shared by all the Jesuits, and by none more than Robert Southwell, who spoke of him as 'the father of his country, to whom must be ascribed whatever good we are here able to do '. C.R.S., vol. 5, p. 319.

[19] This man was Edward Grately.   See Appendix B, *Edward Grately and the Betrayal of the Earl of Arundel*, p. 238.

[20] The Earl's boat was intercepted by a small warship in command of Keloway, a man of such ' notorious infamous life ' that he was taken at his word when he proclaimed that he was a pirate and offered to let the Earl pass free on payment of a hundred pounds.   ' Whereupon the Earl, little suspecting any latent fraud, wrote in a few lines to his sister, the Lady Margaret Sackville, to pay the bearer of the note the sum demanded.'   But Keloway ' as soon as he got the letter, read it and immediately discovered himself, that he was appointed by the Council to watch there for him and carry him back again to the land '.   *Hat. Cal.*, vol. viii, p. 376; *C.R.S.*, vol. 21, p. 109.

Page 15

[21] On 17 May 1586 the Earl was condemned in the Star Chamber to a fine of £10,000 and imprisonment at the Queen's pleasure.   On 14 April 1589 he was arraigned for high treason in the Queen's Bench at Westminster, found guilty and sentenced to death.   ' When the sentence was pronounced ', wrote Fr. Garnet a fortnight later, ' and the crowd saw the Earl coming out of the Hall with the axe-edge turned in towards him—in the trial of nobles this is the sign that the prisoner has been condemned—suddenly there was a great uproar that was carried miles along the river bank, some people demanding what had come of the Queen's clemency that such a splendid and gallant gentleman should suffer condemnation, others passionately indignant that a man who had prayed to God should be executed for that alone.   For among the accusations brought against him, the principal charge and the one on which the whole case turned, was this—he had asked a certain priest to pray for the success of the Spanish fleet; whereas in fact, all his enemies could prove against him and all he had done was this, that he sought that prayers should be said every hour of the day and night in the Tower of London and in other prisons at that time, chiefly, when everyone was expecting a general massacre [of Catholics].'   (Garnet to Aquaviva, 1 May 1589.   Arch. S.J., Rome, *Fondo Gesuitico*, 651.) The indignation of the crowd on this day probably explains why the sentence was never carried out.

[22] The Earl was lodged in the Tower on 25 April 1585.   Four years later, on 14 April 1589, he was attainted on a charge of high treason, and all his honours became forfeited.

[23] Even when he lay dying the Queen refused him permission to see

his wife and children, unless he promised to renounce his religion. He died on 19 November 1595 at the age of thirty-eight after ten and a half years in prison. His funeral, probably similar to that described by W. W. in Ch. 21, cost his frugal Sovereign two pounds. He was buried first in the chapel of the Tower, but removed in 1624 to West Horsley, Surrey, the seat of his widow, and finally to Arundel. On 15 December 1929, he was beatified by Pius XI. *Complete Peerage*, vol. 1, p. 255.

24 Fr. Garnet also kept the Breviary which Fr. Southwell had used in the Tower. Both were lost in the raid on Garnet's London house described by Fr. Gerard. *John Gerard*, pp. 156–7.

25 It is clear from the *Life* (pp. 133, 134) that the Earl held W. W. in high esteem. ' The like grateful mind and great affection he [the Earl] always ever bore and always shewed unto Fr. William Weston by whom he was first reconciled, and for his sake unto the whole Society.' From the Tower the Earl used to send his spiritual writings to W. W. to be corrected (*ib.*, p. 138), and as he lay dying ' he had a great desire to have the assistance of Fr. Weston . . . but it would by no means be permitted, that either he or any other priest should come to him ' (*ib.* p. 114).

3

FLIBBERDIGIBBITS

As soon as Parliament closed, the Act against all priests was promulgated.[1] It commanded them, under pain of death, to leave the kingdom within forty days. Some, thinking it prudent to bow before the storm, obeyed; but the greater number remained to strengthen the spirit of Catholics. At a moment of such grave crisis, there was danger they might fall victim to their fears and become faint-hearted, if there was none left to give the sacraments and preach to them. Moreover, the sudden flight of all the priests was more likely to be interpreted as fear and cowardice than as a determined and concerted policy; and they did not want to give the heretics the satisfaction of seeing their plans prosper from the start. This, in fact, is what would have happened if at the first contact of battle all the leaders of Christ's army had been routed. With victory half in hand the enemy would have been well placed to exact vengeance on those that stayed. In the event he was exceedingly angered at the small number who yielded. By far the greater part determined to stand firm and await the outcome of this sacred conflict.[2]

As far as I was concerned, I thought it would be well to retire by myself to some place where I could judge from my own observation the way things were likely to go. I would be able then to see how Catholics thought and felt: whether they would retain their old loyalty to the faith, search out priests, ask them to their houses and maintain them; or whether they would keep them at a distance and agree to be abandoned by them in a time of such peril. Far better, I thought, that they should invite or summon me to them, than that I should thrust myself on them and have them risk their lives and property for my sake.[3]

However, as I was turning the matter over in my mind, a Catholic gentleman asked me to come and stay with him. He had a large and suitable house in a remote place, about nine miles out of London, so I accepted this offer which fitted in so perfectly with my plan. I took somebody with me to keep me company on the journey,[4] and, to avoid notice, we mounted our horses in the evening after dark. We made the journey safely, and passed the night without incident. I was altogether satisfied—the place was most convenient and our host kind. In the morning I prepared to say Mass. A fine room had been chosen, well suited for it, and the time settled; and I was in the chapel, about to put on the sacred vestments, when a messenger arrived from London. He told me I must leave instantly: it was already known at court that Father Cornelius and I were here—actually we had both been invited, but he had not yet come.[5] What could I do? I was in danger and had to fly, but I had no idea where I might escape with safety. Spies were on the alert everywhere; they were watching the roads and cross-questioning all who passed. For some time I walked up and down in the garden adjoining the house, ready to make off. One man and then another ran up and said that the searchers would be on the spot any minute, and they intended to surround the house and ransack it from top to bottom. I didn't wait a moment longer. Taking with me a man who said he could show me the way to an isolated and dilapidated building, I made off. There I stayed the entire day, peering out frequently to see whether I could catch sight of searchers in the distance. If I did, I was going to make for a wood near at hand and hide there under cover of the trees. That evening a horse was brought to me and I made my escape.

At this time many people, including Catholics, were tormented by evil spirits who would cause fearful disturbance in those in whom they dwelt.[6] But it was difficult to give the sufferers relief by means of exorcism, because usually they let out violent and raucous shrieks during the ceremonies. For all that, it seemed that something had to be attempted, as much for the sake of those who suffered the affliction as from compassion towards the persons who had them in their houses. Indeed there was every reason to have a care for them, for God might be pleased to assist the sufferers and grant them the relief they sought. This He did, and manifestly. Out of many persons demons were cast. The intervention of heaven was undoubted, and incredulous onlookers were astounded. In my own presence and before my own eyes persons were cured and had demons cast out of them; and at the time that these events were fresh in my mind I recorded in letters details that I cannot now recall.[7] Nor, in any case, would they belong to this narrative, though just a few words on the subject will not be misplaced.

There was, for instance, a young Catholic gentleman in the service of the elder Cecil. He had seen many exorcisms on a number of persons, for they had been performed in the house of a relative of his. Later, when the practices became generally known and talk of them reached the court and the Queen's Councillors, Cecil broached the subject with the young man. While discussing the possessed people and the exorcisms, he asked a number of questions, and pressed the young man to tell him honestly how much truth there was in the things people were saying about the demoniacs—whether the tales of them were authentic and trustworthy. Now the young man knew that his master was a persecutor of Catholics and all good people, yet, with his Lord's permission, he told him everything he had seen and heard, and so marvellous was it that he could hardly find words to describe it. Cecil merely laughed. He brushed it all aside as probable fraud and as a series of impostures devised by priests in order to deceive people. At this the young man, with a solemn oath, swore to the truth of all he had said:

' I won't mention other terrible things,' he said, ' but you could actually see the devils gliding and moving under the skin. There were immense numbers of them, and they looked just like fishes swimming here, there and everywhere.'

' You knave. You're all knaves—the whole lot of you.' said Cecil. ' I never want to set eyes on you again. Don't come near my house again—ever! '

But he knew he was wrong. The evidence had disturbed him; and still more had his own conscience. He could not endure to listen further. He was afraid, I think, that such startling testimony to the truth would force open his eyes, and he would have to assent. Or, perhaps, with a conscience already ill at ease, he feared it might add to his remorse.

This may also be the place to tell the story of the pursuivants who came with search warrants to the house where the demoniacs were. Their object was to discover what was going on and who was taking part, and then to arrest any priest or suspect they might find. They chose what they thought was the most likely time for Mass and for the exorcisms; but, fortunately, they spent a long time knocking at the gate—it was a large house encircled by a high wall—otherwise they would have burst in at all the entrances at once and surprised us. Asked what authority they had, they produced their warrants and named the magistrate who had sent them; and it was only then that they were admitted. In the entrance hall, however, they met one of the poor possessed victims. It was a girl. As soon as she saw them, she glared and ground her teeth and said that one of the searchers had a thousand devils hanging on to the buttons of his coat. This scared them. All the mad fury of their first entry was forgotten. Indeed, in their extreme terror they seemed half-dead and became most amenable. They showed no violence whatsoever. Not a thing in the entire house was touched—whether it was because they did not want to or were afraid, I do not know. They looked only at the rooms into which they were taken, although, on their departure, they asked the lady of the house to give surety for her appearance before the Privy Council within a stated period. In point of fact several priests were in the house at the time, some actually saying Mass when the men arrived; but everything was finished and the priests put away in various hiding places before the rogues were allowed in.

Also, I think, I shall mention this: it happened nearly a year later after I had been captured and was in the hands of the heretics.

One day a secret examiner [8] was sent to me in prison to get information.[9] He was an inquisitive man and questioned me in great detail about the incident above. Then, making fun of it, he said he had seen simple people taken in by the same kind of thing done by mere juggling. To end his insolence, I told him of other occurrences of that period, and went on to say that I wished that the Queen had been present or one of her Council to witness the sights, or that they could have taken place in public, for I was certain that there were many people who, given an opportunity of observing the majestic power of the Church over evil spirits and monsters, would see and acknowledge at once the difference between the two religions and award the victory to the Catholic faith.[10] At this he swore a great oath and said that on no account would he like to have witnessed such horrific scenes. He showed, in fact, what little support is to be had from a bad conscience when it is brought face to face with the instruments of God's power.

Page 22

[1] It was entitled 'A Bill for the utter extirpation of Popery, against Jesuits and others'. Introduced into the Commons on 14 December 1584, it received royal assent on 29 March 1585, the day on which the session closed. The last priest to suffer under it was the Welsh Jesuit David Lewis on 27 August 1679, at the time of the Oates Plot. Although Charles II was then too hard-pressed to resist the popular clamour against priests, as soon as the Parliament closed he entered an instruction in the Privy Council Register to the effect that henceforth no priest was to be executed under this Act. Cf. J. H. Pollen, 'The Elizabethan Act that made Martyrs', *The Month*, March 1922.

[2] From the Douai Diaries (ed. T. F. Knox) it would seem that no more than ten priests chose exile, several of whom later returned to England.

Page 23

[3] At the end of April 1585 a conference of Catholic laymen and priests was held at Mr. Wyford's house in Hoxton. The principal representative of the priests was W. W. Among the laymen present were Lord Vaux, Sir Thomas Tresham and Sir William Catesby. There it was 'ordered that the priests shall shift for themselves abroad, as in inns or such like places, and not visit any Papists, especially of the gentlemen, except they be sent for, for this summer season'. It was decided also that all laymen of substance should contribute 100 marks annually to a fund, administered by Lord Vaux, for the support of the priests; and an appeal made in the country for the same purpose. Walsingham received a full report of the discussions from his spy, Nicholas Berden, who was present at the conference; and it was probably on this information that the search for priests in inns and lodgings houses, described by W. W. in Chapter 4, was made later in the year. *C.S.P., Dom. Eliz.*, (1581–90), p. 239.

[4] It is clear from this and other passages that W. W. always moved about with a lay escort. The practice was suggested by Fr. Persons to Mr. George Gilbert as the most practical and heroic form of lay co-operation in the priests' apostolate. Gilbert's own experience is on record in a memorandum which he drew up on this subject for the guidance of Fr. Persons. Cf. *C.R.S.*, vol. 39, pp. 331–40.

[5] The Jesuit, Fr. Cornelius or Cornwallis, whose real name was O'Mahoney, is mentioned several times in W. W.'s narrative. He was born of Irish parents who had settled in Cornwall on the estate of Sir

John Arundell, whose family he later served as chaplain. He was one of the most saintly and successful priests in the English mission. For his Life see Foley, iii, pp. 4 ,3–74.

Page 24

⁶ From here to the end of this chapter, W. W. deals with the somewhat nauseous subject of the exorcisms practised both by himself and a number of the best-known priests in England. It is probable that in a number of cases W. W. was over-credulous and the victim of deception at the hands of malicious or hysterical women.

⁷ Of all the letters W. W. wrote during his two years of liberty only one survives, addressed to Fr. Persons and signed E(dmund) H(unt). About a third of this letter is devoted to an account of the exorcisms. If Richard Mainy, one of the supposed possessed, is to be believed, W. W. wrote a ' long discourse of about a quire of paper of all my pretended trances and visions '. The discourse, if it ever existed, was not brought to light by Bishop Bancroft, when, twenty years later, he examined the victims in an attempt to bring discredit on the Catholic priests. Cf. Stonyhurst MSS., *Anglia*, i, no. 28; S. Harsnet, *Egregious Popish Impostures*, p. 270, sq.

Page 26

⁸ Probably Mr. Bell, a Clerk of the Council, who fancied himself as a theologian and had previously questioned Anthony Tyrrell on the exorcisms, and had dismissed the incidents as ' conjurations '. Cf. *Two Missionaries*, p. 326.

⁹ The enquiry almost certainly concerned the incident narrated by the historian, Fr. Henry More (*Hist. Prov. Angl.*, lib. 4, s. xxv). It was the occasion when the devil, whom W. W. was exorcising, asked his permission to enter the Queen. W. W. refused: ' I wish the Queen every grace of soul and body. She may hold a different faith, but she is still my Sovereign and Queen.' ' Then,' threatened the devil, ' I shall enter you.' ' All right,' answered W. W. ' Do so, if God gives you leave.' The devil then reflected: ' I must have a care for myself. I would be just as comfortable inside you as I would be if I threw myself in a pitcher of holy water.' Fr. de Peralta, who tells the same story, says that the incident was ' public and widely-known and reached the ears of the Queen's Council ', for it was described in full in the records of the exorcism which fell into the Council's hands on the arrest of Anthony Tyrrell. de Peralta adds that ' many think that this was why the Queen never permitted him [W. W.] to be executed.' W. W., he says, always

' wished the Queen long life and happiness and was in the habit of asking Our Lord to give her light and knowledge of the truth, that she might govern well and that things might turn out in such a way that she would be saved ' (f. 220–1).

Page 27

[10] Certainly many conversions followed on the exorcisms. Anthony Tyrrell estimated that no less than five hundred persons were reconciled to the Church by that means: others, doubtless exaggerating, put the figure at three or four thousand (*Two Missionaries*, p. 99). These cures raised a clamour among a section of Catholics for public exorcisms. ' The report of these events is spreading throughout the land ', W. W. wrote to Fr. Persons. ' Very many people are most anxious that [the exorcisms] be carried out in public. But [our enemies] are not such fools.' Stonyhurst MSS., *Anglia*, i, no. 28.

4

WITH SURPLICE AND SWORD

The days that followed the Parliament were bitter days for Catholics and filled with immeasurable suffering. Earlier, indeed, there had been great cruelty. Many had been broken. But now the fury of the persecution burst upon them more savagely still. It was the power held by the Earl of Leicester that was responsible, combined with Cecil's counsel, for these two men were in control under the Queen.[1] Catholics now saw their own country, the country of their birth, turned into a ruthless and unloving land. All men fastened their hatred on them. They lay in ambush for them, betrayed them, attacked them with violence and without warning. They plundered them at night, confiscated their possessions, drove away their flocks, stole their cattle.[2] Every prison, no matter how foul or dark, was made glorious by the noble and great-hearted protestations of saintly confessors, and even martyrs. In the common thoroughfares and crossways watchmen were abruptly posted, so that no traveller could pass peacefully on his way or escape stringent scrutiny. On the same night and at the same hour, now a single town, now several throughout the kingdom, experienced the sudden incursion of secret spies[3]: inns, taverns, lodging-houses, bed-chambers, were searched with extreme rigour, and any suspected person, unable to give a satisfactory account of himself, was put in prison or under guard until morning; or until he could clear himself before the magistrates of the suspicion that he was a Catholic, and, in particular, a Catholic priest.[4] Untrue reports were set in motion that a hostile Armada was being prepared, even approaching England; counterfeit letters were written, purporting to come from Catholics, disclosing plots against the Queen—it was the fashion to believe they planned the Queen's death.[5] Some spies, in fact, went so far as to disguise themselves as Catholics and get themselves arrested and imprisoned in order to confess their guilt and inflame the people's passion against the Catholics, and so have sharp vengence demanded on them.[6]

In London sometimes—I witnessed this myself and listened to Catholics groaning and grieving over it—a report would go round and be confirmed as certain fact, that the Queen's Council had passed a decree for the massacre of all Catholics in their houses on this or that night. Then many people would abandon their homes and lodgings and pass the night in the fields; others would hire boats and drift up and down the river.[7] And a rumour was afoot, supposed to come from the lips of Cecil himself, that he was going to take steps to reduce Catholics to such destitution that they would be incapable of helping one another and, like swine, would be grateful if they could find a husk on which to appease their hunger.[8] In fact, it appeared to me that the prophecy of our Saviour was then fulfilled, ' They will put you out of the synagogues: and whosoever killeth you will think that he doth a service to God.' [9]

I have no misgivings in not speaking here of the arrest of priests and other men, their imprisonment and violent deaths, which took place some in London, some at York, Winchester, Canterbury and other cities.[10] These events have been carefully chronicled in histories of their own, arranged in

order of time, and described in all their circumstances.[11]   It
was then that new prisons were provided and established
—at Wisbech, Ely and Reading—and for the greater part were
filled with high-born and illustrious men.   When the Queen
was asked to make the same provision for women, she is said
to have answered, ' You have had your way with the men.
Would you have me shut the women up too—like nuns in
a convent? A fine thing that would be! ' and she withheld
her consent.   Nevertheless, in Yorkshire there were public
gaols in which the wives of several men of rank were imprisoned.[12]   But this is more properly the place to say a word
about the things that happened to me at this sad time, and
to others who were affected by these trials.[13]

A gentleman I knew wished to have Mass celebrated in his
house. The outside door, therefore, was carefully barred and
the maidservant was given orders to admit nobody without her
master's explicit permission.   Meanwhile, at the top of the
house, the gentleman arranged and prepared everything for
the celebration of the holy sacrifice.   Then, calling the priest
out of his hiding-place, he put on a surplice and devoutly
served the priest's Mass. At his side lay his sword ready for
action.

Mass was almost over when the pursuivants came to the
door and started knocking.   The maidservant, forgetting
her orders, opened the door, and in they rushed. At once
she realised her mistake, and shouted at the top of her voice
that thieves had broken in.   On hearing her call, the master,
still in surplice, snatched up his sword and confronted the men
as they were coming up the stairs to the room where Mass
was going on.   He turned the sharp point on them and drove
them into the lower part of the house.   Then he shut and

barred the intervening door, ran upstairs, removed everything and tidied it away, and hid the priest in a safe place. This done, he took off his surplice and went down again to meet the men.

'Who are you? Tell me,' he said. 'What is it you want?'

'Oh, you don't seem to be the same person,' they said, and they addressed him by name. 'Where's your surplice?'

'What,' he answered, 'I in a surplice? Do you really think I'm one of those people who go about in surplices?'

Then he took out some gold, lined their palms, and sent them away.

And there was a well-born lady who sent to a priest of her acquaintance living some miles off and asked him to her house on a certain day, for she wanted him to give the sacraments to herself and her family. At the same time she begged her husband to be away from home that day, so that the priest would be at his ease in the house and be able to carry out his duties without restriction. From love of his wife—they belonged to different religions—the husband agreed to her wishes. Before he could leave home, however, there was a heavy downpour of rain and he decided to stay indoors. Meanwhile the priest, undeterred by the long journey and the rain, kept his appointment. He arrived wet through by the storm. It chanced, however, that the master himself opened the door to him. Though he guessed at once why he had come, he welcomed him kindly, invited him in and ordered a fire to be lit so that he could dry his clothes; he showed him, in fact, every mark of hospitality. Meanwhile, upstairs, the Catholic members of the household were busy arranging a room and setting out on an altar everything needed for the celebration of Mass, and at the same time were making their own preparation for Communion. But it was not easy to keep it secret. Already the master of the house suspected what was going on. He now approached the priest and asked him directly whether he might be allowed to attend Mass.

'This is a strange request,' said the priest, 'and it is not right of you to make it. Sectarians and heretics are excommunicated. They cannot be admitted to Catholic ceremonies. Sacred things must not be given to dogs.'

But the gentleman would not accept the rebuff. He argued all the more. In the end the priest yielded, for he felt that some good intention must underlie his earnest petition. Nor was his hope mistaken. When the gentleman witnessed everything, the beauty of the ceremony, the reverence of the priest, the devotion of those present, he was overcome. Whether it was terror or awe, I cannot say. But suddenly in the middle of Mass, he became faint, pallid and rigid. Then perspiration broke out all over him and he fainted. His wife ran to his help, and those near him lifted him up from the floor, rubbed his hands and helped him in every way. At last, after a long time, they restored him to consciousness. When Mass and Communion were over, the priest spoke to him.

'Now you have seen for yourself,' he said. 'You have proof from your own experience that you were not worthy to be present; you have suffered the just penalty of an excommunicated man. And you have seen too what a treacherous and uncertain thing life is, how entirely it hangs upon the will of God.'

To such an extent did the gentleman benefit from his experience and the priest's few and emphatic words that he begged the Father to remain with him for a time.

'If you do,' he said, 'I shall be able to listen to you explaining what is good and needful for my soul.'

He was, in fact, instructed in the faith and in the manner of confession. He became a most exemplary Catholic and persevered with great constancy throughout his life. On a later occasion I happened to meet him. It was when he came to visit us at Wisbech, and in his great charity brought us generous gifts.

Also about this time a memorable incident occurred, which was told me by the priest who witnessed it. He had been invited to a Catholic house to give Holy Communion. He had said Mass and was about to give Communion to those present. Among them was a small child, who had watched wide-eyed all that was taking place. At the end of Mass the child went up to his mother and caught hold of her by the dress.

' Mother, mother,' he said.

' What's the matter, child? ' she asked.

' Didn't you see?   Didn't you see? '

' See what? '

' That wonderful little baby,' he answered. ' It was so beautiful. Like nothing you have ever seen before. Uncle, [this was the priest who gave Holy Communion] Uncle put it in father's mouth. Father took it and it disappeared. Oh, what a pity! '

He kept on repeating this, or words like it, again and again saying how sorry he was that the Child was gone.[14]

It so happened that I became a close friend of a young Catholic gentleman who often used to show deep distress at his father's condition. The mother and children were Catholics and others also of the family, while the father continued outwardly to conform to the false religion, though he

knew he was wrong and was running a grave risk by openly
offending God and jeopardising his salvation. The young
man, therefore, asked me to visit his father in disguise and to
find some pretext for speaking with him on the subject of
religion.

' My father enjoys conversation of that kind,' he said, ' and
he likes the company of people who talk about religion.'

I could not refuse such a request, and so I went to call on
him. After friendly greetings and a few words on general
topics, the rest of our talk turned on religion. At the end of a
long discussion, just as I was on the point of leaving, he asked
his son who I was, and said that he would be glad if I came
often to see him. I did this, and we became close friends, and
he would invite me into his library and show me his books.
Among others he took down were Durandus, Medina and
several of the Scholastics,[15] and he would look through them
carefully on the chance of finding some passage which would
justify him in his practice of attending service in heretical
churches. Also he marked certain sentences and asked me
to read them and then solve the difficulties he had constructed
from them, and others he had thought out for himself. Sometimes, also, when he was hard pressed and found it difficult
to maintain his position, he would exclaim and say, ' Ah!
Heretics! Enemies of God! Loathsome creatures! Nothing
is sacred for them. They destroy the law and murder souls!
But never, never will I let them take my possessions from me!
Never will I put myself or my wife and children at their
mercy!'

Now I shall tell you about the end of this man's life—in
other ways he was an honourable person and had many good
qualities; and in his London house scarcely a day passed
without a visit from a priest. Besides this house, he had

another in the country, where he frequently stayed. There he kept a priest, a brother of his, so that if he was suddenly taken ill, he might have a spiritual physician at hand to minister help to his soul. On one occasion, however, when he was making his customary journey from one house to the other, he fell very sick. He was only half way, and he rested at an inn. From there he sent a fast rider to fetch his brother, the priest, from his house. But in spite of all possible haste he was dead before the priest arrived. This indeed was God's way of surprising men in their wisdom.

An almost similar incident I heard of concerned another person who kept his son, a priest, privately in his house against the danger of a sudden death. One day he left to go into a town nearby. There, just after he had heard an heretical sermon, he was seized suddenly with a fatal illness and fell down dead on the spot.[16]

NOTES

Page 31

¹ W. W., with all priests and laymen, ascribed the severe measures against Catholics, not to Elizabeth, but to Burghley and Leicester; for the Queen, as is apparent from his narrative, he had great reverence and some measure of affection. It is interesting that in this year Burghley was exercised to confute what he termed ' the slanders that England had become the *Regnum Cecilianum* '. Burghley to Herle, 14 August 1585, *C.S.P., Dom. Eliz.* (1581–90), p. 260.

² ' Thornes, in Staffordshire, hath driven away hundreds of cattle from Catholics at a time, even all that many householders had, and afterwards turned them out of their houses and kept possession against them, namely Knolles, widow Wade, George Cooke, William Poker, John Coker, Timothy Browne, Mr. Richard Fitzherbert and many others ' (*An Ancient Editor's Notebook*, p. 23, printed in Morris, *Troubles*, Series 3). This book, which consists of factual details of the persecution compiled by an anonymous Catholic probably as a rough draft of a book gives numerous examples of the various vexations described by W. W. in this paragraph. Further instances can be had from the State Papers, 1584. Typical of these cases there is that of Nicholas Tichborne. On 23 October 1585 he petitioned the Council for his release from prison: the small farm on which he made a poor living had been seized by the sheriff's men and consequently he was unable to support his wife and children who were threatened with starvation. *S.P.D., Eliz.*, vol. clxxxiii, no. 43 (3).

³ W. W. almost certainly has in mind the concerted raid made on Catholic centres in London on the night of 27 August 1584. For the occasion special search warrants were issued to at least seventeen officials, and the city divided into areas. None of the principal Catholic homes was omitted. Since many of the places searched were W. W.'s resorts, it is obvious that he is writing here, not from hearsay, but with first-hand information. The certificates of search and the reports made by each party can be read in the State Papers. *S.P.D., Eliz.*, vol. clxxii, nos. 102–115.

Page 32

⁴ So many Catholics or suspected Catholics were arrested at this time that the Justices complained that they had to prolong the sessions to the neglect of other shire business in order to deal with them. In the State Papers there is, for instance, a letter (undated, but listed in the Calendar

39

under this year, 1585) from the Clerk of the Peace in Hampshire, which bears out W. W.'s statement. ' The number of recusants which at every sessions are to be indicted ', he writes, ' is so great that the Clerk of the Peace is driven to spend not only by himself or by his deputy . . . a great deal of time before and after every sessions but also the great part of the sessions itself in drawing and engrossing the indictments, judgements, and processes thereupon . . . whereby the sessions are continued more days than heretofore they have done and almost all other causes and grievances of the shire are omitted . . . without any profit hitherto unto her Majesty by the conviction of the recusants, who are not found to have lands or goods to answer their condemnation and *also without any reformation of any of the recusants hitherto.*' *S.P.D., Eliz.*, vol. clxxxv, no. 83.

[5] In the hysteria caused by the assassination of William of Orange the people were ready to believe in any murder plot, no matter how fantastic. A number of wild statements made by irresponsible adventurers, both at home and on the Continent, were picked up by spies, reported to the Government and given the importance of plots in the popular imagination. For examples, see *C.S.P., Dom. Eliz.* (1581–90), pp. 191, 210, 348.

[6] This is probably a reference to the ' plot ' of Dr. William Parry, whose execution in February 1585 coincided with the passage through Parliament of the savage laws against priests and their harbourers. Cf. Leo Hicks, ' The Strange Case of Dr. William Parry ', in *Studies*, September 1948.

[7] Cf. Ch. 2, n. 21. These alarms, which first occurred in 1585, persisted until after the defeat of the Armada three years later. ' There went then [1588] a rumour very current among the Catholics of London that a sudden massacre of them all was intended upon the first landing of the Spaniards ' (*Life*, p. 81). Nowhere is it stated that a massacre was actually planned, nor is there any evidence that it was. Nevertheless, the fear was not unreasonable or absurd. The formation of Protestant Associations in every county in 1585 was enough to start the alarm, which was intensified by the actual or supposed threat of Leicester at the beginning of 1588 that ' by the end of the year there would be no Catholic left in the country '. *John Gerard*, p. 8.

[8] Cp. Robert Southwell: ' We are made the common theme of every railing declaimer, abused without means or hope of remedy by every wretch with most infamous names. No tongue is so foresworn but it is of credit against us: none so true but it is thought false in our defence. Our slanders are common work for idle presses. . . . If any displeasing

accident fall out, whereof the authors are either unknown or ashamed, Catholics are made common fathers of such infamous orphans, as though none were so fit sluices as they to let out of every man's sink these unsavoury reproaches.' *Humble Supplication*, pp. 40–1.

⁹ The intense persecution in the spring and summer of 1585 recurred after the ' discovery ' of the Babington Plot (cf. ch. 10, p. 80). When more research has been done on these two critical years for Catholics it may be shown that W. W. was right in surmising that the Government was forced to relax its measures in order not to upset the whole economy of the country. In a letter from the Clink on 10 May 1587, W. W. wrote: ' This sudden hurricane [of persecution] brought into instant jeopardy not merely the worldly goods of Catholics, but the security of their very lives. Although it raged several months in its mad fury and in its savagery beyond human endurance, now (so I hear) it is less severe. It is not that they are sparing any Catholic, man or woman, but simply that it is impossible for such a violent disturbance of property not to bring with it great disorder in all parts and the imminent ruin of the whole country.' Arch. S. J., Rome, *Fondo Gesuitico*, 651.

¹⁰ In this paragraph W. W. passes from the events of 1585 to the distress of Catholics in the next five or six years. Between July 1585 and December 1591 seventy-five Catholics, priests and layfolk, were hanged, drawn and quartered. Of these, seventeen suffered at York, four at Canterbury (1588) and two at Winchester (1591).

Page 33

¹¹ The principal books dealing with the persecution of Catholics in England published in the sixteenth century are Fr. John Gibbons's *Concertatio Ecclesiae Anglicanae* (1583), Allen's *Brief History of the Glorious Martyrdom of Twelve Reverend Priests* (1582), Nicholas Sander's *De Origine ac Progressu Schismatis Anglicani* (1585), Robert Persons's *De Persecutione Anglicana* (1582), and Richard Verstegan's *Theatrum Crudelitatis Haereticorum nostri Temporis* (1592). All these books went into numerous editions (there were fifteen editions, for instance, of Fr. Gibbons's book in ten years) and were translated into English, Italian, French and Spanish. In addition, two very popular books were written by Spaniards about the English persecution: Pedro de Ribadenyra's *Historia Ecclesiastica del Schisma* (1588) and Diego de Yepes's *Historia particular de la persecucion de Inglaterra* (1599). The latter is an important source for the history of the English martyr priests. In an interesting letter to Burghley, written from Venice on 10 March 1583, William Parry noted that Fr. Persons's small book

on the persecution ' had raised such a barbarous opinion of our cruelty '
that he could wish that ' it might please her Majesty to pardon the dis-
membering and quartering '. Cf. Leo Hicks, ' The Strange Case of
Dr. William Parry ' in *Studies*, September 1948.

[12] Apart from the common gaol in York where whole families were
confined, there was a special prison at Hull reserved for women recusants.
Cf. J. A. Hirst, *The Blockhouses of Hull.*

[13] About twelve months after the close of Parliament W. W. wrote
to Fr. Persons: ' I am always at work. All my time goes in writing,
in preaching, in offering Mass. From the time of that Parliament which
attempted to shatter the foundations of religion with its savage decrees,
the flow of Catholics into the Church has been greater than ever before.'
(Stonyhurst MSS., *Anglia* i, no. 28.) This was a constant reaction and
was noted also by the Government. For instance, in 1593 when the laws
against Catholics were made still more stringent, Bernard Beard, a Clerk
of the Council, wrote: ' It is said by some that for all the danger of
Catholics and their narrow sifting, infinite numbers run daily into the
Church and are reconciled to the Catholic faith. Good men, making
no account of their lives, hazard themselves to save men's souls.'
S.P.D., Eliȝ., vol. ccxlviii, no. 83.

Page 36

[14] The priest in this story was Fr. Leonard Hyde. He came from a
Catholic family at Denchworth, Berks, and after ordination at the English
College, Rome, returned to England in 1580 about the same time as
Edmund Campion. The incident, which occurred before the end of
May 1585, the date of Fr. Hyde's arrest, is narrated in the Annual Letters
for 1608 (Foley, viii, p. 984). After eighteen years in prison, he was
exiled in 1603: he then tried his vocation as a Carthusian at Mechlin,
and later sought admission to the Society a few months before his death
in 1605 or 1606. Foley, viii, p. 387.

Page 37

[15] William Durandus (d. 1296), a Bolognese canonist and the most
important of the medieval writers on the ceremonies of the Mass. Juan
de Medina (d. 1547), a Spanish writer on ethics and moral theology, who
in W. W.'s time was regarded as a great authority on these subjects.
His works were constantly reprinted in the sixteenth and seventeenth
centuries.

Page 38

[16] This gentleman was probably Mr. Pitts of Iffley. The same story is told in a paper entitled *The Relations of Mr. George Stoker and Mr. Heath concerning Martyrs* (Stonyhurst MSS., *Collectanea M*, f. 193): ' Mr. Pitts . . . being a schismatic, and having two sons Catholic priests in his house, being often desired to come to the unity of the Church, answered that he could when he would ; but as he went into Our Lady's Church at Oxford, he fell down dead.' This was in 1579. Pitts is buried in Iffley Church on the north side of the chancel. He had been a fellow of All Souls and registrar of the diocese of Oxford. Wood, *Ath. Ox.*, vol. 2, p. 585.

Throughout his *Autobiography* W. W. uses the word ' schismatic ' to describe the religious position of men like Mr. Pitts, who believed in the Catholic faith but, lacking the courage to profess it, conformed to the established worship for convenience, not from conviction. W. W. distinguishes this group of non-Catholics both from ' evangelicals' or Puritans and from ' heretics ' or convinced believers in the doctrines of the reformed Church.

5

TWO DAYS UNDERGROUND

A house where I used secretly to be given hospitality was visited once by certain Catholics, who gave a satisfactory account of themselves, both to me and to the head of the family, and said that they wished to hear Mass. After the end of Mass, when the people had left, I stayed on as usual and went upstairs to the room where I kept my books and resumed my work. Not quite two hours later the house was surrounded by a large mob of men. Whether they came on information or on chance, I do not know. But the servant rushed up to my room—I was still there—and warned me of the danger. She made me come downstairs at once and showed me a hiding-place underground; Catholic houses have several places like this, otherwise there would be no security. I got down into it, taking my breviary with me—it was all I had near me at the time, and to loiter would have been dangerous. Meantime the heretics had already made their way into the house and were examining the remoter parts. From my cave-like hide I could follow their movements by the noise and uproar they raised. Step by step they drew closer, and when they entered my room the sight of my books was an added incentive to their search. In that room also there was a secret passage-way for which they demanded the key, and as they opened the door giving on to it they were standing immediately above my head. I could hear practically every

word they said. ' Here! Look! ' they called out, ' A chalice!
And a missal! ' The things were, in fact, there. There had
been no time to hide them, and, in any case, it would have
been impossible. Then they demanded a hammer and other
tools, to break through the wall and panelling. They were
certain now that I could not be far away.

Meanwhile I was praying fervently to God that He would
avert the danger. At the same time I reflected that it would
be better to surrender myself into the enemy's hands than be
dragged out ignominiously. I believed that some Judas had
given information and betrayed me, but, to cover up the
traitor, they wanted my discovery to appear accidental, and
not the result of treachery.

While I was reflecting in this way, one of the men, either
by mistake or on purpose or at the prompting of a good angel,
shouted out: ' Why waste time getting hammers and hatchets?
There's not enough space here for a man. Look at the corners.
You can see where everything leads to. There can't be a
hiding-place here.'

They took the fellow's word for it, and the party abandoned
their plan of search and destruction. It was God's design, I
think, that they should lose all the common sense they possessed, for it was astonishing that men like this, skilled in their
task, should fail to find a place that was constructed with no
particular cunning or ingenuity. And so they gave up, tired
after their search, and went away, taking with them everything they found—the silver chalice, the missal, several books,
and I don't know what else.

The master of the house was thrown into prison, and one
or two others who belonged to the household, which was
small, since, a long time before this incident, he had been
driven from his own home and had rented part of another

house. His wife, too, was—I think—arrested, but they soon released her. She was of noble birth and, on account of her position, they did not like to handle her severely.

The whole of that day I lay in hiding, and the night and day following it as well, almost till sunset. The cellar was dark, dank and cold, and so narrow that I was forced to stand the entire time. Also I had to stay completely quiet, without coughing or making the smallest noise.[1] If they failed to find me, I thought they would probably surround the house and cut off my escape. During those long hours not a servant came to open the door and this confirmed my suspicion that the enemy was still in possession of the house. But something had to be done, otherwise the hiding-place would have become my sepulchre while I was yet alive. I climbed the ladder. For a long time I strained my ears to catch the least noise of voices or passing footsteps. But not a sound reached me. Nothing at all, though I waited for a long time. I was at the top of the ladder, and now I pressed my shoulders against the trap-door which had been shut down on me from the other side. With a great effort, and with prayers to help me, I was just able to push it open. But I was in great fear; if I used too much force, the rung of the ladder might have snapped and given way under my feet. Then it would all have been over. The fall was terrible and I would certainly have been killed.

The servant who had shut me in this place had been taken off to prison; those left behind did not know of it and had no idea what had happened to me. In the end I succeeded; but it took all my physical strength and a great effort of prayer, and for days afterwards my bones were aching.

I stood now at the top of the steps, my head and shoulders visible. There I stayed and listened. Not a sound could be heard, and I began to read the Office of the day from the breviary I had with me. Then, at last, I picked out women's voices. It was the mistress of the house and her nurse and they seemed to be in distress. I heard them calling me, and I concluded that all was safe and the house out of danger. I emerged completely now, but had there been any alarm, I could easily have pulled the door down on top of me and gone down again. As I came right out, I saw that I was covered with dust and cobwebs. I brushed myself clean and made away at once, but at great peril, for, as I heard later, watchers were standing by. Nevertheless, through the goodness of God, I escaped.[2]

NOTES

Page 46

[1] John Gerard, writing of the arrest of W. W.'s companion, Fr. Cornelius, at Chideock, says that the searchers were directed to his place of hiding by sounds of coughing (*Narrative of the Gunpowder Plot*, p. 38). All priests soon became alive to the need to remain extremely quiet during a search. Fr. Garnet, who had much experience, described how the pursuivants ' keeping absolute silence, listened for any sighs, clearing of the throat or any movement on the part of those who they thought were in the house '. Stonyhurst MSS., *Anglia*, i, f. 73.

Page 47

[2] W. W. is not sufficiently circumstantial in the account of this escape to make it possible to identify the house and family. Nor is there any indication of the time it occurred.

6

THE SHERIFF'S DAUGHTER

On another occasion God rescued me from another danger, which was just as great.

I happened to be at the house of a certain sheriff at the invitation of his son-in-law. I had been asked there to discuss religion in the presence of the sheriff's daughter and his sister-in-law, who were both well-disposed towards the faith and were anxious to become Catholics. On my arrival we sat down together—a large group of us—and began to talk on religious questions. Then suddenly a rumour went round the company—started, it was thought, by the sheriff's daughter-in-law (a Puritan)—that an old priest had just arrived at the house and was occupied in a religious discussion in such and such a room. The party, however, continued to listen to me, while my host, suspecting that a trap had been set to have me apprehended, left the room to investigate. It was then discovered that the Puritan lady had, in fact, placed watchers in different parts of the house, so that no matter where I might attempt an escape, men would be posted to arrest me.

In this moment of crisis my host, the sheriff's son-in-law, made a plan which was all but insane, yet, it must be remembered, we were in dire peril and he had little time for reflection. He decided to call together the servants, and with their help force a way for me through the middle of the house, get me safely out of reach of the pursuivants and then put me in a boat—the Thames flowed close to the house—and row me across to the far bank of the river. But he recollected himself in the nick of time, for the plan could not have been carried out without grave hazard—certainly not without violence, perhaps even murder. On second thoughts he resolved to appeal to his father-in-law the sheriff, in person, though the man was a heretic and probably also was commissioned *ex officio* to hunt down Catholics. So, making an act of confidence in God, he went and summoned the sheriff out of the room, where he was engaged in conversation, entertaining his gentlemen guests after dinner. The sheriff, however, made no movement to rise; instead, he went on talking. My host then called him a second time, asking him to hurry, for the matter was urgent. The gentlemen in the room wondered what it could be that was so pressing; the sheriff, however, left the company and came quickly over to my friend, who explained to him that his own daughter-in-law had laid a trap to catch me. I was not (he said) an old man and a priest, as she had imagined, but a young gentleman whom he knew well, making a friendly visit. I had been away several years, visiting places of interest abroad, and it was natural that other people beside himself should want to hear what I had to say about the customs of other countries. His father-in-law listened, and saw that it would be unbecoming if a treacherous action were to take place in his own house under his very eyes and to the discomfiture of his son-in-law.

By now, however, things had reached such a state that the men were actually holding me a prisoner, and another man with me. But there and then, the sheriff ordered his son to be called, asked him where his wife was, and what she was doing at this moment.

'I don't know,' answered the son. The father ordered him to fetch her. He went away and came back saying she could not be found.

'Then go immediately and find her,' said the father. 'I will take no excuses.' At last she came.

'You impudent creature,' said the sheriff. 'What's the meaning of this?' Then she told her story.

'Go at once,' he ordered. 'Call off the men on watch, and all the servants you have posted round the house.'

Then he came down himself, and with him some other gentlemen, and moving across to our room, ordered the door to be opened. I came out looking, I must say, neither the old man nor the priest. I glanced at the company, greeted them all, and was greeted in return by the sheriff. Then I made my way out. That was how I escaped. The gentleman who had asked me to come was standing by, and he turned to his father-in-law: 'Your honour,' he said, 'you can see yourself that this man is not in the least like the person he is supposed to be.'

The sheriff's daughter, however, who was the cause of my coming, was now in a grave predicament, for she was very anxious still to become a Catholic and continued to suffer a great deal from her relatives. They would snatch hold of her dress, undo her neck and look to see whether she was wearing a relic or cross or *Agnus Dei*.[1] Sometimes, too, they would insist on her eating meat on days of abstinence. But all these details I have set down for your Reverence's private reading, so that you can see for yourself how many different accidents can rise out of a single occasion, and the anxieties and troubles it may bring with it.

There is another adventure I had in London which is worth

mentioning. I happened one day to be walking by the shop of a man whom I knew to be a Catholic, and I stopped to have a word with him.

At that very moment a well-born young gentleman came up. The way he greeted me and proceeded to speak to me showed greater reverence than my dress and appearance warranted, for he knew I was a priest. Just then a pursuivant —one of those men who make mischief for Catholics— happened to be in a house on the opposite side of the street. From the extremely civil manner in which the gentleman treated me he guessed that I must be somebody out of the ordinary, and he came down from his room upstairs to see whether he could detect any sign of my being a priest; and if he did, he was going to arrest me. When he got into the road, however, he noticed that I was carrying arms and remembered that he had left his sword behind—he did not know whether he might need it and was afraid to approach me unprovided. He went back, therefore, to find it; and God granted me this short space of time for my deliverance. Our conversation came to an end, and though the young man stayed where he was, I hurried on my way, and by mere chance turned off the main street into a narrow side road. When the pursuivant came out of the house again and across to where we had been standing, I was not to be seen.

' He's gone,' he cried. ' He's slipped out of my hands. I knew he was somebody worth catching.'

' What are you shouting about? ' asked the young Catholic gentleman.

The youth recognised the pursuivant's face. He had seen him before when, on no good errand, he had been at his father's house.

' Who were you talking to? ' asked the pursuivant. ' If

he hadn't been someone unusual, you would never have treated him with the deference you did.'

The youth ignored the question. ' Look,' he said, ' there's no need for all this inquisitiveness. Get away home, and don't be so suspicious.'

Then he said good-day.[2]

Now there was a Catholic married lady whom I knew. She was expecting her confinement and had left home in order to live secretly with another Catholic lady, for she wanted to prevent her child falling into the heretics' hands and being baptised by them. I went to her house to see her. She was young and it was her first child, so I told her of the dangers to be expected in her condition, and suggested that she should go to confession and Holy Communion, to prepare for what might turn out to be the occasion of her death. She listened and decided at once to do as I told her. Assisted beforehand in this way, a day or two later she gave birth to her child very happily and with very little suffering. But after the event her nurse was careless and she caught a fatal fever. As her sickness gained on her, she asked a second time for the sacraments. Finally, her condition became so serious that Extreme Unction was necessary. As this was being administered according to the Church's rite, and to the great comfort and joy of her soul, she exclaimed, not just once or twice but repeatedly, ' I can see my soul. Yes, I can see it—all light and beauty, clearer and brighter than any crystal you can conceive—brighter than heaven itself.' She was favoured also with the vision of celestial spirits, and many times before she gave up her soul she was given such consolation and had such an impelling desire to be with God that the world and all it contained was, as she said, something without substance or worth; repellent, even, in its sordidness. Instead of being frightened by death, she stretched out to welcome it with heart and soul, for she wanted to enjoy the companionship of those holy and glorious creatures. She had no desire to be restored to health, but only to die and be wholly with Christ; and this was all she could speak about, and about the extraordinary splendour of the angels whom she had been privileged to see. She foretold, in fact, the certainty of her death and, I think, its precise moment.[3]

NOTES

Page 51

[1] *Agnus Deis*. Discs of wax impressed with a cross and the figure of a lamb and blessed by the Pope. The *Agnus Dei* is usually worn like a medal round the neck. In origin it goes back probably to the fifth century, and symbolizes Christ, the Lamb of the New Testament. The cross associated with the lamb suggests that its purpose was to protect those who wore it from evil influences as the blood of the paschal lamb protected households of the Jews from the destroying angel. Cf. *Catholic Encyclopedia* (revised edition), p. 200.

Page 53

[2] It was possibly in reference to these two escapes that W. W. wrote in his letter of 1586, ' At no hour are we certain to survive, but as we make no account of living, the expectation of death only puts an edge on our zeal. Twice very recently we almost fell into their hands, but we escaped, for God was pleased to allow their mind and eyes to be cheated. I have lost everything, but " the earth is the Lord's " and we can lack nothing we need.' Stonyhurst MSS., *Anglia*, i, no. 28.

Page 54

[3] This lady was a Mrs. Barnes. A manuscript at Stonyhurst confirms W. W.'s story and adds further details. ' Mrs. Barnes a virtuous gentle-woman died in a very strange manner, with an end answerable to a very rare life. She heard angelical harmony and departed with extraordinary comfort, herself singing with an unwonted but most sweet voice and art more than ever in life she had uttered or learned. After her death in the thick of the feather-bed there appeared so perfect a white cross as if it had of purpose been made by art, to the great admiration of all, and continued a long time.' Stonyhurst MSS., Grene, *Collectanea M*, f. 149a; cp. *An Ancient Editor's Notebook* (Morris, *Troubles*, Series 3), p. 56.

7

JOHN THE WATERMAN

It was also about the same time, I think, that this authentic story was told about a certain man who, in worldly reckoning, was a humble person, but who in God's judgment—we may well believe—was an outstanding and predestined soul. John was his name, and he earned a mean livelihood by rowing his small boat on the river Thames.[1] One day some men who looked and were dressed like merchants—so he thought—approached him. They were, in fact, common thieves. And when they asked whether they could hire his boat and services, he was glad of the chance of earning a little money. But no sooner had they got into the boat than they ordered him to row out to a ship that was lying in the river at anchor. They had chosen their time well. No watchman was on board, and they removed the merchandise from the ship unobserved, loaded it on to the small boat, and pulled off. They did their work very secretly and cleverly, and began to congratulate themselves.

God, however, who has ordered all things to work for the good of His elect, did not allow the deed to go undiscovered for long. The men were tracked down and put in prison; and so was John, for he was recognised as the man who had been with them and had provided the boat, and was consequently arrested at the same time. When they were brought to trial, the thieves pleaded guilty and were condemned to death. But John urged his case, protesting that he was innocent, that he had merely let out his boat to earn his charge of a couple of crowns. The plea, however, did not save his life. He was condemned to the same sentence as the thieves.[2]

The verdict given, they were all committed to prison. Within a few days they were to be executed. But in that very place where he expected nothing but death, he found his way to a better kind of life. In order to earn a mouthful of bread for himself, he used to carry mugs from the cells of prisoners who were locked up, to a tavern inside the prison, set up for the use and convenience of the inmates. Now a priest, who was a close prisoner in the same prison, happened to notice him.

'Where are you off to, John?' he asked. 'Why all this hurry with the mugs? A few hours and you'll be hurrying quite another way.'

'Sir,' he said, 'please give me some money, just one crown.'

'What good can a crown do you?' the priest asked. 'This time to-morrow you'll be setting out for the gallows.'

'I am hoping to be reprieved, or, at least, to have my execution postponed,' he answered. 'But I need a crown, and I haven't got one. If only my wife had the money, she could pay a lawyer to draw up a petition.'

'I understand,' said the priest. 'But you can have no idea how the law works, if you imagine all your troubles can be settled as simply as that. Get rid of your silly hopes. If I were you, I would give what time is left to thinking about my salvation in the next world.'

Then he began to explain the importance of the Catholic faith and the confession of sins, pointing out at the same time the error of all those who renounced the ancient teaching of the Apostles and the Fathers for their personal fancies and crazy dreams. John listened eagerly to all he said—and with his heart as well as his ears. Then, unburdening himself, he said, ' Tell me more, I want to know about these things.'

Accordingly the priest continued his instruction. John listened with increasing attention, and, the grace of God assisting him, he was convinced. So the priest arranged that on the next day, the date fixed for the execution, John should meet him in a certain place and make his confession. In the meantime he should examine all the thoughts and actions of his past life.

Nor was he remiss in doing exactly as he had been told. Moreover, he kept his appointment to the minute. Everything was done to the satisfaction of both. And the priest warned him that for the future he should not attend any heretical meeting or church or sermon or service that was held in contradiction to the teaching and practice of the Catholic Church. John pledged his word to obey.

When the time for execution came, the criminals were summoned to a sermon and to receive communion before they were led off to the gallows. The other poor men submitted without protest. John was the only one who stayed behind. An order was sent for him to appear. He refused. They sent a second time. Again he refused. They tried to cajole him, then they commanded him, threatened him.

' Get away,' he said. ' I'll have nothing to do with your religion. In the course of my life I've practised it enough. No, more than enough. But it has done me no good. You can use force if you like, but you can't make me go of my own free choice. I'm not one of yours. Take those who want your religion and ask for it, but leave me alone. I'm not coming.'

They saw his resolution and realising that both threats and tricks had failed, they left him and went through the heretical service with the rest.

When it was over, all of them, including John, were led out to the gallows. The others died heretics, as they had lived. But before the rope was placed round John's neck, an evangelical Minister urged him to stir up a strong faith within himself and to bear testimony to it. But John answered that he would have no truck with their belief. In his great blindness of heart, he said, he had professed it right up to this day. But now he was full of sadness and remorse at this. He was a Catholic now, and in the Catholic faith he would die. He held it for a certainty that in that faith, and in no other, was salvation and eternal life to be sought and found. Moreover, he was altogether innocent of the crime brought against him; he knew nothing of the snare that had been laid for him; he had let out his boat with the sole purpose of doing a job and earning a livelihood in the way he had chosen to earn it from his boyhood.

'Now leave me alone,' he said. 'Don't harass me further. I am innocent. I die a Catholic. You are wasting your efforts if you go on trying to convert me.'

But the Minister, and others who were with him, continued talking a great deal. They promised to pardon and grant him his life, if he would change his mind on his religion. But their efforts were unavailing. He remained steadfast and full of courage, and persevered unto death, carrying away a double crown of innocence and of faith.[3]

NOTES

Page 56

1 Before coaches became the common means of transport, the Thames was the principal highway between the Tower and Westminster. John Taylor, the London ferryman and poet, conjectured that ' the number of watermen, and those that lived and were maintained by them, and by the labour of the oar and scull, betwixt the bridge of Westminster and Gravesend, could not be fewer than 40,000.' *Shakespeare's England*, vol. 2, p. 154.

Page 57

2 At this time persons accused of even ordinary felonies were not allowed the assistance of counsel. At the Guildhall, moreover, juries were notoriously prejudiced and the administration of criminal law more brutal than in any other place in the realm. *Shakespeare's England*, vol. 1, p. 170.

Page 59

3 In his *Historia Provinciae Anglicanae* (lib. 4, s. 16), Fr. Henry More tells the same story, and adds, without giving his authority, that the priest who instructed and received John was W. W. himself.

8

A TRAIL OF SINGING CAKES[1]

I have not been able to discover for certain whether it is at this time or a little later that I should place the following incident. It occurred to Father John Cornelius during the celebration of Mass, and it is this.

A certain nobleman had fallen from the profession of his faith and with considerable remorse of conscience had persisted in error for a number of years. Eventually he became fatally ill. Fully realising in his last moments the extent to which he needed a priest's assistance in order to obtain forgiveness of his sins and receive the last viaticum, he commanded a reliable servant to seek high and low for a priest and bring him to his bedside. The servant searched everywhere; he did all he could, but still he failed to find one. It was certainly a case for pity, and the nobleman's suffering was greatly intensified, since the peril of his eternal salvation caused him far greater anxiety than his imminent death. However, he did what was in his power—more he could not do. He called together his whole family, and in their presence he made a public profession of the Catholic faith. He asked them to be his witnesses in the day of judgment, that he repented of his faithlessness and his fall into error; that he was a Catholic and wished to die one; and that there was no way, outside this faith, of saving one's soul.

While he was making this speech, or shortly after it, he breathed his last.

Some days later, while Father John was celebrating Mass in the house of Sir John Arundell (his wife was the mother of the gentleman who had just died), the man appeared to him, completely encircled in flames.[2] The priest recognised him by his bald head which was clearly visible in the midst of the fire—his baldness extended to the crown of his head—and asked him why he was in this state and what he wanted. The man explained who he was, and said he was suffering greatly, but hoped nevertheless for salvation. He begged the priest's prayers, and the prayers of all those present. Then he disappeared. I cannot recall exactly whether or not those present at Mass were said to have heard low and muffled voices and seen on the altar an object which shone with extraordinary brightness. But the Father did tell them of his vision, to make them pray more fervently for his soul; and he also explained how, when the man had given up hope of finding a priest, he had confessed all his sins to a faithful servant exactly as he would have done in confession.[3]

Once, a certain Catholic asked me to go to the house of his father, who was a schismatic. On the road we called at several Catholic homes, and in my own poor way I did what I could to help them. I encouraged them and I gave them the sacraments, for this was our work.

After our arrival we spent several days in the house without any noticeable benefit; I mean, as far as the purpose for our visit went. But during my stay I got to know a certain gentleman—his home was nearby—and we became friends. I gained his confidence, and it transpired that he had once been a Catholic, but had fallen away through the strain of circumstances. His physical strength was now beginning to fail, and he was much afraid that if he did not take the opportunity my presence offered, he would not merely lose his life, but his eternal salvation as well. He decided, therefore, to throw aside all his anxiety and fears; he would beg God's mercy, put his trust in Him, return to the Church, and confess his faith steadfastly. With this in mind he called me over to his house: or, rather, I think I went of my own accord and uninvited, not once but several times, always looking for a suitable place and occasion for my purpose.

His wife, however, was an uncommonly inquisitive lady. She kept a close watch on all his actions and on all the people he saw. She had, I think, some suspicion of her husband's intention, and was afraid he would jeopardise all his possessions—his wife, his property, his entire family—making wreck of them all. Consequently she would not let him out of her sight. She followed him everywhere to prevent him taking any such rash step.

Nevertheless the man stood resolute. When he saw that nothing could be done in his own house because of the difficulties made by the wilfulness of his wife and her perverseness, he found some pretext for making a visit of courtesy to my friend, a man of wealth and breeding like himself. He was thus able to see me, and while we were walking in the garden I heard his confession, for this seemed the best way of averting the suspicion that was bound to arise if we had a long conversation together in a room apart. It was this that had caused his anxiety—there were busybodies all around and he had a large household, both men and women.

So in this way he made his confession. We were both satisfied, and we gave the remainder of our time to planning some means whereby he might be able to receive the Sacra-

ment of the Eucharist. Though it proved most difficult, he
would not let the matter drop on that account. Neither his
own house nor my host's was suitable, and every other place
we considered had its inconveniences. In the end, we arranged to meet at a nearby market town—barely three miles
away—and we decided on a certain inn for the purpose. With
my host's son to keep me company, I set out for the town on
horseback—I had said Mass in the house in the early morning
and had placed the Blessed Sacrament in a pyx which I carried
suspended round my neck.

On entering the inn, we chose the best room we could find.
It was large and fairly well furnished. Then, on the pretext
of being engaged on some business, we spent the time, almost
till mid-day, walking backwards and forwards from the
market-place, waiting for the gentleman. When the time
was up, and he had sent no message to say that he had been
delayed or prevented from coming, and there was still no sign
of him, I told my companion to prepare to receive Holy
Communion. He just had time to do this when, the very next
moment, a man knocked violently on the door of the room.
I enquired who was there. There was no reply. He knocked
a second time, more violently. My companion was still on
his knees, making his thanksgiving to God. I opened the
door. And there stood a most unwelcome guest—a
pursuivant.

Immediately the thought crossed my mind: what evil
demon has driven you here? For I saw the badge of his office
fastened, as usual, on his breast. Then I enquired what he
wanted, expecting only that he would seize hold of me and
take me prisoner.

'I am looking for a suitable lodging for the King,' he
said, 'and this is the best room in the whole house.'

I was surprised to hear him mention the word king—I had heard of no new king. The Queen was still alive. So I asked him what king he meant.

'Antonio,' he said, 'the King of Portugal. He has been forced in here on his way from France. He is making straight for court.' [4]

And he added, 'If you wish, you can stay where you are. We will find another room for him.'

'We will be glad,' I said, 'to make way for such an important guest. Besides, we shall be leaving in a few hours in any case, as soon as our business is done.'

Then he wrote the king's name on the door of the room, and went away.

Meanwhile a messenger arrived from the man who had made the appointment with us, explaining the reason why he had been unable to join us at the agreed time and place. He had had a sudden and violent attack of bleeding in the nose which had left him utterly weak and exhausted. But he asked us to come on market-day the week following and he would certainly be there, if Providence did not prevent him. The week passed. We all assembled. We did quickly what we had come for; and then went our way again.

On this journey an incident occurred which brought us into considerable danger. It used sometimes to happen that in Catholic houses there were no altar-breads for celebrating Mass, and for that reason the principal benefit of our ministry was lost, for we could neither celebrate Mass nor distribute Holy Communion. As a precaution against this inconvenience, I thought it would be well to obtain some altar-breads and carry them about with me. As we had no suitable case to put them in, my companion arranged them and wrapped them up, quite securely as he thought, in a linen cloth which he happened to have with him. With the constant jogging of the horse, however, they shook their way out and gradually, first three or four, then a large number dropped out and lay scattered on the public road for the space of nearly half a mile. We did not notice the accident until we had turned off the narrow road into the open country fields, for our entire way had lain between deep banks and hedges on both sides. But the wind was blowing strongly now. It lifted the altar-breads high into the air and scattered them over the fields. Only then did we notice the mishap. At once we realised the danger. We had to come to a quick decision, and with some risk to ourselves we did what we judged best. As I was riding the faster horse, I galloped back to the spot where they had begun to fall, and started gathering them up. My friend did the same, quickly collecting the rest that had fallen intermittently on the stretch of road between us. In this way, with God's help, we completed the task. Had we left them to lie there under the eyes of all passers-by, the Catholics of the neighbourhood would have been in considerable danger, and there would have been a hot and close pursuit for us, particularly as the altar-breads had not fallen in deserted and lonely lanes, but along a village street and by the cottages of country workers. About twenty or more lay in a single heap in front of the door of a house which, as I was told afterwards, belonged to the parson of the village. It was a piece of good fortune for us that it happened at harvest time when nearly everyone was out-of-doors working in the fields.[5]

NOTES

[1] 'Singing cakes' was the contemporary Catholic word for altar-breads.

Page 62

[2] The nobleman in this story was John, ninth Baron Stourton, one of the twenty-four noblemen who condemned Mary Queen of Scots at Fotheringhay. He died on 13 October, 1588. After his father, the eighth baron, had been condemned for murder and hanged in March 1567, his mother married Sir John Arundell of Lanherne. Their chaplain was Fr. Cornelius, and it was in their house in Clerkenwell that this incident took place. *Complete Peerage* (ed. 1896), pp. 254-5.

[3] W. W.'s account of Fr. Cornelius's vision is based on hearsay: an eye-witness, Dorothy Arundell, half-sister of the deceased Lord Stourton, gives more details. ' One day my mother, Lady Arundell, begged Father Cornelius to offer up Mass for the soul of her son John, Lord Stourton, which he consented to do. When at the altar he remained a considerable time in prayer between the consecration and the memento for the dead. After Mass he made an exhortation on the words, *Beati mortui qui in Domino moriuntur,* and then told us that he had just seen a vision. Before him was presented a forest of immense size, in which all was fire and flame, and in the midst he perceived the soul of the deceased Lord. . . . Father Cornelius wept much in relating his vision to us, and all the household, who to the number of about eighty persons were listening to him, united their tears with his. The server of the Mass [John Carey], afterwards a sufferer for the faith with Father Cornelius, saw and heard all that passed in the vision; but as for myself and the rest of those present, we only perceived, while it was manifested, a glimmering reflection like that of live coals on the wall against which the altar stood.' Dorothy Arundell, *MS. Life of Fr. Cornelius.* Cf. Foley, iii, p. 445.

Page 65

[4] This curious encounter would have occurred at the end of May 1586, when Don Antonio, the pretender to the throne of Portugal reached London from the Netherlands (*C.S.P., Simancas* (1580-6), p. 582). Antonio, who was played as a pawn by Elizabeth in her dealings with Spain, was alarmed at this time because the Queen appeared anxious to come to terms with Spain (*ib.,* p. 584). He was now hurrying to London to get printed a book full of arguments ' to lead the Queen to aid him with 10,000 men for the recovery of Portugal ', *ib.,* p. 589.

Page 66

[5] Presumably this was the hay harvest in June, and not the corn harvest of August, for the next incident W. W. recalls is his meeting with Fr. Garnet and Fr. Southwell, which took place in July 1586. We know that W. W. was in Bucks with Richard Bold in June (cf. *inf.*, p. 95) and it is likely, therefore, that the singing cakes incident occurred in the Chilterns. Cf. *C.Sc.P.*, vol. viii, p. 699.

9

MASS AND MADRIGALS

Some days after I had got back from this journey, I was told that two of our Fathers had arrived in London. This news made me very happy. Although the persecution at this time was very severe [1]—many were executed, houses sacked, and through the length and breadth of the entire kingdom Catholics were hunted down and imprisoned—still it was a great consolation to me, in the midst of all these anxieties, to have faithful and brave companions in my perils.[2] So, putting everything aside, I went at once to the inn where they were staying.

They were Fathers Henry Garnet and Robert Southwell. We greeted one another and embraced, and had dinner together at the same place.[3] The following day—there was no security at all in London, either at inns or private houses—we left the city, and went out nearly thirty miles to the home of a Catholic gentleman, a close friend of mine.[4] His household was delighted at our arrival and so pleased to see us that, as it turned out, we could not have desired or imagined a more affectionate or cordial reception. This man had once attended the royal court and had been given over to courtly interests. He had been, if I am not mistaken, chamberlain to the Earl of Leicester, whose position at the time was paramount.[5] At least, he was one of his intimates, loved by him and in his highest favour. But while still a young man he had grown very weary of this life. Being then familiar, to some extent, with Catholicism, he was aware that the manners and corruption of the court were in complete contradiction to the sincere and upright life which the Faith inspired. He determined, therefore, to break with it altogether, to leave the court and find some place where he could live in the manner of a solitary, far removed from worldly splendour and remote from all enticements to sin. He knew, of course, that he could not do this without running counter to the wishes of the Earl—there was no detail of his life, however secret and hidden, that he did not know—yet he placed the salvation of his soul before any temporal hazard. He thought it best to be resolute and make the break once and for all, since he realised he could not dally without serious danger, perhaps irremediable hurt to his soul. So, with his wife, family and servants, he settled in a country mansion well out of the city and away from the crowds. However, he made it an open house for all priests and Catholics who passed that way.[6]

This change of life gave deep offence to the Earl of Leicester —nor was it surprising, considering the kind of person he was. Offence, perhaps, is too mild a word. He became completely hostile. Fired with hatred, he treated the matter almost as a crime, something which he could not overlook without exacting reprisal. Nor did this fail to follow. A short time afterwards, when the plot to kill Mary, Queen of Scots was contrived, this Catholic gentleman's entire establishment was overturned; and, with his wife and several members of his household, he was taken off to the Marshalsea prison in London. Sentence of death would certainly have been pronounced against him had not the Earl's unexpected death —brought about, it was said, by poison administered by his wife—removed the enemy from the scene.[7] When this

happened, contrary to everybody's expectation, the fierceness
of the persecution against this gentleman, our host, relaxed,
and he was released from prison. The remainder of his life
was spent partly in Ireland, in exile from his country and
friends.[8]

On reaching this gentleman's house, we were received, as
I said before, with every attention that kindness and courtesy
could suggest. We met also some gentlewomen who had
come there to hide; and altogether we were eight days at the
house. We were very happy, and our friends made it
apparent how pleased they were to have us. Indeed, the place
was most suited to our work and ministrations, not merely
for the reason that it was remote and had a congenial household
and company,[9] but also because it possessed a chapel, set
aside for the celebration of the Church's offices. The gentleman was also a skilled musician, and had an organ and other
musical instruments, and choristers, male and female, members
of his household. During those days it was just as if we were
celebrating an uninterrupted octave of some great feast.[10]

Mr. Byrd, the very famous English musician and organist,
was among the company. Earlier he had been attached to
the Queen's chapel, where he had gained a great reputation.
But he had sacrificed everything for the faith—his position, the
court, and all those aspirations common to men who seek
preferment in royal circles as means of improving their
fortune.[11]

Father Garnet sometimes sang Mass,[12] and we took it in
turns to preach and hear confessions, which were numerous.
Nearly the whole of the morning passed in this way. (I
should mention also that we had with us the domestic chaplain,
a man who deserved well of this distinguished and saintly
family, for not long afterwards he became a most illustrious

martyr of Christ.[13])   The afternoons we gave to other business
and to conferences. The new arrivals explained the instructions
they had brought from our Father General in Rome,[14] and,
on my side, I told them what I knew about conditions in
England.   Then we discussed our future methods of work
and the prospects that lay before us.[15]

Thus, during these days, we talked together on questions
of this kind. Then I gave them the names of Catholic houses
where they might go and make their residence, and arranged
for reliable guides to take them there.[16] I myself went off
immediately to Oxford. An urgent call had come from a
family that was in great distress and needed comfort and
whatever advice and assistance I could give. This done, I
started back for London. But half way there, I spent the
night at the house of a Catholic gentleman. I knew him well,
and his whole family, and his place was most suited for a
project I had been turning over in my mind for some time.
It was to withdraw a few days from my ordinary work and
dealings with people and devote myself without distraction
to prayer. This would enable me to refresh my spirit, exhausted as it was after such unremitting occupation and
anxieties, for now I could leave my business a short time to
the hands of the two Fathers.[17]

With such a perfect house for the purpose, I decided not
to let the opportunity slip, for the mansion was very remote,
situated in the middle of a park stocked with rabbits and deer,
a delightful place with pleasant fields and woodlands.[18] But
God had not destined me for this lovely and enchanting
retreat, but for another which was to prove better suited to
prayer and spiritual exercises of every kind, and which, also,
was to endure longer.

This is what happened. The second or third day after

my coming, two Catholics arrived and informed me that I must leave at once for London. Some people were waiting to see me and there was business to be done. They themselves did not know what it was, but they mentioned the name of the house where I would be told everything I needed to know about the people and their business. So I set out the next day, hoping I would be able to return in a short time. The two men kept me company. They were both of them gentlemen and Catholics of distinction—in fact, we all knew them as honourable and trustworthy men. It is my duty to say that, lest anyone conclude wrongly that I was in any way the victim of their fraud or double-dealing.

On reaching London I bade them good-bye, and set out immediately for the house where I was to get information about the people who had asked for me.[19] On the way I frequently looked behind to see whether I was being followed by any suspicious-looking person. Then, as I was approaching the house, I saw a man chasing after me;[20] but as he had no sword or weapon of any kind, there was no reason, I thought, to fear him. I knocked at the house, and as I stopped for a moment in front of the door, he turned and brought his hand down on my shoulder.

' In the Queen's name,' he said, ' I arrest you.'[21]

' Take care,' I retorted, ' and be sure you're not making a mistake. Why on earth should you think I am the person you're after? '

' I am making no mistake. You're the man I want. Your name is Edmunds,' he said, ' the priest and Jesuit.'

' Well, you are right so far,' I said, ' but where's your warrant to arrest me? Let me see it. If you have no warrant, I am no prisoner of yours.'

He put his hand into his jerkin and pulled out a sheet of

paper containing the names of a large number of Catholics, who, I think, were listed for arrest. My name was not one of them.[22]

' This warrant,' I said, ' gives you no authority whatever. My name's not on it. If you have got nothing better than that to produce, I have every right not to give myself up.'

While we were disputing, a butcher passed along the road driving two oxen in front of him; I think he was taking them to slaughter. There were only a few houses in the street, though it was near the city, and a few other buildings. The butcher saw us arguing. He guessed what it was about, and told me to submit to authority, otherwise he would lay me out on the ground with the stick he carried on his shoulder.

In the middle of all this, an old woman came and opened the door of the house—she had heard me knock, but she was in time only to see me being taken off. In fact, she was the solitary witness of the incident, and consequently she was forced later to appear at my examination together with the owner of the house. But, as far as I could learn, she suffered no harm, although if they had actually taken me in they would not have escaped. Indeed, it had been my constant prayer to God that when the time came for me to be taken by my enemies, no one should suffer hurt on my account.

Page 69

[1] In the first six months of this year seven priests, all of them secular clergy trained at Douai, had been condemned for their priesthood and executed at Tyburn, York, and in the Isle of Wight. On Ladyday Margaret Clitheroe had been pressed to death at York for ' harbouring priests '. But the special severity described by W. W., as we can now see from documents (cf. *C.R.S.*, vol. 2, pp. 241 sq.), was due to the systematic clearance of the London prisons, which began in June, to prepare the way for the ' discovery ' of the Babington Plot in August. It is not surprising that W. W. did not realise either at the time or later what was happening, for the truth about the Babington Plot only began to leak out to the public, and then only to a very limited extent, in 1590.

[2] Garnet and Southwell embarked at Boulogne on 6 July. A more unpropitious day could scarcely have been chosen. It was the day that Anthony Tyrrell, who had attached himself to W. W. during the previous month, offered his services to Burghley as a spy only two days after his capture. On the 6th also the Government ordered a general search of Catholic houses and a special watch to be kept on the ports. Finally it was the day that Anthony Babington, as was alleged, wrote the famous letter to Mary, Queen of Scots, designed to involve her in the Plot. On this last point it is worth noticing here that Southwell, who began in 1590 to get inside and largely reliable information, learned and believed that this critical letter ' was brought him ready penned by Pooley from Master Secretary [Walsingham] ' (*Humble Supplication*, p. 21). If this indeed is true, it would explain the mystery that so puzzled Fr. Pollen, as to how the dilettante Babington, who was so easy-going and so disliked handling ciphers, was able to decipher Mary's letter and compose, encipher and send off his long reply in one day.

[3] This was probably on 13 July (cp. p. 77, n. 10). After dinner at the inn W. W. removed Garnet and Southwell for the night to his own lodging, probably the house lent him by his friend, Mrs. Francis Browne, in Hog Lane, on the boundaries of Bishopsgate and Shoreditch. The same night or next morning Babington called—it was the last time he saw W. W. His statement to Walsingham—' I myself might have seen them [Garnet and Southwell] '—suggests that the two priests were in another room while W. W. was having the conversation with Babington which he describes in ch. 12. It was on this day, the 13th, that Poley, who was keeping close on Babington's tracks, had been ordered by Walsingham to discover the whereabouts of the newly arrived Jesuits. It is to the

credit of Babington, who had come to seek W. W.'s advice, that he did not inform Walsingham of this encounter until the 19th, by which time all three Jesuits were in comparative safety in the country (cf. p. 77, n. 10).

⁴ Richard Bold of Bold, near Prescot, Lancashire.

⁵ Richard Bold appears to have joined Leicester's household some time after 1577. Between 1584 and 1586 he changed his residence from Lancashire to a house two miles upstream from Marlow, on the borders of Bucks and Berks, at a place described as Harlesford (*Stanley Papers*, vol. ii, p. 191). By the reckoning of Leland's *Itinerary* Harlesford or Hurley would be exactly thirty miles from London. *C.Sc.P.*, vol. viii, p. 699; Lodge, *Illustrations*, vol. 2, p. 449.

Page 70

⁶ Bold, who had been sheriff of Lancashire in 1576, was probably an example of a border-line squire like Richard Shireburn of Stonyhurst, a Catholic at heart but conforming for expediency. In a list (1582) of suspected Catholics in his house there is a ' Richard Smith, priest '; and it was reported that Catholics flocked to his mansion for Mass ' at such time as other men were in church '. In 1584, however, when the Protestant Association was formed under the Earl of Leicester's leadership, Bold joined with nine other Lancashire gentlemen. Cf. J. S. Leatherbarrow, *The Lancashire Elizabethan Recusants*, passim.

⁷ All Catholic sources are agreed that Leicester, a wholly unprincipled man, developed a fierce hostility to particular Catholics, like Richard Bold and Christopher Blount, whose loyalty he had once possessed. Bold himself was found guilty of treason without solid ground. He was presumably released in September the following year, after Leicester's death. Cf. *inf.*, ch. 11.

Page 71

⁸ Bold had returned to Lancashire by 1590 (*C.R.S.*, vol. 4, p. 202). He may have been one of those ' sundry English Catholics ' who were reported as having crossed to Ireland in 1592. He died in 1602. His family remained Catholic for many generations.

⁹ W. W. was familiar with many Catholics in this area who probably formed part of the company gathered to greet Garnet and Southwell. Apart from William Byrd who lived at Harlington, there may well have been present Sir George Peckham of Denham, a brother-in-law of Fr. John Gerard and a cousin of Richard Bold's; James Gardiner of Fulmer, a ' receiver of priests ', whose sister was a friend of the Queen;

Lord Compton from Wooburn, who is mentioned by Tyrrell as a man 'greatly influenced' by W. W.; William Fitton of Bailes, who had been recently reconciled with his family: he exchanged letters with Byrd on the subject of music and was arrested with Bold in the following September.

[10] Robert Southwell says that he was hoping 'we should have sung Mass with all solemnity accompanied by choice instrumental and vocal music, on the feast of St. Mary Magdalen (22 July). This however was put off until the next day, and I could not spend it there, being called elsewhere.' W. W.'s 'octave', therefore, can be dated 15–23 July 1586.

[11] William Byrd was engaged at this time in setting to music the poems contained in his *Psalms, Sonets and Songs of Sadness and Piety*. He was not struck off the roll of the Queen's chapel, as W. W. suggests, but he certainly suffered for his religion. This meeting was the beginning of a life-long friendship between Garnet, a keen musician, and Byrd; and probably gave Southwell, the poet, the chance of making himself familiar with the new forms of English verse, which were then current in manuscript form. Cf. E. H. Fellowes, *William Byrd*; Morris, *Two Missionaries*, pp. 141–5.

[12] One of Byrd's three Masses might well have been sung on this occasion; it is impossible to date their composition. Cf. E. H. Fellowes, *William Byrd*, p. 53.

Page 72

[13] This was Robert Dibdale, who was executed on 8 October following this meeting. He was a close friend of W. W.'s and had practised exorcisms with him at Sir George Peckham's house at Denham, where he had been chaplain until the place was searched in June 1586. He then moved to another house in the same area, probably, as W. W.'s narrative suggests, that of Mr. Bold, who had recently settled at Harlesford. Cf. J. H. Pollen, *Lives of English Martyrs*, vol. 1, pp. 234–50.

[14] The instructions, dated 24 March, 1586, are printed in the Appendix to the *Letters and Memorials of Fr. Robert Persons* (C.R.S., vol. 39, p. 355). They provide for the appointment of Garnet as Superior should W. W. be captured, state the extent of the faculties given for confession, etc., and conclude: 'If it should become necessary to flee the country, they may go wherever they please; but they are not to go to Scotland, except after consultation with our Fathers there, nor to Ireland, except after consulting Fr. Weston.'

[15] It is difficult to exaggerate the importance of this conference,

Plans were here made for covering the whole country with Catholic centres. ' There are three or four counties together ', wrote a priest to Allen on 23 July, ' as yet unfurnished with priests . . . the tops have been left and only the lower boughs dealt with ' (*S.P.D.*, *Eliz.*, vol. cxci, no. 26). Ten years later, in spite of Government attempts to shatter the system, the plans laid by W. W. at this conference had provided in every county a network of Catholic establishments served by more than three hundred priests.

¹⁶ Garnet went either to Harrowden, Lord Vaux's seat in Northants, or to Mrs. Brooksby's, Vaux's daughter, at Shoby in Leicestershire to organise centres in neglected counties; Fr. Southwell went to Vaux's house at Hackney to provide for the priests coming into England from the seminaries and despatch them to centres established by Garnet. In the next ten years scarcely a single priest entering England was not assisted in this way (cf. *John Gerard*, p. 221). It was a natural development of the work initiated by W. W. and Lord Vaux in the crisis of March 1585 (cf. *sup.*, p. 28, n. 3). The Jesuits both at this time and later were on the terms of the friendliest co-operation and understanding with the seminary priests (apart from a few renegades) who gladly accepted their unofficial leadership until the appointment of an archpriest in 1598. Hitherto there had been chaos. Priests coming into England, without any station to go to, had drifted into London where more often than not they had been picked up by spies and imprisoned.

¹⁷ It is a fine tribute to the work done by W. W. that, in spite of the failure and indiscretion of some of the early Jesuits in England, Garnet in his first letter after this meeting was able to write: ' So high is the opinion our friends have of the Society that we are forced to hide the fact that we are members of it, lest the whole of Jerusalem be disturbed.' Garnet to Aquaviva, 30 July, 1586. Arch. S. J. Rome, *Fondo Gesuitico*, 651.

¹⁸ Nicholas Berden, one of Walsingham's cleverest spies (cf. *C.R.S.*, vol. 21, pp. 66–93), complained on 21 July that W. W. had been allowed to escape from the house of Mrs. Francis Browne at Henley Park. Evidently Berden was wrong on this occasion, for W. W. was then at Mr. Bold's with Garnet and Southwell. Fr. Morris (*Two Missionaries*, p. 146) presuming that Henley Park (four miles from Guildford on the Surrey-Sussex border) was at Henley, Oxon, makes it the place of W. W.'s retreat. It was probably at Bradenham, four miles north-west of High Wycombe, that W. W. rested. This was the seat of Lord Windsor, the brother of W. W.'s close friend, Edward Windsor, who was later arrested in connection with the Babington Plot.

Page 73

[19] This may have been the house in Hog Lane, close to Bishopsgate, which had been lent to W. W. by Mrs. Francis Browne. W. W. was reported to be living there in May 1586.

[20] This would be John Sheppard, the keeper of the Clink (cf. *inf.*, p. 140). Berden, who was with him, was the man who recognised W. W. but he kept out of sight, for he was not known to be a Government agent and continued for some time after this to masquerade as a devout Catholic. Eventually his treachery was exposed, and with the intention of entering ' a more public way of life ', sought and obtained through Walsingham's favour the office of purveyor of poultry to the Queen. *C.S.P., Dom. Eliz.* (1581–90), pp. 468, 478.

[21] W. W. was captured on 3 August outside Bishopsgate, where Berden and Sheppard were lying in wait to arrest Babington and Ballard who, at that moment, were hiding in Poley's house in the same area. W. W. may be right in saying there was no double-dealing. Certainly the letter of Francis Mills, Walsingham's principal agent, reporting W. W.'s arrest, makes it clear that it was unplanned. ' One thing this afternoon, about five of the clock, is fallen out besides our expectation. Berden and Sheppard, the Keeper of the Clink, being together here about Bishopsgate espied Edmonds, the Jesuit, and he was presently arrested by Sheppard alone . . . his weapon being taken from him.' Ballard was arrested in Bishopsgate the following day. *C.S.P., Mary Queen of Scots*, vol. xix, no. 14.

Page 74

[22] These were all Babington conspirators, and included many of W. W.'s friends and acquaintances. *C.R.S.*, vol. 2, p. 253.

10

DAYS OF DISTRESS

I was arrested, then, in the way I have described. But instead of putting me at once into prison, they shut me up in a private house opposite the common gaol. There they locked me behind several doors, and gave out that I was a Puritan. This was to be my abode for a number of weeks. No examination took place and no indictment was framed against me.[1]

The principal agent responsible for my arrest was a certain person who held a minor office at court.[2] He was by nature a cunning man and had a considerable talent for deception. Fairly closely attached to Secretary Walsingham, he served him in the capacity of spy and from time to time received from him, so it was said, large sums of gold and silver to expedite his work. He had wormed his way into the intimacy of a group of Catholics who lived in and about London, and used often to entertain them at his house with lavish hospitality. Thus he came to be accepted by their society on terms of intimacy, and they considered him an honourable and religious man. When they went to Mass, the sacraments or sermons, he would keep them company. He knew exactly what to do, and no suspicion fell on him.[3]

By these Catholic practices, then, and by his friendship with men of fine character, he had won esteem, and, turning it to advantage, attached himself to me. He was anxious for me to treat him with much greater familiarity than I wished, and he made such fulsome promises and put himself so completely at my service that I began to form suspicions of him. His house, rooms, keys and chests—he offered them all to me and gave me free access to them. Whether at home or away, he gave me to understand that if ever I was in danger or times were difficult, I could seek a safe refuge in his house. If I should want to send letters or money abroad, he had no doubt at all that he would be able to arrange for their despatch from any part of the coast.[4] These wild and extravagant promises, as I was perfectly aware, could never have been made with sincerity by any good Catholic—it was not in his power, when the country was so disturbed and hostile, to promise or even attempt such things, still less accomplish them. So gradually I began to keep the man at a distance, and, as far as I could, prevent him seeing me—although, of course, I knew that such action gave me no guarantee of safety. Even so, I could not keep aloof for long without his demanding to know with great insistence the reason why I was avoiding him. It was very clear that he was offended; and his attentions to me began to cool. What harm he later contrived against me I am unable to say. But it was commonly said that this was the man who betrayed me; that ten days before they captured me he had stationed secret watchers for me at the London gates, and had given them a personal description of me,[5] so that they could arrest me as I came by. And that was, in fact, what happened.[6]

But to return to my story. They imprisoned me in a room by myself, and for greater security shut in a guard with me. After two or three nights, at midnight, I heard the bells pealing all over the city. As this was most unusual, I asked my guard the reason for the bells. The city, he said, was celebrating the capture of certain Papists—traitors who had made a dastardly plot to assassinate the Sovereign and to bring in the Queen of Scots. They were going to declare her rightful heir, and to storm and fire the city of London. They had schemed, also, to make the Jesuit Edmunds—meaning me, for I was then called Edmunds—bishop of the city.[7]

' A ghastly plot,' he said, ' but God has brought down these machinations on the heads of its leaders.'

Then he named several gentlemen I knew and claimed that they were responsible for the plot. It was easy, of course, to see that a great deal of what he said was completely fictitious, but I felt certain that at the centre of it all there had been some kind of conspiracy.[8] And I knew that the heretics would turn it to their utmost advantage and, unless Providence intervened, would use it without any scruple whatever to persecute Catholics with extreme severity, perhaps even bring them to utter ruin.[9] This made me forget the fate awaiting me personally which, I thought, could be only death in a most brutal form. Our cause was in peril, and every kind of anxious thought troubled the peace of my soul. I knew the extent to which hatred of the Catholic faith inflamed the heretics. Nothing was to be hoped for at their hands, except lies and deceit and savagery of every sort; no mercy at all for any person or object. Now that they possessed this pretext—it did not matter to them whether it was genuine or false or, as it was later proved, actually fabricated by themselves—they would go on raging in their mad frenzy against Catholics.

My mind was rent by the tumult of these reflections. And so the night passed. The morning came, and a sadder day.

On one side of my room was the public road. On the other,

the river Thames.[10]   Throughout that day and, I think, for several days that followed, great crowds gathered in the street cheering and making merry. They piled up masses of wood and set fire to them, then stood around, talking wildly all the time against the Pope, the King of Spain, against Catholics and the Queen of Scots; and, not least, as you can guess, against the Jesuits. I listened to all this and watched it through my window, for they lit a bonfire just below it; and I could not help a feeling of sorrow for them, and of distress at our own straits.[11]

On the other side of the river the sight was more terrible still. Catholics, tied hand and foot, were ferried along the river, up and down between the Tower of London and the tribunals—I think the distance was almost a mile and a half between the Tower and Westminster where the trials were held. It was easy to notice when these men were taken along the river in boats, for you could pick them out by the uniforms and weapons of the soldiers, and you could see the vast hustling mob of spectators and the countless people who took off in light boats and followed them the entire reach of the river.

For the space of at least six or seven weeks this was my daily spectacle. During all that time the trials were conducted, death sentence pronounced on many gentlemen and the executions carried out.[12] But for all those seven weeks no action was taken against me: there was no examination, no interrogation, though in the opinion of nearly all the heretics it was I who was reckoned the instigator and principal person in the whole tragedy. So I was at a total loss to find any reason for the delay and for the peace which they allowed me. Every hour of every day I expected to be transferred to the Tower, where they held the other prisoners in chains and subjected them to torture.[13] I could only presume that they were anxious first to have ready at hand all the information they could extort by torture from their other prisoners, and then, at the end of the tragedy, to produce me as a prize-piece convicted and condemned beyond dispute by the evidence of all these men. Thus they would be able to show triumphantly, and for all time, that Jesuits contrived the death of princes. As I was to learn afterwards, during the space of an entire year no one who was taken and racked was not closely questioned about me, as to whether I knew of the plot or had given advice. And my own guard made no attempt to conceal this. He told me, several times, that he expected any day that I would be taken to the Tower for examination.

Page 80

[1] The reason for W. W.'s confinement in a ' private house ' and for the announcement that he was a Puritan is given in a letter of the spy, Francis Mills, to Walsingham: the Government was anxious that none of the conspirators ' should know what has become of him ' lest, ' being missed ' by them they should disperse in alarm (*C.S.P., Mary Queen of Scots*, vol. xix, no. 4). Had W. W. been taken to a public prison, Babington, whose movements were being closely watched by the spy Scudamore, would have fled immediately he got the news. It was only two days after W. W.'s arrest that Babington in fact gave Scudamore the slip and escaped into St. John's Wood. He was arrested on the 14th.

[2] W. W. is here referring to Robert Poley, who was in the service of Walsingham's daughter, Lady Sydney; although in fact, it was not Poley, as W. W. thought, but Nicholas Berden who was principally responsible for his arrest. Berden had been given the task of watching W. W., and it was he who identified him in the road outside Bishopsgate.

[3] Cp. Robert Southwell: Poley ' was the chief instrument to contrive and prosecute the matter, to draw into the net such green wits as . . . might easily be overwrought by Mr. Secretary's subtle and sifting wit. For Poley masking his secret intentions under the face of religion, and abusing with irreligious hypocrisy all rites and sacraments to borrow the false opinion of a Catholic, still fed the poor gentleman with his master's baits, and he holding the line in his hand, suffered them like silly fishes, to play themselves upon the hook, till they were thoroughly fastened, that then he might strike at his own pleasure, and be sure to draw them to'a certain destruction.' *Humble Supplication*, p. 18.

Page 81

[4] Poley may have known that W. W. was worried about the loss of his letters to Fr. Persons. ' There are few enough men who can be relied on to carry letters, and even these do so at infinite risk ' he had written to Persons in the previous year (Stonyhurst MSS., *Anglia*, i, f. 28). Presumably Poley had arranged to have W. W.'s correspondence intercepted on the south coast as he had done Morgan's. F. S. Boas, *Marlowe and his Circle*, pp. 37–8.

[5] Poley's description of W. W. has not survived. Richard Bold who was examined in connection with the Plot calls W. W. ' a tall man with a down[ward] look ' (*C.Sc.P.*, vol. viii, p. 689). Tyrrell adds that he was wearing, on his visit to Bold's in June, a ' doublet and hose of yellow canvas lined with black '.

6 For the fullest account of Robert Poley, see F. S. Boas, *Marlowe and his Circle*, pp. 30–55. From the references to him in *Leicester's Commonwealth* he would appear to have been more closely associated with Leicester than with Walsingham, at least at the start of his mysterious career. His first step in the process of ingratiation which W. W. describes, was to form a close friendship with Christopher Blount, a young Catholic soldier closely attached to Leicester (cf. p. 76, n. 7). By means of Blount, Poley got an introduction to Thomas Morgan, Mary's agent in Paris, who recommended him to the Queen as a Catholic ' much disposed to see some happy and speedy reformation ', viz., her establishment on the English throne. It was only in June 1586 that he was introduced to Babington as a man of influence who could obtain for him a licence to travel abroad. Although at this time Poley was actually living in Walsingham's house, where Sydney was now residing, and was considered ' in vehement suspicion ' by a number of Catholics, he successfully deceived Babington, who offered to take him on the Continent as his travelling companion and pay all his expenses. To the end Babington trusted him, and in the affectionate farewell note before his flight to the woods, addressed him as ' sweet Robin '. As a ' blind ' Poley was arrested when the Plot was exploded and put in the Tower for a time, but soon released.

Page 82

7 On a list of ' Prisoners after the Babington Plot ' drawn up in September 1586 there is a note after W. W.'s name—' promised to have been made Bishop '. The story appears to have been invented by the spy, Berden. *C.R.S.*, vol. 2, pp. 253, 257.

8 The pattern of the Babington Plot resembles closely that of the Gunpowder Plot, twenty years later. With the exception of Ballard, Savage and Babington himself, all those executed were fine young men and it is likely that they had agreed to nothing beyond another romantic attempt to rescue Mary Queen of Scots (cf., p. 100). The real villains of the piece were not these gentlemen, nor even the professional spies like Poley and Berden, but those renegade Catholics behind the scenes who played on both sides, as conspirators and as informers, notably Thomas Morgan and Gilbert Gifford, and probably also William Gifford, who, as Conyers Read observes, emerges from the conspiracy ' with a dark stain on his character '. There is evidence that Ballard, too, had been a Government spy, but after his first confession on the rack he seems to have made a good end, encouraged by the Jesuit, Fr. William Creighton.

[9] Cp. Robert Southwell: ' Thus is your Highness drawn by these indirect courses to use your unwilling sword . . . and put in ungrounded fears of their disloyalty who are of themselves so far from defiling their hearts with any treasonable thoughts, that their heaviest enemies had no other means to dismount them from their best deserving, but by violently constraining them to evil by these sinister inventions.' *Humble Supplication*, p. 25.

Page 83

[10] As W. W. speaks later of crossing the river for an examination, it is probable that he was confined in one of the houses, close to the Clink on the south bank, which were used as private lock-ups. The road on which he saw the bonfires would be Southwark Street.

[11] ' Upon the discovery of this dreadful plot . . . the city of London made extraordinary rejoicings, by public bonfires, ringing of bells, feastings in the streets, singing of psalms and suchlike . . . whereof the grateful Queen thought fit to take public notice by a letter to the Lord Mayor and aldermen ' (Strype (ed. 1824), vol. iii, part 1, p. 607). Writing on 10 May the next year, W. W. recalls the same scene in more detail: ' The imprisonment and butchery of Catholics . . . was the occasion of triumphant rejoicing. In the midst of our calamities the bells were rung throughout the city, sermons and festivals held, fireworks set off, bonfires lit in the public street—a customary and unmistakable manner of manifesting public joy—and with one cry the whole people exulted and clapped their hands over the wretchedness of the papist traitors.' Arch. S.J., Rome, *Fondo Gesuitico*, 651.

[12] The trials were conducted on 13, 14 and 15 September. W. W. is probably referring also to the preliminary examinations of the individual conspirators which started on 8 August and ended on the eve of 5 September.

Page 84

[13] It is uncertain whether any of the conspirators were tortured apart from Thomas Bellamy (cf. *inf.*, p. 104) and probably Ballard also (cf. J. H. Pollen, *Mary Stuart and the Babington Plot*, p. clxxx). W. W. may be speaking from knowledge; and it is not improbable that others were racked in the Tower.

11

THE MAN BEHIND THE GRILL

After the whole business of the plot had been thoroughly
sifted in all its aspects, and the men who were found guilty
sentenced to death and executed, only then was my case dealt
with.[1] But, considering the times, it was soon despatched;
for in all their most detailed examinations of the prisoners there
was nothing they could find against me. In despair, so to say,
of extracting anything, they decided on lenience. However,
they did submit me to examination. And they brought up
the names of all the men who were said to be the instigators
of the conspiracy, and asked me whether I had known them
or given them advice or received word of their attempted
plot or known anything about it? And other searching
questions of this kind. I denied emphatically, as was true,
that I had known the slightest thing—either about the execution or the plan. And as there was nothing more serious of
which they could accuse or convict me, they stopped questioning me on this subject and turned to another.[2] I had persuaded
a certain gentleman to withdraw the military assistance he was
giving to the Earl of Leicester in the unjust war he was
waging with the heretics of Flanders against the King of
Spain.[3] (The gentleman in question had served the Earl with
a large equipment of horses and men furnished at his own
expense.[4]) I had argued with him, so they said, and spoken
at great length to demonstrate the injustice of that war. And

the examiner went on to mention the place where the conversation had occurred; [5] how he had given me his own horse
and brought me back to his house; [6] and how I had preached
a sermon there before a group of gentlemen; and he quoted
the text of Scripture on which I had preached and sections
and odd sentences from the sermon.[7]

As I listened to this I could not help being astonished.
A great part of what he said was true. Of course, he had
inserted a number of false statements. This I had no difficulty
in demonstrating, and I took advantage of it to show that
there was no guarantee his other assertions were not false—a
man who had no hesitation in telling lies could not be trusted
not to lie in everything he said.

'Don't imagine,' he said, 'that you are going to save yourself this way. Your logic and sophistries will not protect you
from the law. We shall get the truth out of you by force.'

Then he turned to other subjects that had no direct bearing
on the point. With much curiosity he asked me many
questions about exorcisms, and the way we had cast out devils
from men's bodies by use of the Church's ceremonies. There
had been much talk on the subject and it had been widely,
almost universally, discussed. After this he departed for the
day.

The following day he was back. ' See,' he said, taking out
a piece of paper from his doublet, ' here is a confession written
in the man's own hand. There's no evading this. Everything
I asserted, everything I questioned you about, is true. Are
you still going to prevaricate and refuse to admit it? '

Then he began to read out a long list of statements from
the gentleman's confession.

' Look,' I said, ' why go on questioning me, if you've
already got the confession of an accused man? What's the

point of pressing further? If he says he's guilty, that he spoke with me, gave me hospitality; if he says I made this or that statement about Leicester or the war in Flanders, go and settle the matter with him. A criminal's confession against himself is worth more than a crowd of witnesses. Let his blood be on his own head. I know nothing about it. I cannot confess. If he accuses me on any score, then you know more about it than I do. But if you hold anything against me which I am bound to admit—that I am a Catholic, for instance, or a priest, or a Jesuit—then say so and prove it; and it will be for me either to defend my case or to admit the charge.'

When he saw he could get no information from me, he left. I knew, or suspected rather, from certain indications that the whole business had been faked; that the man had made no confession at all.[8]

As he was a very rich person and had large revenues,[9] they had fabricated the entire story in order to bring the gentleman within the grasp of the law, which forbids subjects—under penalty of death and confiscation of property—to have any dealings with priests or Jesuits. It was on this pretext that they intended to take his property, and, if they so wished, his life also.

Actually at that time the man was not a Catholic, though he was well disposed towards the faith.[10] As he had been very anxious to see me and discuss matters touching his soul and conscience, I had agreed, but only with some reluctance and at the entreaty of friends who knew him well and had influence over me.[11] He was married to a Catholic, and others of his household belonged to the faith, and he had a mansion several miles from London. It was there that he had taken me. I had said Mass in the house, heard confessions and preached to the

Catholics. The gentleman was not allowed in to Mass, but he had attended the sermons.

This, however, was not the end of the proceedings. After one or two days they took me out of the room where I had been confined all this time with my guard, and conducted me to a private house on the far side of the river.[12] Here they worked through a whole list of charges. It was a long and rigorous examination.

I thought that in bringing me out into the open they were going to produce a number of traitorous witnesses and get them to testify that they had seen me in the gentleman's company and preaching in his house. But when I reached the place, they did not treat me like a criminal. Instead of making me stand in front of them with my head bare, answering their demands like a suppliant, they placed me at the head of the table above the examiners themselves. Then they invited me to speak and answer questions with my head covered. At first I was disinclined to accept. But they pressed, and I sat down.[13] Still, I was not such a fool as to think they were honouring me by this gesture, for I knew well how they loathed even the mention of the word Jesuit or priest.

Happening to lift my eyes, I noticed above the dais opposite me a grill in the wall, covered over with a curtain. Immediately the thought occurred to me that they had placed a spy there. I was looking straight at him, and he would be able to identify me as the man they charged with carrying on a secret correspondence with the accused gentleman. My suspicions were not far-fetched. Later, the whole ruse was uncovered, and it transpired that he was responsible for this betrayal. Until then he had been in prison; but afterwards he was given his liberty. They did not want to produce him openly as a spy now and have him charge me to my face.

Had they done this, he would have been recognised at once, and would no longer have been in a position to do us harm. He would have been of no further use to them, whereas, in fact, he continued to serve them and do grave injury to countless persons, and to himself, most of all.[14]

So here they asked me many questions about the conspiracy of Anthony Babington and his companions; also about the Queen's supremacy, the authority of the Pope, the papal dispensation for the marriage of Henry VIII with his wife, Catherine; and about the Queen of Scots and heaven knows what else. But these arguments were all the old ones, and the evidence brought carried no more weight than previously. Then, after completely exhausting these topics, they sent me back to prison. There I stayed for five months. Every day I expected either to be taken out to public trial or sent off to the Tower—in spite of their finding me innocent and free from any charge connected with this conspiracy. But in law the fact that I was a Jesuit was sufficient for the death penalty, though usually they did not press this when they could seize on some accusation which would inflame popular hatred.

Everything, they thought, was going well; exactly as they had hoped. So immediately they gave their entire attention and effort to staging the trial of the Queen of Scots. All the preparations were made; the details arranged; the judges appointed; couriers despatched and the sentence executed at Fotheringhay where she had been kept in the closest custody; and the whole iniquitous business was completed in a very short time.[15] As for myself, I stayed here, as I said, most anxious about my fate and the fate of us all. Unceasingly I prayed to God that He would turn to some good effect this monstrous and savage persecution.

Then one day, while I was sitting down in my distress, I happened to cast my eyes to the far part of the room. There I saw a scrap of paper being pushed through a dark crevice. Only the day before, close to this very place, I had heard a considerable noise, evidently made to attract my attention by the man who was now pushing the paper through. I picked the paper up—the man had noticed the time of the guard's absence—and read: *Write back. Say who you are. Tell me anything you want done or anything you need.* He had wrapped a pen inside the sheet, but the messenger had dropped it on the way; or perhaps he had forgotten to enclose it. Anyhow I examined every cranny in the room, looking for something I could write with. Eventually I found a flower. It was dry and withered; but I chewed it with my teeth and was able to extract just sufficient moisture to write distinctly enough for a person to read. I said only what was barely essential. The next day I watched the guard, and when I heard the friendly noise at the crevice, I handed back my reply.

This had been arranged by the contrivance of some Catholics in the neighbouring prison, and you cannot realise what consolation it brought me, and what use and convenience it proved, for in this way I received news, which I so much desired, of things happening in the world outside.[16]

After a short time this channel was blocked, and all correspondence in this way. But another method was hit upon and developed, which proved even more convenient, not just for letters, but for receiving and posting other things as well.

At this time two priests who were together in prison were taken out to trial, sentenced to death and executed.[17] It was a period of very great confusion for us all. Every road, cross-way and port was watched night and day, and sealed off so effectively that no person could pass without the most rigorous examination.   Lodging-houses,   private   homes, rooms were searched and examined with minute thoroughness; neither friend nor acquaintance could escape without being forced to give an account of himself.[18]   In this way many priests were captured, and Catholics filled the prisons throughout the country.[19]

Page 88

[1] The 'confessions' of all the conspirators were completed by 5 September. Between the 13th and 15th they were tried in two batches and similarly executed on the 20th and 21st in Lincoln's Inn Fields. 'For more terror' the hangman was given instructions, to which the Queen was party, that the young men should be disembowelled alive. When the cruelty of the butchery caused a revulsión of popular feeling, the Government published an official statement that the Queen herself was disgusted and had given orders for a more merciful execution of the second batch of conspirators. A. G. Smith, *The Babington Plot*, pp. 239–42.

[2] This and other examinations make it clear that the Government never suspected W. W. of complicity in the Plot. From the start Walsingham realised that any attempt to involve such an obviously innocent and respected priest would recoil on himself and probably lead to the exposure of his own 'double-dealing'. In fact, as Southwell points out (*Humble Supplication*, p. 23), Walsingham instructed his agents that they were to keep the 'conspirators' away from wiser and maturer priests like W. W. who might 'see through so many mists as he by his instruments had already cast before their eyes'; or, as Southwell says again, using a different phrase, they were to 'keep the thread out of their hands that soon would have unwound it to the bottom'.

[3] This is Richard Bold, mentioned in ch. 9. W. W. has separated his story concerning him into two halves, and treats one half as though it had no connection with the other. In this he cannot be blamed, for the events of these few months were very complicated and he is not attempting a full account of the conspiracy which, he says (p. 99), had already been done by Southwell.

[4] Richard Bold's name occurs on a list of horsemen at the Hague serving under the Earl of Essex on 10 January this year. E. M. Tenison, *Elizabethan England*, vol. vi, p. 45.

Page 89

[5] There are two accounts of the conversations, one in Richard Bold's examination (*C.Sc.P.*, vol. viii, p. 700), the other in Anthony Tyrrell's second confession (*ib.*, p. 654). According to the first statement it took place while W. W., Bold (not at that time a Catholic) and Tyrrell were riding over Hounslow Heath the previous June on their way from London to Harlesford, where W. W. had been asked to perform some

exorcisms. Bold merely says that W. W. tried to dissuade him 'from proceeding any further' in the wars in the Netherlands; and that he answered that 'by the grace of God he would go thither again to the Earl of Leicester, and that if he found the expense to grow greater than he could well bear, he would return home again. Other speeches than these, either touching reconciling, or any other matter of state or religion, there passed none.' Tyrrell is more detailed, but at the same time very untrustworthy. He places the conversation after dinner in Bold's house, when 'F. Edmunds [W. W.] persuaded Mr. Bold to be reconciled to the Church. He [Bold] protested that with all his heart he desired it, but he was so entangled in my Lord of Leicester's affairs that as yet possibly he could not. He said he would make all the speed he could to begin again, and then he would wind himself out of Leicester's fetters. He reported that he hated him from his heart. . . . And many other hard speeches he gave out of the Earl.' As W. W. remarks, probably 'a great part [of this report] was true'.

⁶ At Edmund Peckham's request, Bold had lent W. W. a horse, and Peckham, Bold, Tyrrell and W. W. mounted, after breakfast, outside the White Hart in St. Giles. *C.Sc.P.*, vol. vii, p. 699.

⁷ W. W. 'sitting on a stool, as all the rest did, began a discourse with a text in Latin out of Scripture . . . [and] went forward and discoursed of faith, and that we ought to believe the pastors sent from the true Church'. (*C.Sc.P.*, vol. viii, p. 700, Bold's Examination.) Neither Bold nor Tyrrell give the text which W. W. used, but Tyrrell adds that there were present 'Mr. Bold, his wife, and one other gentleman and his wife of Hertfordshire' (*ib.*, p. 654).

Page 90

⁸ W. W. was right in suspecting forgery. Bold's statement contains nothing incriminating beyond the fact that two persons unnamed had visited his house and performed some ceremonies.

⁹ In 1590 Bold was reported to be still a man of 'fair and ancient living'. *C.R.S.*, vol. 4, p. 202.

¹⁰ Bold was not a Catholic at the time of W. W.'s visit to his house in June; he may have been reconciled the following month, when he was W. W.'s host. Cf. *sup.*, p. 76, n. 6.

¹¹ Principally at Edmund Peckham's request. *C.Sc.P.*, vol. viii, p. 699.

Page 91

¹² This was probably Ely House, the London residence of Sir

Christopher Hatton, where Babington and the other conspirators had
been examined before trial. J. H. Pollen, *Mary Stuart and the Babington
Plot*, p. clxxiii.

[13] Presiding over these examiners was probably Sir Christopher
Hatton. He was well known among Catholics for his courtesy to priests,
so much so that he was suspected of being a crypto-Catholic himself.
By inviting W. W. to keep his head covered he was acknowledging him,
in the convention of the day, as his social equal. Hatton had treated the
Scottish Jesuit, Fr. William Creighton, with similar courtesy (J. H.
Pollen, *Mary Queen of Scots and the Babington Plot*, p. 168). Actually
Hatton, as Fr. Hicks has shown, was working all the time, through the
agency of an apostate spy, Solomon Aldred, for disunion among Catholics, and for this end had been in secret negotiation the previous year
with the authorities of the Inquisition in Rome. 'An Elizabethan
Propagandist' in *The Month*, May-June, 1945.

Page 92

[14] Most probably this was Anthony Tyrrell. As with Bold, so with
Tyrrell, W. W. does not gather in one place all that he has to say about
him. At this time Tyrrell was in the Clink, serving there as a spy. It
was he that informed on Bold (cf. *sup.*, p. 95) and did 'grave injury'
to 'many other' friends of W. W. The unmasking of his treachery
is described in ch. 15.

[15] On 11 September the commission of thirty-six judges, peers and
privy councillors met at Fotheringhay for the trial; but when they were
about to pronounce judgment Elizabeth called them back to London.
The guilt of Mary was then debated for six days in Parliament. On
12 November both Houses petitioned Elizabeth for sentence and
execution. Elizabeth again hesitated. On 1 February she signed the
warrant. It was despatched on the 3rd by the Privy Council without
the knowledge of Elizabeth. On the 8th Mary was executed. When
London got news, it celebrated with bonfires and banquets in the streets
for a week, as it had done on the discovery of the Babington Plot.

Page 93

[16] We know the subject of this correspondence and how innocent
it was from Anthony Tyrrell's *Confessions*. The priest was Fr. John
Lowe, an old friend of W. W.'s, who had been associated with him in
the practice of exorcisms. Young and Burghley allowed these messages
to pass between the two priests in the hope that W. W. would incriminate
himself. 'I observed [to Mr. Young]', writes Tyrrell, 'that the chief

dealer with Fr. Edmonds was a good priest named Mr. Lowe, and how Mr. Lowe did write him many letters, as occasion served, about his necessary business and received answers . . . I think verily they did import the state of the whole house, how the poor prisoners might find money to pay for their commons, to get relief to preserve themselves from famine, hunger and cold: other State matters I protest I knew none to be treated by them. I would, besides that, be always prying into Mr. Lowe, his chamber, among his papers, to pick out what I could find that might concern Fr. Edmond's overthrow, and with much ado I found at the last only two writings of his own hand; the one concerned the answer that a Catholic might make to the Oath of Supremacy if it were tendered to him, and the other was of matter that now I remember not, but sure I am that they could not hurt or prejudice the least hair of his head for any harm that was contained in them. Yet the one I sent to my Lord Treasurer, and the other I did give to Justice Young.' *Two Missionaries*, p. 409.

[17] John Lowe and John Adams. They were executed at Tyburn, together with Robert Dibdale, on 8 October 1586. All three were W. W.'s friends and had been associated with him in the practice of exorcism. From Tyrrell's *Confessions* it is clear that the first two were selected for execution by Justice Young on the advice of Tyrrell, who was chagrined at his failure to implicate W. W. in Babington's plot, and recommended instead the execution of Lowe and Adams on the ground that they exercised most influence over their fellow-Catholics in the Clink. *Two Missionaries*, pp. 411–12.

Page 94

[18] Cp. Southwell's description. 'All highways were watched, infinite houses searched, hues and cries raised, frights bruited in people's ears, as though the whole realm had been on fire, whereas in truth it was but the hissing of a few green twigs [viz., the Babington Plot] of their own kindling, which they might without any such uproar have quenched with a handful of water.' *Humble Supplication*, p. 22.

[19] In a letter of 21 December 1587, Southwell referring back to the earlier part of the year, wrote : ' from the beginnings of our griefs until this day there has been nothing so outrageous '. On 2 October 1586, Burghley had drawn up a memorandum for a thorough enquiry into recusancy throughout England. Starting in January 1587 there were searches, organised county by county, covering the whole of England and filling all the county goals with Catholic prisoners.

12

ANTHONY BABINGTON

This seems, perhaps, as convenient a place as any to insert something about the attempt made by Anthony Babington. I base it partly on a book written by Father Robert Southwell, which contains a brief account of the whole conspiracy; partly, also, on my own knowledge and observation.[1]

Babington was a gentleman. In property, income, establishments and the rest he had considerable wealth. He was young, not yet thirty, good-looking with a fine presence, quick intelligence, enchanting manners and wit. Moreover, he was well-read, and had a love of literature uncommon in men of his class. He had spent a large part of his life travelling abroad, in Paris and other cities on the Continent, for the sake of seeing places and understanding foreign ways. When in London he drew to himself by the force of his exceptional charm and personality many young Catholic gentlemen of his own standing, gallant, adventurous and daring in defence of the Catholic faith in its day of stress; and ready for any arduous enterprise whatsoever that might advance the common Catholic cause.

This group, however, was unable to escape Walsingham's attentions—so wrote Father Southwell, whose little book (I am told) has now been printed; and I wish your Reverence had seen and read it, as I did, immediately after it was completed in manuscript and circulated among a few friends.[2]

Now Walsingham knew that if he could only contrive some wicked stratagem to implicate these young men in a foolhardy plot there was nothing which would do more to enhance his reputation for craftiness.[3] Besides putting a stigma on the Catholic cause, it would bring in rich spoils from their property. This man Walsingham, therefore—his whole character was set for every kind of fraudulent and deceitful dealing— introduced one or two of his agents, hypocrites I should rather call them, into this group. With deep dissimulation they were to pose as Catholics and, after long and intimate intercourse, make show of devoting themselves without reserve to God and to every undertaking that touched the holy faith: then leaving aside lesser issues they were to propose for consideration the culminating enterprise of all.[4] This was not, as the heretics made out and proclaimed, the death of Queen Elizabeth, but the release from prison of the Queen of Scotland—who, next in line to Elizabeth, was reckoned the lawful successor to the kingdom—and her safe conveyance into France, to her near relative, the Duke of Guise. They were convinced that this was not a particularly hazardous task, and reckoned it would strike terror into the heretics and at the same time cause them much heart-searching, lest the French, now in possession of the legitimate successor, should collect and equip their forces and, by armed strength, restore her—at least after Elizabeth's death—to her rightful kingdom.[5]

This was the plan underlying the whole venture and conspiracy. With this aim a number of journeys were made into Scotland and into France, and the execution of the plot in all its details was revealed and discussed with the Duke of Guise (or so they thought). But the wretched men—they were blindly and woefully deceived—were caught up in an

inextricable mesh of intrigue; for the authors of the fabrica-
tion got hold of another man and suborned him to imper-
sonate the Duke of Guise and to promise the assistance they
sought from the real Duke. To this man, then, they unbur-
dened their confidences and secret designs, and rushing
precipitately into hasty and rash discussion came to their
ruin.[6]

This, as well as I can remember, is what Father Southwell
says. For myself I can add a few details to the story from
what I saw and understood of it. Very frequently I had
occasion to talk intimately with this gentleman, Anthony
Babington, and discuss many things with him.[7] He had an
acute mind and, for a young man, remarkable intelligence
and judgment. As he had a great desire to visit foreign
countries, he took pleasure in hearing me talk from time to
time about all I had seen and knew. But before starting out
on his tour, he was anxious to visit his home and family, who
lived a long way from London.[8] Everything was ready for
the road—horses, coach and all—when he asked me to keep
him company on the journey. At the same time, he hinted
I might achieve something for Christ and the Church with his
friends and relatives. But in spite of the attractive bait of
spiritual profit which he dangled before me, I judged it wiser
not to join him. Other good reasons apart, the ostentatious
splendour in which he had decided to travel did not seem to
me sufficiently in keeping with my purpose, namely, the saving
of souls—though it was altogether fitting for him in his
position.[9]

However—such is the changing lot of human kind—all
these plans of his were shattered a few days later. Walsingham
summoned the man. He asked him many questions about the
Queen of Scotland, expostulated severely, said he knew every

detail of his designs, and, if he chose, could reveal many secrets; and he claimed, for instance, certain information that frequent letters had passed between him and the other party. In conclusion, he used threatening words, commanding him to love his own country and become a faithful subject of the Queen. How Babington defended himself, I do not know; but he did so as best he could. Finally, Walsingham sent him away, very dejected (I think) and tormented and anxious over the issue of many things.

A few days passed and he summoned him again. He reiterated all he had said about the Queen of Scotland, but with less rancour, using gentle words to soothe him; he was a man of parts, he said, richly gifted in body and mind, and could make his mark in the state, deserve well of it, in fact, if he chose to give it his talent and ability; and for his part, he promised to bring him to the notice of the Queen and obtain an audience for him. 'Be confident,' he said, kissing his hand with affection, 'have no hesitation. Talk as freely as you wish about the matter. It will make for better concealment.' And he spoke about many other things, trying to win him over. But for what purpose, I do not know; for already (I would have thought) he had him well entangled in his net by those earlier devices I mentioned above.[10]

Every single one of these things Babington told me with his own lips, and, as I listened to him, I became profoundly sad. I knew only too well that Walsingham was a master in the art of deception and was able always to accomplish exactly what he wished. 'You will be well advised,' I told him, ' to put away all idea of this expedition. The business cannot be despatched as quickly and easily as that. There is no way I know which will get you out of the snare set for you. If you accept his offer, you deny your religion; if you hold him off and reject his advances you expose yourself to inevitable death; and you cannot dissimulate and waver between the two without endangering your salvation; nor, if you did, would you keep for any length of time your Catholic name among Catholic gentlemen.'

'No one,' he answered, 'no one who has ever known me will ever suspect that I am anything but a Catholic, even if, occasionally, I have acted and spoken rather more freely than I should.'

'You are a Catholic,' I said, 'and you always will be. Nobody doubts that; nor will they, so long as you continue to act in the manner that people rightly expect of a Catholic. On the other hand, if you take a chance and say or do anything which Catholics are afraid even to suggest to their most loyal and close friends, you cannot avoid suspicion and a bad name.' [11]

That was my last conversation with Anthony Babington. From that day I did not see him again. In fact, had the opportunity offered, I would have been happier not to see him. Not that I was afraid of him or of anything he might do, for he was always a most honourable youth and most faithful to his religion. Nor did I have any fear that Walsingham might deflect him to perform the smallest action which would discredit a Catholic; but it was clear to me that I could not safely continue on familiar terms with men of this type.[12] It was impossible, if I was to keep the rule of the Society and concern myself merely with matters of religion, not with those of state; for he would be certain to ask my advice on many questions and give me secret information.[13]

Afterwards the affair became public. The plot was uncovered, its leaders captured, and the rest, scattered over different parts of the kingdom where they considered they had the best chance of survival, were hunted to death. Anthony and four others fled to a neighbouring wood, and there tried to hide. But they were hard pressed by hunger. As they did not dare to come out, Anthony sent to a nearby house that belonged to a Catholic lady, the same Mrs. Bellamy whom I mentioned earlier. He despatched a ring to one of her daughters, and begged her by that token—she knew the ring, for it was set with costly jewels—to send him and his companions food. She did as she was asked; it was dangerous, but affection and pity overcame her terror.[14] Yet they could not escape long.[15] They were captured and with them Mrs. Bellamy, her daughter and two of her sons, both of them young men. All were segregated and consigned to different prisons.

One of these two young men, Thomas, was tortured in the Tower of London and died on the rack, though the heretics gave it out that he had strangled himself.[16] The second, Jerome, was condemned to death at the same time as Anthony and the other accomplices, and was executed. Their mother was shut up in the Tower. There, after a few months, she died wasted with sorrow and with the squalor and filth of her imprisonment. If one thinks only of this present life, her end was miserable: but, as I see it, it was glorious: no less than a martyr's and no different from it.[17]

NOTES

[1] This is Southwell's *Humble Supplication to Her Majesty*, in answer to the Proclamation of 18 October 1591, which branded all missionary priests as agents of Spain and personally dissolute. Southwell's book, written before the middle of December the same year, was an attempt to break through the ring of Ministers and reach the Queen herself. His thesis was that time would show Catholics to be natural defenders of the monarchy, in opposition to the revolutionary element already prevalent among the Puritans. In order to rebut the charge of disloyalty, Southwell describes the Babington Plot at length, listing the few Catholics engaged in it as against the large number of *agents provocateurs*. Much of Southwell's information came probably from Paris, where Gilbert Gifford had been arrested in 1588 and many of his papers discovered. Some of the details given by Southwell may well be inaccurate or dubious, but in general outline his account is far closer to the truth than the version put out by the Government.

[2] The only printed edition of the *Humble Supplication* was published posthumously in 1600, under curious circumstances described by Fr. J. H. Pollen in *The Month* (January 1902, pp. 93–6). It bears the date 1595, a deliberate falsification by the Appellant priests, who, against the wishes of the Jesuit Superior, Fr. Garnet, produced the book for their own controversial purposes. On the last page Southwell states his intention of having it multiplied in manuscript copies. There is evidence of two of these copies: one captured by Topcliffe in August 1596 (cf. *Hat. Cal.*, vol. vi, p. 311), the other (possibly the same) sent by Francis Bacon to his brother Antony, with a note recommending him to make a copy of it. Cf. Christopher Devlin, ' The Patriotism of Robert Southwell ', in *The Month*, December 1953.

[3] Cp. Robert Southwell: ' And as for this action of Babington, it was in truth rather a snare to entrap them than any devise of their own, since it was both plotted, furthered and finished by Sir Francis Walsingham and his other complices, who laid and hatched all the particulars thereof, as they thought it would best fall out of the discredit of Catholics and cutting off the Queen of Scots.' *Humble Supplication*, pp. 17–18.

[4] Speaking of Robert Poley, one of the agents to whom W. W. here refers, an anonymous but well-informed contemporary writer says ' He was continually with Ballard and Babington, he heard Mass, confessed and in all things feigned to be a Catholic, and still learned his

lesson of Mr. Secretary [Walsingham], whom they should draw into the plot, what plot they should lay, and what course they should take that might best serve the turn, for which all this device was intended.' Stonyhurst MSS, *Anglia*, i, no. 70, ' General Heads of Persecution in England.'

[5] There were two distinct threads in the Babington Plot. One was a plot to murder Queen Elizabeth, hatched by Gilbert and George Gifford, using John Savage as their instrument. But since all the men, except possibly Savage himself, were either agents of Walsingham or had an understanding with him, this cannot be taken very seriously. Southwell asserts that two gentlemen pensioners were assigned to keep an eye on Savage, who was allowed to hang about the Court. The other thread is that of the romantic young men, Charles Tilney, Chidiock Tichborne and others who were seduced by Babington. W. W. is almost certainly right in saying that they had no other idea beyond that of rescuing Mary Queen of Scots. But since Walsingham in England and Thomas Morgan in France were controlling the two ends it was easy for the Government to entangle both threads and show that both groups were involved in the one plot. The whole affair will become clearer when it is finally established that Morgan himself had some sort of understanding with the English government.

Page 101

[6] This seems to be a misunderstanding of Southwell's *Humble Supplication*, or else it is information that W. W. gained independently. Southwell says nothing about this incident, but he does say (p. 34) that Gilbert Gifford, pretending to come from the Duke of Guise, tricked Chateauneuf, the French ambassador. There is no suggestion of ' impersonation'.

[7] Certainly, during the time W. W. was in touch with Babington, there was no question of a plot to murder Elizabeth; and there is no need to doubt Babington's declaration at his trial: ' Yea, I protest, before I met this Ballard I never meant nor intended to kill the Queen; but by his persuasions I was induced to believe that she was excommunicate, and therefore lawful to murder her.' Cobbett, *State Trials*, vol. I, p. 1138.

[8] Babington's home was at Dethwick, in Derbyshire, about three miles south-east of Matlock.

[9] It was probably Fr. Heywood's acceptance of such an offer a few years earlier that gave rise to the malicious gossip that he habitually rode round in a ' coach accompanied with many and in costly apparel ... [like] a legate *a latere* '. *C.R.S.*, vol. I, p. 112.

Page 102

10 Babington had three interviews with Walsingham, not two, as W. W. states. They took place on 29 June, 3 July and 13 July. It was after the second and third that Babington visited W. W. At the third interview Walsingham, who had learned through Gilbert Gifford of the coming of Garnet and Southwell, demanded that Babington should give proof of his loyalty to the Queen by discovering the whereabouts of the two Jesuits. The date of Babington's second visit to W. W. was probably 14 July, for he reported to Walsingham, ' They landed on the downs. Two of them [Garnet and Southwell] are Jesuits. They are in London very close '. And he added a sentence which suggests that the two priests were actually on the premises while he was talking to W. W. ' I myself might have seen them; but in regard they are suspected to be dangerous men, I durst not without knowledge of Mr. Secretary's faith and pleasure.' Clearly W. W. was wise to avoid Babington's company after this meeting. *C.Sc.P.*, vol. viii, p. 598.

Page 103

11 Walsingham had promised Babington a free pass to go and live abroad in return for his services in betraying the two newly-arrived Jesuits. Babington now enquired of W. W. how far he could lawfully go in giving information about them, provided it did them no harm. W. W. gave Babington advice on general lines, and immediately arranged to leave London with Southwell and Garnet.

12 Probably at the time W. W. last saw Babington (about 19 July) vague news of a plot had already leaked out. Writing to Rome on 25 July Southwell reports, ' At the Queen's Court they say there is a business in hand which, if it succeeds, will mean ruin for us, but if it fails, all will be well.' *C.R.S.*, vol. 5, p. 308.

13 W. W. takes the most plausible view he can possibly do of Anthony Babington. It seems certain that Babington, in the hope of saving his own life, incriminated his companions. On 6 July he had ostensibly given up the Plot and was hoping to go abroad on a free pass from Walsingham. It was then that George Gifford, Gilbert's cousin, brought him a letter from Mary, Queen of Scots. That same morning Babington wrote a long missive about the six gentlemen ready to ' despatch the Queen ', and giving details of the plot to murder Elizabeth. It was Mary's answer (the postscript, at least, if not other parts of the letter, was forged) which led to her execution. The most kindly interpretation, therefore, would be that Babington was playing a double game.

Page 104

[14] It was for this action that Jerome Bellamy was indicted. At his trial he confessed that he had brought them [Anthony Babington, Robert Barnwell and Henry Donn] meat into the woods and lodged them in his house. Cobbett, *State Trials*, vol. I, p. 1154.

[15] Babington, disguised as a farm-labourer, his hair cropped and his face smeared with walnut juice, was captured in the barn close to Mrs. Bellamy's house. There was said to be an underground passage, perhaps a disused sewer, connecting the barn with the house. W. Done Bushell, *The Bellamies of Uxenden* (1914), pp. 3, 13.

[16] As in the case of other prisoners who died under torture or as a consequence of it, the Government gave out that Thomas Bellamy had ' hanged himself in the Tower '. *C.R.S.*, vol. 2, p. 257.

[17] Mrs. Bellamy was committed to the Fleet prison on 14 August 1586, and was later transferred to the Tower. Her name appears on a list of prisoners there, dated 25 September 1586. She escaped execution only by a flaw in the general indictment in which she is called Elizabeth Bellamy. Before proceedings could be resumed on the amended indictment made out against Catherine Bellamy she had died in the Tower. *C.S.P., Dom. Eliz.*, vol. cxcii, no. 49; vol. cxcv, no. 34.

13

RETROSPECTIVE TALES

Since this serves as a good place to mention one particularly memorable event, I should not pass it over. It happened in the house of this same gentlewoman, Mrs. Bellamy, a short time before these tragic events occurred.

A plant started to grow in the ceiling of one of her rooms, just above the height of the head, between the principal beam and the mortar work. (It is customary to cover the ceiling of houses on the inside with a smooth layer of mortar or gypsum spread over a solid framework of wood.) It seemed at first to be a herb, but later it began to look more like a shrub, with leaves; then it showed flowers and, finally, bore fruit, like berries. It struck root and grew between the mortar and an old rafter where there was no sap or moisture whatever; and after it had come into leaf and flower, it bore its fruits, just five altogether. It was no sudden occurrence—here one moment and gone the next. It lasted many months, and she showed it to her neighbours, who were all amazed, and rightly so, when they saw it.

The lady was delighted with this new and prodigious plant. She visited it daily and showed it to all who called at the house. Some months later, however, she went as usual to see it and found that it was beginning to droop and wither: its roots were loose and it seemed as though it might fall from the beam. Turning to her daughter-in-law, who had also come into the room, she said, ' What is this, daughter? I fear I shall lose my plant and all its berries.'

As she spoke she raised her hand, intending to straighten the shrub and set it back into place; but before she could touch it the whole thing fell into her hand. It was strange, and she wondered what it meant, afraid it might be a portent for her and her children. And with reason, too. For only a few days afterwards those five young men were captured. And it was this, as some maintained, which was forecast in the miraculous manifestation of the five fruits. Just as she had sustained them with food and provisions while they were wandering in the woods, so their plight, as it were, descended upon her head, to the ruin of herself and her family.[1]

Certain things escaped me in the narrative of (I think) the year 1586, that is, a short time before I was put in prison. They are not of great consequence—but still, they are not too trivial to be passed over altogether.

After I had visited several other places, I sought hospitality once at the house of a certain Catholic. He was a very old man, his hair completely white. He was at least an octogenarian. Before Henry VIII destroyed and did away with the monasteries, he had been in the employment of the abbey of Glastonbury, either as a servant or as the holder of an administrative office in some department.[2] At the overthrow of the house all its most sacred treasures and consecrated possessions were dispersed in a profane manner among the people, and fell into sacrilegious hands. In addition to other things which the old man was able to seize and save, as it were, from the conflagration was a certain cross, venerable and hallowed not so much for its material interest—though it was worked with gold and valuable gems—as because it encased the remains of revered saints. Its principal relic was one of the nails with which our Saviour Christ was fastened to the Cross, and an almost immemorial tradition held that it had been brought to England by St. Joseph of Arimathea and his companions. Through successive generations it had been passed down from hand to hand and finally it had become the recognised property of the monastery of Glastonbury where there was also a tradition that the body of St. Joseph had been translated several hundred years after his death and preserved with much veneration.

This old man, as was right, kept the nail with great reverence for many years. In time, however, Jewel—the pseudo-bishop of Salisbury—came to hear of it, and with exceeding high-handedness obtained the Queen's authorisation and took it from him.[3] What use he made of it or where he placed it, nobody knows, so I was unable to see the nail; but he showed me the case made of linen in which it had been preserved. The material was soft and still retained the impression of the nail distinctly enough for its dimensions to be clearly seen. As far as I could judge, it was about one foot in length and a finger in breadth towards the top. The head was not broad; lower down, however, it was rather wider than in the other parts, tapering gradually to a bevelled point with four, per-haps five, distinct corners.[4]

He told me also of a remarkable miracle worked by the reliquary containing the nail, or, perhaps, by the cross I mentioned—I cannot remember clearly which it was. It had occurred a short time before I met him and was corroborated by the testimony of nearly all the neighbouring people. The story concerned a certain boy, who had some large and deep wound which had been healed by its simple touch.

The old man's house was three or four miles from the

ancient monastery, but barely a mile from the place which, according to tradition, St. Joseph of Arimathea and his companions had chosen for their dwelling. This was on a high hill, and its old foundations and broken fragments of masonry can be seen there to-day.[5] He told me how occasionally he would visit it out of piety and devotion, climbing up, not on his feet, but on his knees;[6] and how he would take with him the cross and the reliquary containing the nail—' my protection,' he called it, ' against the molestation of spirits.' Indeed, it was possible to hear there the groanings, sighs and wailing voices of people in distress, so that he thought it must be a kind of approach or vestibule for souls passing into the pains of Purgatory.[7] As a constant religious ceremony he kept a lamp suspended and always burning in a part of the house which looked towards the hill. All these stories and many others the old man told me, so that I stayed with him two days or more, entertained and enchanted by his conversation far more than I had expected.[8]

On leaving him I went a few days later to another house which belonged to a well-born Catholic gentleman who brought out for me a New Testament, a big volume in parchment. It was written entirely in large letters of gold, with most elegant capitals and occasional ornamental characters in blue. The initial letter of each chapter was most delicately and artistically decorated, and its workmanship was very old; but through bad preservation, I think, several entire leaves at the beginning had deteriorated and others had perished altogether. Seeing that its present place was unsuitable for such a treasure, and insecure as well, I asked the gentleman to let me have the book and he gave it to me. But for the present I suggested that he should guard it carefully for me, and in a short time I would see that it was removed

to safer keeping. But before I could arrange this, I had been
arrested.

Much about this same time a certain Catholic in extreme
distress at his own sins fell into a state of despair, and resolved
to take his own life. At his first attempt he thrust a dagger,
which he carried about with him, into his belly. The wound
was severe, but not mortal. At the time he was riding in
company on the road, seated in the saddle. In his pain from
the wound he leapt off his horse, pretending he was going to
do something of another nature. But his fellow-travellers
saw streams of blood spurting from his body and ran up in
amazement. They carried him to the nearest town where he
could be cared for. There the wound healed, and he went
back to his family in good health. Four years later, if my
memory is not at fault, he was afflicted once more with the
same mental disease or melancholia, and decided to settle the
matter once and for all in some place where nobody could
disturb him. He was then staying in a very large house, and
he took himself to its farthest and most secluded corner, there
to carry through his deadly purpose. Remembering a rusty
and corroded knife, which several years before he had concealed there in a cranny, he brought it out and began slicing
up his belly into pieces till his bowels gushed forth. In the
pain and torments of death he let out piercing and blood-
curdling shrieks. Eventually, at the other end of the house,
his cries were heard. They rushed straight up, and what a
ghastly sight they saw: a man spattered all over with his own
blood and entrails, shouting and yelling for a confessor. By
a happy chance there was one in the house, and the life of that
desperate soul was prolonged just sufficiently for him to make
a full and complete confession of his sins before he expired.[9]

NOTES

Page 110

[1] There is another account of this phenomenon in the manuscript *Catalogue of Martyrs* (p. 48) at Stonyhurst. Though briefer, it gives some details omitted by W. W., and suggests that the room under the rafters was Mrs. Bellamy's private oratory, for 'while kneeling in her chamber, directly over her head, out of an old post there sprang up a flower with four pendants at it. She lifting up her eyes by chance, saw it and being amazed thereat called her daughter to see it also. The same flower, not long after, fell upon her head, the which she took and put into a box. It is at this time in England and hath been seen by many of good credit.'

[2] This journey to Somerset was made probably in the summer of 1585. The text gives no explanation of it. W. W. may have been making a pilgrimage to Glastonbury, but it is possible also that he was calling on Fr. Persons's mother, if she was still living at that time in the West Country. Fr. Garnet and Fr. Southwell later took care of her, referring to her always in their letters by the code name of 'the old woman'. *C.R.S.*, vol. 2, *passim*.

Page 111

[3] John Jewel, Bishop of Salisbury 1560–71, the leading controversialist among the Elizabethan clergy, abominated what he termed 'the scenic apparatus of divine worship', and dismissed the crucifix as 'a little silver cross of ill-omened origin'. At the same time he was, in Anthony Wood's phrase, a man of 'exquisite erudition in theologicals', his principal work, *Apologia pro Ecclesia Anglicana* (1562), being accepted as the best exposition of the Anglican position in theology. His pupil, Richard Hooker, esteemed him 'the worthiest divine that Christendom had bred for some hundreds of years'. F. O. White, *Lives of Elizabethan Bishops*, pp. 111–2; A. Wood, *Athenae Oxonienses*, vol. 1, p. 393.

[4] At the end of his visitation of the dioceses of Salisbury and Bristol, Jewel wrote to his friend, Peter Martyr (2 November 1559), 'It is almost impossible to conceive what a crop, perhaps I should say, thicket of superstition had grown up in the dark days of Mary. We found everywhere votive relics of the saints, *nails with which Christ had been pierced* (as some infatuated people believe), and God alone knows what tiny fragments of the sacred cross.' *The Works of John Jewel* (Parker Society, 1850), p. 1216.

Page 112

⁵ Fr. William Good, an early English Jesuit (died 1586) who had been brought up at Glastonbury, records the belief of many of the monks that St. Joseph of Arimathea was buried at Montacute or Hamdon Hill (Hamhill), a sharp pointed hill four miles to the west of Yeovil, on the top of which stood the ruins of a chapel until the eighteenth century. There is no doubt that W. W. is confused about his distances. Cf. Dom Aelred Watkin, 'Last Glimpses of Glastonbury' in the *Downside Review*, Winter 1948–9, pp. 76–86.

⁶ 'To it [the chapel] for half a mile well near men ascended on the stone stairs fetching a compass round about the hill.' Thomas Gerard, *Description of Somerset* (1633), ed. Bates (Somerset Record Society), p. 98.

⁷ There was a tradition dating from Celtic times that a passage to Purgatory was to be found on the summit of Glastonbury Tor. It was associated with the legend of the king of the underworld, who was said to dwell there, and it was the origin of St. Patrick's Purgatory. Later the tradition may have become attached also to Brandon Hill. Cf. Aelred Watkin, *loc. cit.*

⁸ Fr. Edward Maihew, the Benedictine historian who was a contemporary of W. W., mentions this old man. 'I remember when I was passing by that hill [Brandon] I heard from trustworthy persons about a certain old man who lived not far from that place who, in the reign of the heretic Queen Elizabeth, used often to visit the site, and was in the habit of praying at a certain spot there on his bended knees.' (Armitage Robinson, *Two Glastonbury Legends*, p. 67.) Thomas Gerard, speaking of the chapel at Brandon, ' where was found one of those nails which fastened Our Saviour to the Cross ', mentions a ' gentleman not far off '; doubtless the same old man, who (as Gerard wrongly asserts) kept the nail ' and after sold it for a great sum of money to be transported beyond the seas '. *Description of Somerset* (1633), p. 98.

Page 113

⁹ If this was a well-known incident, it may have suggested to Spenser the lines in his ' Allegory of Despair ':

> In which a rusty knife fast fixed stood
> And made an open passage for the gushing flood.

Faerie Queene (1590), Book I, Canto IX, stanza 36.

14

MIDNIGHT IN THE CLINK

After five or at most six weeks (I am going back now in the chronological order of my narrative) there was no further talk of transferring me to the Tower. In none of the confessions had they found any pretext for charging me with complicity in the intrigues or actions of the conspirators. I was therefore removed from the custody of the private house and put in the public prison commonly called the Clink, where my cell-companion was a priest called Nicholas Smith.[1]

I remained here in fairly close confinement for rather more than a year.[2] Besides criminals and thieves,[3] to say nothing of Puritans, there were many Catholic priests in this prison,[4] gentlemen of quality, men of middle means, women, and some who were little more than boys.

Not to mention other cases of injustice—and it shows how iniquitous the heretics could be—I met here a lay Catholic with his wife and two children, who had been apprehended and imprisoned several years before on the ground that he was a priest.[5] Also, among the Puritans, there was a preacher of considerable notoriety—you might almost describe him as a prophet—who one day was found by a Catholic in a corner all by himself poring over a small book, trying hard to master it. When asked what the book was, he answered most reluctantly. Then grudgingly he showed an ABC, containing the elements of the alphabet. For eight years or more he had been studying it industriously, but had been unable to make even enough progress to form the letters into words, still less into sentences.[6]

This prison was a much more convenient and congenial place in many ways for, from time to time, I could benefit from the kind services and conversation of the Catholics—though, of course, only through chinks in the walls of my cell.[7] Sometimes, also, we were able to fix a time and place for Mass. Then secretly in the middle of the night we would lower a rope to the room below, which was occupied by Catholics, and draw up the sacred vestments. Early in the morning, when Mass was over and before the other prisoners and the warders were awake, we would let down the rope again in the same way.[8]

One thing also occurred which was an exceptional and immense consolation to me. On the night of our Saviour's nativity, all the Catholics of the prison were gathered with me. Each came first to confession. Three Masses were then said and there was not one of them who did not receive the Body of our Saviour Christ in communion. Finally I spoke with each of them in turn and sent them away safely. There was no mishap. Your Reverence would indeed have been amazed at their devotion, and the skill with which they arranged everything. One of them, in the days when he was a heretic had been a keeper of Catholic prisoners. His ingenious cunning covered a wide range of practice, and with other accomplishments he was most clever at picking the locks of our doors and closing them again. He went round every cell in order, unfastening each door. Then he opened mine, and they all entered and through the whole of the night we celebrated the feast.[9]

The greater part of this year passed for me in the constant

expectation of death. And although, as several people told me, the Queen herself had stated that she was satisfied that Edmunds—meaning me—had taken no part in the conspiracy, yet rumours were going round all the time and constant talk reached me that on such and such a day I would be taken out for public trial, and receive the capital sentence. So frequently, almost daily, was this news brought to me that I passed my days and nights thinking prayerfully about death. There were some Catholic friends of mine who took up my case with the gentlemen of the court and the Queen's close circle. But no one, no matter how high he stood in royal favour, was bold enough to intercede for me. 'If he were a common thief,' one of them said, 'or a murderer or buccaneer, or something of the kind, I would not hesitate one moment to obtain a pardon, or at least to ask for it. But where it is a matter of a Jesuit, I cannot; I am afraid to ask.'

Others too tried to buy me out of prison with money, or get me a pardon or safe-conduct. But when I came to hear of this I wrote immediately to Father Robert Southwell asking him to use every means he knew to stop it. It seemed to me a dishonourable course—a course particularly alien to the Society, so many of whose members were daily risking their lives for the salvation of souls in so many different parts of the world—for a paltry sum to tarnish in a shamefaced manner the confession of my faith. Also I felt I would not be able to look men straightly and confidently in the face again, if I was branded and marked, as it were, with the stigma of pusillanimous, not to say ignoble, conduct. It was not that I did not shudder at the thought of death, nor prize my freedom. I was very much afraid, and I would have welcomed my liberty gladly and with open arms. But the thought always obsessed me, that it was a despicable method of liberation, particularly unworthy of those times in which so many martyrs had been killed for their faith.[10]

While I was here, I also received letters encouraging me to martyrdom from the same Father Robert and from Father John Cornelius,[11] both of them now martyrs of the Society. For what purpose God has kept me safe up to now, I do not know. But He, who has kept me, knows; and I pray that He, whose will it has been so far, may continue to preserve me.

The magistrates often visited this prison and held frequent investigations and enquiries.[12] Once when one of them entered the cell of a certain priest to search it, either he or his attendant let fall some altar-breads on to the floor, and then, as though he knew nothing of the deceit, turned round and pointed to them.

' So this is what goes on here,' he said. ' It's got to stop. And probably this isn't all. I should think it means there are other things hidden here, contrary to the rules and regulations of the prison.'

Then immediately he started to search. He made straight for the place where all our altar furnishings were hidden with the silver chalice. A single board was raised and everything was exposed and carried off. The fact was that the place had been betrayed by a man who from time to time had been allowed in to say Mass. With him my narrative will deal more fully later.[13]

Not satisfied with this haul he passed on at once to my cell. He had a preliminary look round, and then began shifting things from their place, and examining every part of the walls with extreme care. ' Sometimes,' he said, ' I find chalices hidden between the brickwork or in the fireplaces.' As he said this, he drew out a dagger hanging at his side, and began probing with it.   But he was disappointed, though actually, at that very time, I had a silver chalice lying under the hearth, and all he had to do was to lift one brick, and he would have seen the cavity beneath the grate.   On top of it was lying a pile of faggots, and it was an excellent hiding place, for when the brick was replaced and sprinkled with ash, nobody would suspect it unless he were told beforehand.

While I was being harassed by these constant irritations and the unconfirmed reports that I was to die, an official sent for me one day to my prison, and I was taken off to a house where a number of commissioners and examiners had assembled.   A notary was with them, and each item on which I had been previously examined, with the single exception of the Babington affair, was gone over again.   What was my name? I was asked.   What sort of people were my parents?   Where was I born and educated—in England or abroad?   Where had I studied for the priesthood?   Where ordained, and where had I done my first priestly work?   Who had sent me back to England?   What places had I stayed at?   Who were the people I knew?   Where had I said Mass?   Whom had I reconciled to the Church?   What persons' confessions had I heard?   All these questions I answered briefly and without difficulty.   Whenever I could confess the truth without injury, I did so, as was right; but where a moral obligation prevented me from confessing I denied simply that they had any right to press their questions, and said that I could not answer them without sin.   At first, however, they brought out a Bible in the vulgar tongue, and wanted me to swear on it that I was answering them truthfully and sincerely on every point.   I rejected the book.[14]

'But you will swear on a copy of Jerome,' one of them said, ' if we bring it down? '

'No,' I replied. 'I will not swear on that either, or on anything whatever. You are laymen, and I am a cleric. You have no right to force an oath on me or bring me to count. I have a privilege and I am exempt. I claim benefit of clergy.[15] And you have no need to make all this fuss about an oath. I am ready to do anything you wish save what my conscience forbids. Any statement I make to you is as firm as my oath.'

This was only the beginning. Unless my memory is at fault, they passed on to other items. They questioned me about the lawfulness of Pius V's bull excommunicating the Queen. What did I think of it?

'I have never seen the bull,' I said, 'and I have never been told all that is in it.'

At this they pressed me a great deal and persisted in an effort to get some statement out of me. But they failed.

This was the time when there were constant rumours of the Spanish fleet, and great dread and anticipation of it. Even then it was said to be equipping in Spain to sail the following year.[16] They went on, therefore, to ask me many detailed questions about it. Did I know anything about the expedition? Had I any news of its approach? Was I involved at all in the plans? What would I do when it touched the English coast? On which side would I stand? Who would I come out for?

I answered, Yes, I had heard the rumours, but I had received no letters, no secret communications. I had nothing on my person, I had done nothing which might give them ground to convict me. Nor was there anything they could reasonably fear from me. As for which side I would take, in the first place as I did not know the reasons for the war, I could not properly discuss the question. But, even granted that war had been declared with the object of restoring the Catholic religion, or avenging some wrong, or for any other cause whatsoever, just or unjust, I was unwilling and I was unable to stand in arms and fight.[17]   It was not my profession.

'We know that already,' they said. 'But what would you counsel others to do? Which side would you advise them to take, presuming that they came out to fight for religious reasons?'

'You can be certain,' I answered, 'that in an emergency such as this I should do nothing that conflicted with my religion. Here and now I can state that. But what my conduct would be when the time came, I cannot say. The shifts of men's opinion are incalculable. There is no sense, or right or justice in branding me a criminal because of something I *might* or *might not* do.'

But they did not stop at that. They teased the matter inside out, turning over different modes of expression and formulas for possible contingencies, situations that sometimes arose and could not, therefore, be ruled out as altogether improbable. They would lay down some hypothesis and demand a straightforward and plain answer. And, exactly as if the case had been actual, they would certainly have seized upon it and made it a matter for conviction.

So this examination was prolonged for three or four hours. And the questions touched many points apart from the above: in particular, the death of Mary, Queen of Scots. To what extent, they asked, had it been a catastrophe for the Catholic body, bereft now, as at last they were, of the final hope they had of ruling the country and seeing prevail the religion which they clung to and loved with such passion?[18]

This, in summary, was the drift of their questions and my answers.

I was then sent back to my prison. There I devoted myself entirely to my former practices of prayer and meditation on death. Every moment I expected a summons to stand my trial and receive sentence. This, in fact, was the rumour abroad, and it was what everyone expected.[19] Naturally the Catholics were anxious to know in detail all the items on which I had been examined, and I met their wishes by passing through the chinks and holes in the walls a written account of what had passed. Other prisoners, there and elsewhere, expected to be treated in the same fashion and thought it likely they would be asked the same questions.

Nevertheless, with all the tribulation, persecution and even death which the Catholics suffered daily, three of our keeper's own family were converted to the faith;[20] also an assistant warder; one very old man and a young girl, who left her former employment and henceforth gave devoted service to Catholic masters.

NOTES

Page 116

¹ Fr. Nicholas Smith, whom W. W. knew before his imprisonment, was related to Fr. Southwell's cousins, the Copleys. It was at Lady Copley's house, Gatton, Surrey, that he was arrested on 11 September 1586, along with Lady Copley herself and her daughter. Fr. Smith had joined the Jesuit noviciate at Sant' Andrea with Fr. Southwell but had been obliged to leave on account of his health. He rejoined later, dying in Lincolnshire in 1630 at the age of seventy-two. Foley, vii, part 2, p. 719; *C.R.S.*, vol. 2, p. 268.

² From September 1586 to January 1588.

³ Felons detained in the Clink and other prisons were a constant source of irritation to Catholics. ' All the robbers, murderers and other malefactors who are detained in the same prisons are set on against their Catholic fellow prisoners with insults and curses in the hope of greater favour and impunity for their misdeeds, and daily prevent them from sharing in the alms, bread and other things sent to the prisons.' Letter of 1584 quoted in *Memoirs of Fr. Robert Persons, C.R.S.*, vol. 4, p. 140.

⁴ In a prison list drawn up in November 1586 there were ten priests then in the Clink, including Anthony Tyrrell. *C.R.S.*, vol. 2, p. 268.

⁵ This was John Launder, with his wife Anne. He was committed to the Clink on 18 June 1584 and his wife, who had been imprisoned in the Hull block-house, reserved for women recusants, followed him there on 22 March 1586. When Anne was first apprehended at York in 1577, John, an attorney, attempted to defend her at law and was told by the Earl of Huntingdon that there was ' no law for Catholics '. Both died in the Clink, Anne in 1589, John on 26 January 1591. They had seven children. Probably W. W. refers to the two youngest who would have been cared for by their parents in the Clink. *C.R.S.*, vol. 22, p. 14.

Page 117

⁶ This Puritan was Samuel Mounsey. His name occurs on a list of prisoners in the Clink made out in April 1584, where he is described as a Brownist (*S.P.D., Eliz.*, vol. clxx, no. 10). The book which he had been studying for eight years was most probably Richard Huloet's *Abcedarium Anglo-Latinum pro Tyrunculis* (1552) which, as Thomas Fuller says, was ' a book of low and general use for the common people, who then began to betake themselves to reading . . . so that many who had one foot in the grave had one hand on their primer '. *Worthies of England* (ed. 1643), p. 158.

⁷ John Gerard described his removal from the Counter in Poultry

to the Clink as a ' transference from Purgatory to Paradise ' for the same reasons given by W. W. He also gives an account of midnight Mass in the Clink and of the Good Friday ceremonies (*John Gerard*, ch. 12). The Catholics in the Marshalsea, a stricter prison, were equally ingenious. Walsingham's secretary concluding a report of a celebration there on 22 July 1586, writes: ' Your Honour sees how well these kind of prisoners are looked to by their keepers.'

[8] All this time W. W. was being watched by Anthony Tyrrell, who reported on him to Burghley and Richard Young: ' Father Edmunds and Mr. Smith, the priest [he writes] being placed together in one chamber. . . . I informed how they had Mass every day, how many were let in and how often times unto them, how they made exhortations and preachings at times unto companies and who they were that heard them.' *Two Missionaries*, pp. 418–9.

[9] Writing to Rome four days before Christmas 1586, Southwell speaks of the comfort W. W. gave to his fellow Catholic prisoners in the Clink. ' In prison [W. W.] is devout and steadfast, so much so that he makes imprisonment more pleasant to those in chains, and less fearful to them that are free.' *C.R.S.*, vol. 5, p. 310.

Page 119

[10] Details of one attempt to obtain W. W.'s release in 1587 are given in the *Life of the Earl of Arundel* (p. 27). ' When he was first taken and put prisoner in the Clink, the Countess of Arundel went in disguise to visit him, and offering by means of money to procure his banishment, as was usual in those times, his answer was, that he was not committed to prison for money, so neither would he be released by money, but expect that either God or they by whose authority he was deprived of his liberty should of their own accord set him free.' It appears that W. W. came to this decision in consultation with Fr. Garnet, who wrote to Persons on 29 October 1588: ' About William [W. W.] and Ralph [Emerson] we have already explained that he could be bought out of prison for a small sum of money. In the case of William, we have not approved of such action up to now. Since he has as it were gained for himself an eminent and illustrious position he is exposed to everyone's gaze, and it would look shameful for the shepherd to fly from his flock —a sordid transaction indeed to sell the bonds of Christ for the wretched price of fake freedom.' Arch. S.J., Rome, *Fondo Gesuitico*, 651.

[11] Fr. Cornelius was captured on 14 April 1594, at Chideock Castle, Dorset, after saying Mass for Lady Arundel. While he was held prisoner in the house of Sir George Trenchard, sheriff of Dorset,

he received a visit from Sir Walter Raleigh who spent the whole night with him in an attempt to clear his religious doubts. ' He [Raleigh] was so pleased with the Father's conviction and reasoning and with his modest and courteous manner, that he offered to do all he could in London for his liberation, and this although the Father had gently reproved him for his mode of life and conversation.' Fr. Cornelius, however, was executed at Dorchester on 4 July 1594. Fr. Gerard writes that 'he was so famous in preaching that all Catholics followed him, as children do their nurse when they long for milk '. Foley, iii, p. 462.

[12] The purpose of these raids was often the extraction of payment in kind from the poorer prisoners, who apart from the money demanded for their maintenance, had, in addition, still to pay the fine for non-attendance at church; they were often forced therefore ' to give the furniture which they had for necessary uses in prison, such as beds, books and other things of the sort, to make up the money. . . . The Knight Marshal [consequently] visited all the prisons and took away whatever he could find, either in ready money or in clothes or any other stores.' Letter from England (1584) quoted in *Memoirs of Father Robert Persons, C.R.S.*, vol. 4, p. 141.

[13] This was Anthony Tyrrell. He himself admits that this search and ' the finding out of some secret places which, without discovery [i.e., betrayal] could not easily have been known ', was the final act which caused W. W. and other priest prisoners to shun Tyrrell as a traitor. *Two Missionaries*, p. 440.

Page 120

[14] If a Catholic, particularly a priest, swore on the Protestant version of the Bible, it was assumed that he recognised it as a faithful translation in all its parts. Examiners were always trying to extract this recognition from eminent Catholic prisoners. Cf. *John Gerard*, pp. 96–7.

Page 121

[15] W. W. is here questioning the right of civil examiners to exact an oath from the clergy. Before the Reformation a cleric in England could be tried by lay judges only after he had been defrocked by the ecclesiastical courts. The system still prevailed in Rome and Spain, where W. W. had been living for more than twelve years. He seems to have taken the board by surprise, for they proceeded in their examination without insisting further on an oath.

[16] The first reports of preparations for an invasion reached England in December 1585 and were confirmed eight months later, shortly before

W. W. was arrested. It was then that the first counter-measures were taken: the houses of recusants were searched for arms and orders were issued for the mustering of footbands. In August 1586 there were rumours that the French had landed in Sussex and in the following month a report that the Spanish fleet had been seen off the coast of Brittany. Tension then subsided until the summer of 1587.

Page 122

[17] From his reply it is clear that W. W. was asked the famous ' bloody question '—what would he do if the Pope declared war with the avowed object of re-establishing the Catholic faith in England ? It was a hypothetical question framed by Burghley with the purpose of trapping Catholics into a reply which could be construed as disloyalty to the Crown. Cf. *John Gerard*, pp. 235–6.

[18] Thomas Pound, mentioned later in W. W.'s narrative, was at this time a prisoner in the White Lion in Southwark. He records how his keeper, in a similar manner, tried to learn from him what effect the Queen's death had on the morale of Catholics. ' Out of my window ', he writes, ' I saw the bonfires and banquets in the streets for our King's [James I] mother's death; a justice there saying to me in derision, at sight of her picture in my chamber, that he was sorry for the loss to all the Papists of so good a friend.' *The Rambler*, New Series, vol. viii, *Biographical Sketch of Thomas Poundes*, p. 27.

Page 123

[19] After W. W.'s name in a list of prisoners drawn up in December 1586 is the note in the hand of Thomas Phelippes, Walsingham's agent: ' to be kept, if not hanged '. It is clear that at this time Walsingham, for whom the list was made out, had not decided W. W.'s fate.

[20] ' Fr. Weston succeeded in winning over the keeper; and he converted him and his wife and young daughter. Thus it became easy for people to come in numbers to see and converse with him.' Fr. de Peralta (f. 220) is clearly wrong in implying that these conversions took place at Wisbech. The office of keeper in the Clink seems to have changed hands frequently. One of this keeper's successors was in his turn converted by John Gerard. Cf. *John Gerard*, pp. 101–2.

15

A DISCUSSION WITH DR. ANDREWES

About the same time and in the same year I chanced to hold a disputation with a University Doctor called Andrewes.[1] He was a man of considerable repute among them, and he is now, I hear, the pseudo-bishop of Ely. I was summoned, then, from prison and escorted to the place appointed for the disputation.[2]

'We want you to talk with this learned gentleman,' said the man who had given the order to call me. 'Explain your views to him. See, in turn, if he will make any impression on you. No one will interfere. You can put your questions and difficulties to him, just as if you were alone together.'

'If this disputation is intended for my benefit,' I said, 'I do not see how I can allow it at all. I have no doubt or uncertainty, great or small, in any matter of faith. Discussions of this kind should be held in universities or in places where the public can gather. Then the truth, plain and uncorrupted, can be set forth and all its sham substitutes exposed so that the people who are now caught up in error can see and understand it, naked and stripped of lies.'

'No,' he said. 'That is not the way to proceed. It would give you a chance to seduce any number of persons. But if you so wish, then seven or eight of your folk can come here to my house, and the same number from our side. There will be space for them—if not here, then somewhere else. And you can have your books too.'

'But who are to be the judges?' I asked, 'and who is going to listen? For unless the judges and listeners are chosen from both sides, the truth will be suppressed and buried. However,' I went on, 'arrange for the people to come as you suggest. But see that you bring in reliable notaries, who will act for both sides, and record faithfully every syllable, statement, and argument of both parties. You will not find it difficult to get them. There are sure to be many persons who will be glad to come forward and have some function to perform.'

This did not, however, meet with his approval. 'You can go off now,' he said, 'and have your discussion together. Nobody will disturb you.'

At this he left and shut the doors, leaving us alone.[3]

I told Andrewes I had no need to take instruction from him, as from a master and doctor, when I had the faith and authority of the Church to teach me. But if he wanted to put any questions to me, since we were alone, I said that he could ask them.

The discussion turned on sacramental confession and the interpretation of Scripture; possibly also on other subjects, but I have no clear recollection of them now. Certainly many points must have been raised, for we were there about four hours. Regarding the first two questions, he admitted in the end quite frankly that he did not allow the capricious and blundering construction of private persons in the inter-pretation of Scripture. Similarly on confession, he did not deny its use, even its lawful use, and admitted that among his own people the custom was not altogether unknown. This doctor, as I think, was one of those Puritans who allow some form of confession, and his frame of mind, as some held, was not altogether opposed to the Catholic faith.[4]

It would take a long time to put down the remainder of our conference, and I pass it over more readily because, apart from these two topics of confession and Scripture, the details of the rest have escaped my memory.

At first I did not know the reason for this meeting. I thought it most strange to be summoned to a private disputation of this kind, with no witness and no arbiter. But two days after I had been sent back to prison a complete stranger came to see me. He had the keeper's permission, but whether he was a Catholic or heretic, I do not know. All that I can say for certain is that he was friendlily disposed and intended me a kindness.

'It is possible,' he said, 'that no one has told you the reason for your conference with Andrewes. There were two priests present at it. They were placed very close and were able to overhear every word that was said. So affected were they that they almost broke out of hiding. In fact, they were on the point of confessing their inconstancy, and wanted to make an open profession of their faith and return to their senses there and then, after their lapse into error.' Fear of torture and death had made these men waver in their faith.[5] One of them (if I am not mistaken, and I do not think I am) later suffered martyrdom for the faith.[6] The other was

---

Explanation of illustration: After the possessed person has been carried into the Church (A), a Friar preaches to the people (B) and the Bishop offers Mass (C). With the help of a notary the Bishop then examines the devil (D), who reveals that his name is Beelzebub (E); the Bishop then raises the Sacred Host in his right hand and conjures the devil to leave the possessed person (F), but at this Beelzebub cries so raucously (G) that the Church fills with townspeople, in whose presence the remaining rites are carried out (H to M). Finally the devil gives up the struggle and a thanksgiving service is held (N) in the presence of the civic officials (O). All Beelzebub's companions follow their master into flight (P to S) and the ceremonies conclude with the blessing of the sick (V).

DEO

ET SVMMO IESV-CHRISTI VICARIO
IOCHANNES BOVLÆSE PRESBITER
ET CIVIS LAVMDVNENSIS PAVPER
COLLEGII MONTIS-ACVTI PARISIENSIS

1566

La Croisée de l'Eglise.

La Nef de l'Eglise toute pleine de peuple.

AN EXORCISM AT LAON

according to the ritual later introduced into England by
Father Weston and the Douai priests.

DR. JOHN REYNOLD

DR. LANCELOT
ANDREWES

Anthony Tyrrell, about whom I promised earlier to say more. This is his story.

This other Anthony was captured a short time before Babington, and confined in the prison called the Poultry.[7] He possessed little resolution, and soon began to vacillate. He was tempted partly by the flattering promises of the heretics and the hope of obtaining freedom; partly, also, he was fearful of the torments of death and torture. Now in the same prison with him were a number of Catholics.[8] They were most observant and thought it a bad sign that so many heretics came to see him and have long conversations with him. They discovered also, after some time, that he received and kept by him a number of heretical books, an English Bible and Calvin's *Institutes*. This further confirmed their suspicion that his courage was declining.

Some months later he was transferred to our prison, where, at that time, I was kept in strict custody.[9] Here also was a large number of Catholics in bonds, most of them in connection with the case of that noble youth, Babington.[10] All these people, as reasons for just suspicion multiplied on every side, began either to shun the man's company altogether or deal more guardedly with him. First of all, when there was no necessity whatever, he continued to wear lay clothes.[11] Then at table, when he was the only priest present in a large company of lay Catholics, he could not be persuaded to say grace. They noticed also his breviary—how the tabs and markers for the office of the day were never in position.[12] And, again, his too intimate dealings and intercourse with heretics rather suggested that all about him was not as right and holy as became a priest, or as befitted a person who was in prison for his faith and under the observation of so many heretics and Catholics alike.

In the end he ceased to deceive. A short time after this he shook off both his prison bondage and his religion, and, going over to the heretics, he was granted his liberty.

Now, just at this time, a Catholic who had been sharing his cell began to reflect carefully on the man's character, and he decided to make a minute examination of the room to see whether he could find any of his possessions or any letters and papers written by him. And he hit on a place where he had concealed several letters of William Cecil and his own replies, all torn into little pieces.[13] These he brought to me and asked me how we could use them, in order to have him convicted on this irrefutable evidence—for he had always done his utmost to conceal his duplicity and not be shown up for his sin against religion. I instructed him to lay out the pieces on the table, fit them together, and then stick them with glue. We could then read them and send them to the Marshalsea prison where, among other prisoners, there were several priests. We would tell them to call the man up, and, first and above all else, expostulate with him about his treachery in conspiring with heretics, and at the same time use every means in their power to persuade him to return to his profession. If he was obstinate and persisted in denying his crime, then they should produce Cecil's letters and his own, and shut his impudent mouth by showing him the plain evidence against him.

So the priests summoned the man to call on them.[14] They did their best to get him to see with his own eyes the heinousness of his sin against God, against his fellow men and against his own conscience. But he did not seem in the least disconcerted by what they said. So they then showed him the letters, written in his own hand and he admitted he was the liar he had been proved. Convicted now, he promised to return to the Church, renounce his pact with the heretics, and do serious penance. Furthermore he undertook, so far as he was able, to repair the injury he had done to others by his actions and accusations. All this indeed he did. And in a long screed he revealed all his former frauds and the reason for his collapse.[15] He also exonerated many persons from his wicked and unjust accusations; and, for myself, he cleared me completely of many aspersions.

This scandal, however, had spread far and wide. Nothing was more talked about or eagerly awaited than Tyrrell the priest's public recantation of the Catholic faith. The place and date fixed for the renunciation could not have been more suitably chosen: it was to be at St. Paul's Cross on the occasion of the public sermon to the people. The day came. At the appointed time John Reynolds mounted the pulpit.[16] Taking as the subject of his sermon a perfidious priest's recantation of his faith, he assumed he was going to score a striking triumph. Anthony Tyrrell went up at the same time; but with a very different purpose. Far from intending any action against the faith, he proposed to retract and abjure his errors. There, in front of the people, he would confess his treachery and the causes of his fall, and, after expressing his grief at his sin, promise that, no matter what time was left to him to live, never again, in speech or deed, would he offend against religion. He faced the people. He began to address them.[17] Instantly the heretics realised that the occasion was being turned against them. They seized hold of him and dragged him forcibly from the pulpit.

But Tyrrell had a second card. As it was impossible now to give a complete and detailed explanation of his conduct, he took out a sheaf of papers from his jacket. These contained a full statement of his case, and he scattered them among the crowd so that they would have a chance to snatch and read for themselves all they had been prevented from hearing. Indeed, he had guessed that he would never be suffered to go through with his sermon to the end. And in place of his address, which, as it happened, was cut short, he had prepared this leaflet.[18]

From the pulpit he was rushed hurriedly to prison.[19] There he was put behind bars, fastened with iron chains, and tormented in a thousand different ways. What am I to say now? Unable to endure this harsh treatment, he threw everything over again. He succumbed to Satan's wiles and surrendered a second time to the heretics, lured by excessive love of liberty and the hope of obtaining pardon. After his release, he came back again to his Catholic acquaintances, full of moans at his inconstancy. But as there now appeared slender hope that he would be able to live in England without getting trapped again by heretics, they arranged for him to pass the rest of his life abroad, safely established among Catholics and remote from all temptation. But he would not rest. He returned—the wretched and wayward man—a few days later, and joined up again with the heretics.[20] As one of their ministers he served their sacrilegious tables almost to extreme old age.[21] Finally, as I have recently heard, one of his brothers, a Catholic and very devout man, by his constant warnings and fervent prayers brought him back to God and His Church, the most secure anchorage of salvation. To make his conversion sure, he went abroad into Belgium where he died at peace with the Lord and at one with the Church.[22]

Page 128

[1] At this time the famous Dr. Lancelot Andrewes was thirty-two, about four years younger than W. W. After gaining a great reputation for his catechetical sermons at Cambridge, he had been appointed chaplain to the Earl of Huntingdon, President of the Council of the North. In this post he is said to have won over many waverers to Protestantism. As the sequel to this story shows, it was hoped that Andrewes by confuting W. W. would ' convert ' two priests who were listening to the discussion in secret. Although, as Fuller says, ' the world wanted learning to know how learned this man was ', W. W. got the better of him on this occasion.

[2] Fr. de Peralta rightly places this discussion in the first weeks of W. W.'s confinement in the house near the Clink. de Peralta, f. 219.

Page 129

[3] W. W. was clearly anxious to prevent false or biased reports of the conference circulating among the public, as had happened in the case of Campion's debates with his even more distinguished Anglican adversaries. W. W. won his point, for it was agreed that the discussion should be a private one between himself and Andrewes.

[4] W. W.'s observation is exact. By Lent 1600, when Dr. Andrewes preached at Court, he had advanced to a still more Catholic position on the subject of confession. ' His text was the 20th chapter of St. John, the 23rd verse, touching the forgiveness of sins upon earth. He said that contrition, without confession and absolution, was not sufficient; that the ministers had the two keys of power and knowledge delivered unto them, that whose sins they remitted upon earth should be remitted in heaven. The Court is full of it, for such doctrine is not usually taught here.' *Sidney Papers*, vol. ii, p. 185.

Page 130

[5] ' The reason of the discussion was that a Catholic priest had promised them [viz., the Council] that if they could convince Father Weston, he would join their sect, and so he was hidden behind some curtains during the whole time of the discussion. But the Doctor was convinced and confounded in the debate and the priest animated and confirmed in the Catholic faith.' de Peralta, f. 219.

[6] Fr. Edward James, who was then in the Marshalsea. He is the only priest in a London prison at this time who vacillated and later suffered martyrdom. When he came to the gallows at Chichester on 1 October

1585, he was deliberately kept back to watch his companion, Fr. Ralph Crockett, suffer in the hope that he would yield at the sight of his execution. J. H. Pollen, *Lives of English Martyrs*, vol. 1, pp. 496–7.

Page 131

[7] Tyrrell was captured on 4 July 1586 and committed not to the Poultry, as W. W. says, but to the Wood Street Counter. *C.R.S.*, vol. 2, p. 253.

[8] Among the Catholics in the Wood Street Counter was Fr. Richard Dryland, who was later with W. W. at Wisbech and presumably gave him these details. Tyrrell had been in prison a month when his old ally, Ballard, and the other conspirators were arrested. This so alarmed him that he turned informer, bearing fatal but false witness against his fellow-priests (cf. *sup.*, p. 98, n. 17). On the instructions of Young he continued to hear confessions and say Mass in order to keep his credit among his Catholic fellow-prisoners.

[9] Tyrrell was transferred to the Clink on 13 September on Young's instructions. *C.R.S.*, vol. 2, p. 273.

[10] A list of these prisoners is printed in *C.R.S.*, vol. 2, pp. 268, 271.

[11] It was the custom among Catholic priests to wear the clerical soutane in prison. Cf. *John Gerard*, p. 94.

[12] 'I thought it booted me not to pray', writes Tyrrell himself referring to this time, 'and yet without prayer I thought the devil should have too much power over me. The sign of the Cross and other customs of the Catholic Church I had laid aside, and yet at times fear forced me to use them.' *Two Missionaries*, p. 434.

Page 132

[13] Tyrrell himself preserved one of these letters from Cecil and copied it into his Autobiography; it concluded with these words of patronage: 'Your dissimulation is to a good end, and therefore both tolerable and commendable. I pray you therefore persevere therein, as I will persevere in goodwill. In haste.' The letter was written on 23 September 1586, and signed, 'Your loving friend, W. Burghley'. *Two Missionaries*, p. 419.

[14] Tyrrell at first refused to answer the summons of his fellow-priests in the Marshalsea, but suspecting 'some further discovery of myself besides that of the Clink, but not knowing what it could be, I determined to go'. On entering he was 'lovingly saluted' by Fr. Lewis Barlow, a priest whom he had betrayed, who with friendliness 'did break unto me these matters, telling me of the letters that had been written with

mine own hand '. Tyrrell first ' denied a great while any such matter, but in the end one or two of my brethren were called in, who showed me mine own handwriting, and the matter it did contain, which when I did see, my purpose of persisting in obstinacy relented '. *Two Missionaries*, p. 444.

Page 133

15 This is Tyrrell's Autobiography edited by Fr. Persons and published in *Two Missionaries*. It deals with his fall and treachery up to the time of his meeting with the priests in the Marshalsea.

16 The choice of John Reynolds, who was considered one of the best preachers of the day, shows the importance given to Tyrrell's recantation. ' There wanted not concourse of people from all parts, and many of the Council and nobility were also present to hear so rare a comedy.' *Two Missionaries*, p. 489.

17 Southwell, who was probably an eye-witness, gives the opening sentences of Tyrrell's speech. After the people had been called upon to recite Psalm vi, Tyrrell mounted his pulpit and began: ' It has been given out that I have come to this gathering in order to renounce the ancient faith which I sucked in with my mother's milk and which I have always cherished from my tenderest years. But today I shed the most bitter tears, and will always do so, because at times I have pretended in a most ungodly way to profess a faith which I knew was false. Standing here I proclaim myself a member of the Roman Catholic Church and I embrace its faith from my heart. God's good spirit has inspired me to return to it and with God's help I am ready to die for it and I shall think myself happy if at such a price I can atone for the grievous sins I have committed.' This was as far as he was allowed to proceed. Southwell to Aquaviva, 22 January 1588, the day following Tyrrell's abortive sermon, Arch. S.J., Rome, *Fondo Gesuitico*, 651.

Page 134

18 This leaflet was printed the next year in Fr. John Gibbon's *Concertatio Ecclesiae Anglicanae* (1589).

19 Fr. Persons gives a more detailed account of this incident. ' After he had uttered a few lines at the beginning . . . all began to cry *Crucifige* upon him, and to pull him from the pulpit; at what time he cast abroad his papers. . . . All was in marvellous hurly and burly. . . . The people had heard three sermons in one hour, all contrary the one to the other; the first of the preacher in praise and credit of Tyrrell; the second of Tyrrell in derogation of the preacher; the third of Justice Young

threatening death to those that should believe Tyrrell. But the concourse of the people was so unruly as Tyrrell was carried away on men's shoulders to the gaol of Newgate. . . . The Protestants crying out vengeance on him, and he weeping bitterly and knocking his breast, and affirming that he had done nothing but upon mere force and compulsion of his conscience; and the concourse was so great about the prison as they were forced to change him within two hours after to the Counter where none came to him but Topcliffe and Young.' *Two Missionaries*, pp. 496–7.

[20] W. W. is wrong in placing Tyrrell's visit to the Continent after his sermon at St. Paul's. The order of events is this. After his reconciliation in the Marshalsea Tyrrell had a temporary lapse, during which he acted for a short time as a spy in Norfolk. He then came back to his Catholic friends in prison ' full of moans at his inconstancy '. They reconciled him a second time and subscribed fifty pounds to get him safely abroad. But Walsingham, knowing he had written ' fifty sheets ', viz. his Autobiography, exposing Burghley and Young, set his spies to track him down. Tyrrell however eluded them, crossed the Scottish border and took ship from Leith to Germany in May. He appears to have stayed on the Continent only long enough to despatch his ' fifty sheets ' to Persons when he returned unaccountably to England and gave himself up. It was then that Burghley arranged for him to preach at St. Paul's the sermon which W. W. describes above. Cf. Christopher Devlin, ' An Unwilling Apostate ' in *The Month*, December 1951.

[21] After nine months in prison Tyrrell again weakened and preached a recantation sermon at St. Paul's on 8 December the same year (1588), taking as his text Matthew 12, vv. 43–4. In return Burghley rewarded him with two small livings, Dengy and Southminster, in Essex, and a concubine, ' for wife by reason of my priesthood she could be none '. He makes his last appearance in 1601 when he made depositions before Bancroft concerning the exorcisms he had practised with W. W. fifteen years before.

[22] This is confirmed by a note—*mortuus est poenitens*—after Tyrrell's name in a list of apostate priests in the Archives of the old Chapter. Cf. Christopher Devlin's article, ' An Unwilling Apostate ' in *The Month*, December 1951. This is the best summary of Tyrrell's character and career.

16

DEVILS GALORE

The year '88 now broke, and with it came tense expectation, and large-scale preparations by sea and land to meet the Spanish fleet.[1] It was reported to be approaching in immense strength, and the Queen's Council reckoned it would be of little avail to meet foreign arms with arms, if they did not take timely measures against internal dangers. And since they held the whole name and race of Catholics in perpetual suspicion, they made provision, insofar as the situation allowed, for a large section of the priests and noble lay-folk to be herded into remote prisons. They feared that, given the opportunity, they might go over to the enemy.[2]

The decision was made public. The first to receive the order were the priests held in London prisons: not all of them, but some only of that large number, and among them myself. Accordingly a messenger was posted to me in the name of the whole Council. ' It is the Queen's pleasure,' he said, ' and the Lords' of the Council, that you should go to Wisbech castle in a few days' time.' [3]

' At whose expense? ' I asked.

' Your own,' he said.

I was, however, allowed two or three days in which to visit, in company with my keeper, various friends and obtain from them everything I needed for the journey, so far as they could provide it. Actually I had all the money I required, but

I gladly took advantage of this permission in order to gratify a number of people who wanted very much to see and speak to me, but had not dared to come near the prison.

The next day, therefore, I changed my habit for lay clothes and went out. First of all I visited the Catholics confined in other prisons, priests and laymen alike, and on my side as much as theirs it was a source of great joy and happiness.

While I was busy visiting my friends, a messenger came to me from a certain illustrious and noble lady, asking me on no account to leave her out of my calls before my departure.

'I can easily arrange that,' I answered. Then I added, 'But I have my keeper. Wherever I go, he accompanies me and never lets me out of his sight. He will certainly not allow me to go anywhere without him.'

'No. That will not do,' said the messenger. (The lady was of more than ordinary nobility.) [4] 'See if you cannot get free of him for a few hours. Come by yourself, if you can arrange it. If not, do not trouble yourself further.'

'There's no harm in trying,' I said, 'but I do not think there's much chance of my succeeding.'

I left the place—it was a prison—and went on my way to visit some other people. As soon as we were alone together, I turned to John (that was the keeper's name).[5]

'I have just received a message from a friend,' I said. 'He wants me to see him, and he won't take any excuse.'

'Of course you can go,' he answered, 'whenever you like. Go now, if you wish.'

'But I don't want you to come and stand over me all the time,' I explained.

'Impossible,' he said. 'I'm not letting my eyes off you.

I have special orders to guard you most strictly. That's my task. If you slip out of my hands, it is I who will suffer. I fear I cannot let you go alone.'

'Already,' I said, 'you've had some experience of me. You know the kind of man I am. You have seen that I can be trusted, that I am not the sort of person to betray anyone who has done me a kindness.'

Then I took out an angel [6] (it is a gold coin worth twenty reals).

'Take this,' I said. 'I'll see that you get something out of it, even if you don't ask for anything. It's yours for the permission.'

'I daren't,' he said. 'I daren't.'

He had scarcely gone another six steps, when he said, 'Tell me when you'll be back, and where I can find you after you have seen your friend.'

That was the effect of a little gold.

'It's for you to say what suits you,' I replied. 'Any time and any place will be convenient to me.'

Perhaps these trivial details may seem unimportant, but my reason for mentioning them is that this was how I came to see Father Robert Southwell and have a very long conversation with him, and also to visit other illustrious persons. Moreover, I was given the opportunity of comforting and assisting a soul in acute distress. [7]

This man, a Catholic, was staying in a heretical house. His keeper had given him leave to come to London on important business, for he had been confined in a country prison a long way out of London. He had now caught some lingering disease and was suffering severely; in fact, he was not far from death. The woman who looked after him in his sickness was a Catholic, and she had been all through the city searching everywhere for a priest to aid him in his extremity. She had failed to find one. Then she had sent me a message telling me of the man's danger, and asking me, if I could possibly arrange it, to come and attend him, for he was almost at his last gasp. So I availed myself of my liberty, bought with a paltry piece of gold, and went to his bedside. I explained that I was a priest—for I was wearing lay clothes— and had come to hear his confession.

'If that is what you have come for,' he said, 'it's no use. The time for confession is over.'

'What,' I said, 'you mean to say that you are not a Catholic? You ought to know what you should do, particularly now. You believe that this is your last hour. Then make a good and complete confession while there is yet time, so that if any guilt remains from the sins of your past life, you can rid your self of it.'

'I repeat,' he said, 'you have come too late. The time for all that is past. Judgment has taken place; sentence is already pronounced. I am condemned and handed over, for good and all, to the devil. I have no hope of forgiveness.'

'What nonsense,' I said. 'There's no bigger mistake you could make. No one, as long as there is life left in him, no one can say he is cut off from God's goodness, or so abandoned by His grace that when he craves and beseeches God's helping mercy it is refused him outright. You know—your faith teaches you—God's mercy is infinite. It is mightier than all our sins and all the wickedness and power of the devil. There is no bond imaginable that He cannot break; no excess of crime that He cannot overcome and conquer by His goodness and grace.'

'Can't you see,' he said, 'the room is full of devils? Yes, here where we are. They're in every nook and cranny. In

the ceiling, in the walls. A thousand. More. Terrible
black devils, with fearful faces. They mutter and terrify
me. They go on and on. They never stop. They're savagely cruel. They say they'll drag me down to the bottom
of hell. I have the cursed creatures inside me. In my
bowels. I am full of them. They claw me to pieces. They
tear me in all directions—torture me, body and soul, with a
thousand torments. It's not as if I were going to be snatched
away instantly and smothered in pain. I seem to be hurled
into hellfire already. Clearly God has abandoned me. He
has barred me for ever from all hope of mercy.'

I trembled as I listened to this, and to many other similar
things he said. At the same time I saw clearly that death was
drawing near. He would take no counsel. Nothing I could
say would move him. There was no one I could ask for
advice. In silence and suspense I tried to think what best
to do. Then—I think it must have been God who suggested
it, as the result seemed to show it—this very good way of
dealing with him occurred to me.

' Look,' I said, ' you may be damned. I am not going to
ask you to make a confession. But just recollect yourself a
moment. Answer briefly. Don't worry yourself at all. Say
' yes ' or ' no ' to the questions I ask. That's all I want you
to do. Nothing more. Just answer simply. There is no need
for anything else.'

Then I started going through the Commandments, taking
them in order. First, had he denied his faith? ' Now look,'
I said, ' don't torment yourself. Simply say " yes " or " no ".
That's all.' So, as he affirmed or denied each point, we
proceeded in sequence to the fourth and fifth Commandments.
Had he killed anyone? or stolen? or fornicated? and so on.
As he replied more calmly, I asked, ' What are the devils

like now? How do you feel? Are you suffering much?' [8]

'They are quieter now,' he said. 'They don't seem to be raging so much as before.'

'Lift up your heart and think of God,' I told him, 'and we will go through to the end.'

Then in the same way I went on to question him in order, covering what remained. Then I asked him again: 'How are things now?'

'All the agony in my soul has gone,' he answered. 'The devils are keeping their distance. They are throwing stones. They are making dreadful faces, threatening hideous things. I don't see how I shall escape them.'

And so I soothed him gradually and helped him to recover himself. With every moment he gathered more and more control, till in the end he made an excellent and exhaustive confession of his sins, satisfactory both to himself and me, after which I gave him absolution.

'Do you see anything now?' I asked. 'Are the devils troubling you still?'

'No, not at all,' he answered, 'they have all fled. Not a trace of them is to be seen, thanks be to God.' [9]

I gave him a few words of comfort and strengthened him against his temptations, in case they returned. Then I left. But I promised him that I would be back to see him the next day, when I would bring him the most Blessed Sacrament. Meanwhile he was to prepare himself carefully for such a surpassing mystery.

The whole of the same night he spent most peacefully, with no molestation whatsoever. The next day, in great tranquillity and peace of soul, he received the Holy Sacrament, and a very few hours later, without any disturbance, he breathed forth his soul and gave it back to God.[10]

Before the man died I asked him what it was that had driven him into such a despairing state of mind.

'For many years,' he said, 'I was kept in such and such a prison. The cause was my Catholic faith. But I did not cease to sin. Rather, I concealed my sins and hid them from my father confessor. The devil convinced me that I had to seek pardon and help from God, not through confession, but by penance and austere living. Therefore I used either to make an insincere confession or no confession at all, and found myself cast into this anguish of soul and most tormented state.'

Page 139

¹ W. W. probably refers to news of the preparations in hand to receive the invasion fleet in Flanders, where canals were being widened and deepened and new dockyards constructed. There was a general expectation of the armada in the summer of 1587; and in August two hundred and twenty Spanish ships were reported off the Scilly Isles and the fleet mobilised. It was only in the second half of this year that Walsingham was able to organise a spy service in Spain and receive more reliable information. *Acts of the Privy Council*, vol. 15, p. 192.

² This decision followed the lines of policy laid down in a memorandum drafted in December 1586 by Walsingham, who distinguished between two classes of priests, the more ‘ learned and politic withal and of great persuasion ’ and others ‘ simple, having more zeal than wit or learning ’. The former, such as W. W. and his companions, were to be ‘ sent on to Wisbech or some other such like place where they may be under honest keepers and be restrained from access and intelligence ’, and thus cease to be of service to their fellow-Catholics, even in prison. Conyers Read, *Sir Francis Walsingham*, vol. 2, pp. 312–5.

³ This was probably a few days after 7 January 1588, when the Council, meeting at Greenwich, issued a warrant to the keeper of the Clink, to deliver W. W. to the Queen’s messenger, George Cobham, and at the same time authorised Cobham ‘ to be provided of post horses and sufficient grade of men ’ for conveying W. W. and the other selected prisoners to Wisbech. *Acts of Privy Council*, vol. 15, pp. 331–2.

Page 140

⁴ This was almost certainly the Countess of Arundel, who was then living at Arundel House in the Strand. It was there also that W. W. would have seen Fr. Robert Southwell, her chaplain.

⁵ Presumably John Sheppard, the keeper of the Clink, who had assisted Berden in W. W.’s arrest.

Page 141

⁶ The angel, an English coin, was worth about ten shillings; the Spanish real, sixpence.

⁷ These were very busy days for W. W. In a letter of 22 January 1587 Southwell speaks of the unique affection which the Catholics of London had for W. W., and he adds: ‘ Before his departure he was allowed to visit others and others to visit him. So many requests did he receive to call on people that it would certainly be unbelievable if

there were not proof of it.   And this very high opinion of his saintliness
is indeed his due, for he is a true Israelite, prudent as the serpent and
simple as the dove.   God grant that we may follow in his steps.'   Arch.
S.J., Rome, *Fondo Gesuitico*, 651.

Page 144

[8] In Fr. de Peralta's account of this incident, which, he claims, W. W.
narrated to him in 1605, the devils, at this stage of the dying man's
confession, 'withdrew into the next room and from there threatened to
kill him if he persevered in his confession'.   In other details the two
accounts are identical.   de Peralta, f. 219.

[9] Delusions of damnation and the like, described here by W. W.,
are characteristic of agitated melancholia.   The sin of despair is not
involved, since it is a question of mental, not spiritual, disorder.   However, the visual hallucinations are not characteristic of the psychosis,
so it is arguable that the condition of the man was complicated by an
extreme degree of malnutrition brought on by his long imprisonment.
E. B. S.

[10] On his deathbed, ten years later, W. W.'s friend, Fr. Jasper Heywood, was similarly afflicted.   However, he dealt with the devil's
assaults in a more robust manner.   'You are going to hell', the demon
insisted, 'because you have been unorthodox in your teaching.'   'Liar!'
Fr. Jasper shouted back, 'I have suffered imprisonment and exile for
the orthodox faith, and now I am dying an exile for its cause.   What
about all those years in the pulpit, when I battered down heretics who
blasphemed against it?'   This was too much for the devil, who left
Fr. Jasper to die in peace.   Henry More, *Hist. Prov. Angl.*, lib. iv,
s. xi, p. 134.

17

THE MAN WITH BRASS BOWELS

Although the incident just narrated does show what strange effects can be produced sometimes by a mind terror-struck at the consciousness of sin, yet the next story gives the point solid confirmation. On the occasion when, for her entertainment, the Queen made a progress through the county of Norfolk,[1] all the nobles and gentry in that county vied with each other, to the limit of their wealth and connections, to entertain her as lavishly as they could and receive her with all magnificence and pomp: some to win her favour, others not to lose it; and yet others—principally Catholics—not to rouse further displeasure of the sovereign or quicken her hatred against them. At the end of the tour she received fulsome felicitations. Festivals were held. Triumphs were staged. And she left. But just when they were all waiting to receive thanks and favours for the services they had given, she commanded all the Catholics, who so far had not obeyed her injunction to go to church, to go henceforth under pain of imprisonment and heaven knows what else. This caused great perturbation, and all of them deliberated gravely what course they would be best advised to take.

I will mention no other case here, apart from this. Although I never had any previous doubt about it—I had it first on the testimony of a large number of witnesses—later on I heard

everything I am going to tell you from the man himself
when he came to see us at Wisbech.[2]

'That proclamation of the Queen,' he said, 'did not
touch me lightly. On the contrary, it lay like a load on my
mind. It was not a matter merely for myself, not just a
question of imprisonment. My wife, my children, my whole
family and fortune were concerned. At a single blow all
would be gone together. Yet, if I submitted, I would have
to face perpetual disgrace in the eyes of decent men: and not
that only, but infamy and the stigma of cowardice as well,
and, before God, the assured and inescapable jeopardy of my
soul. And on top of it all,' he continued, ' came the entreaties
and prayers of my friends—friends, that is, who regularly
set more store by the things of this world than by those of
God. They exaggerated infinitely the importance of these
passing possessions, and insisted how rash and regrettable
it would be to refuse to purchase immunity from disaster by a
single visit to church. Finally,' he said, ' I was timid. I saw
the best course, and followed the worst. I decided, just once,
to rig my conscience, and throw my scruples to the wind. The
feast day came when I had to be present. Immediately I
entered the church—it was quite foreign to me, a novelty
which I had shunned already for many years—my bowels
began to torture me. A fire seemed to kindle in them and in
a few moments flared up. The torment was acute. The
flame rose right into my chest and the region of my heart,
so that I seemed to be steaming and boiling in some hellish
furnace. And it did not stop there; it mounted to my head
and rose so high above it, that from time to time I raised my
hand to see whether it was a real flame that I felt. At last all
my intestines seemed one furnace of fire. I was at a loss
what to do, for I no longer had strength enough to endure

the flames. To go out and leave the pestilential meeting when its business was only half through would avail me nothing, or rather place me in an even worse position than before.'

So he held on, doing violence to himself to master his agony, until the profane prayers were ended. Outside the church, so it seemed to him, he was carrying about within himself an unendurable hell. Afflicted with a searing thirst, he entered the first tavern he saw, and ordered a drink to be brought. And—this may seem incredible—he emptied to the dregs so many mugs one on top of the other, that he put down about eight gallons in all. And he felt no discomfort or nausea. It was like pouring water into a raging furnace; all the liquor was immediately taken into his stomach and absorbed. Yet, in spite of this, the secret fire was not extinguished, and he got no relief. In desperation he returned home, with a justifiably sad heart and countenance. His wife looked him all over. She saw he had altered altogether and asked him what was wrong. What had he done? He told her, therefore, his whole sad story from the beginning— what had happened to him at the heretical meeting and the acute physical and mental anguish he had been through. Now she was not only a good Catholic but a sensible woman also. She comforted her husband in every way she knew; she soothed him with wise words and with hope of better times, and, what was most important, ordered a priest to be called in at once, in order that the inpouring of the grace of the Holy Spirit might, better than any medicine, heal his soul's distemper and deep distress. With every day his condition became easier and less acute. Finally, he was totally restored to his former good health.[3] After this, he visited the pseudo-bishop of the place and told him how, to

meet the wishes of the Queen, he had compromised his conscience and been to church. And he explained all that had
taken place there. ' I desire you to know,' he said, ' that not
only do I regret what I have done, but I am determined never
to do it again. You can do or command anything you wish.
That is my resolve.' But the tale the man told did not stir
the bishop at all. Neither did he commiserate with him nor
show him the slightest sympathy. But, there and then, he
clapped him into prison.[4] And with a brave heart he suffered
there for four whole years, not minding so much the lack of
personal freedom as the loss of his home and family.[5]

As it is to the point, I should not omit this story either.
It was told me to by the wife of the same man, a Catholic
lady well deserving of her religion. It concerns one of her
sons.[6]

This son—he was the child of a former marriage—was
summoned by a certain officer of the public peace and
examined about his religious beliefs. Without faltering he
confessed himself a Catholic, with the result that for three
whole days he was kept foodless in the man's house. It was
his purpose to subdue and wear him down to such an extent
that he would be forced to eat flesh meat on days forbidden
by the Church. When this failed he sent him to the University of Cambridge and placed him in the hands of a most
cruel tutor, who tried every device and deceit he knew. He
threatened him fiercely, but no violence would force him to
church. The boy resisted and refused resolutely.[7] Then he
started flogging him—every day, most savagely, till the lad
nearly went out of his mind. But his mother heard of it and
came to see her son. On entering the room she found him
lying in bed, sick and barely conscious. Then she saw his
shirt, stained all over with blood, and the red cuts and weals

on his flesh, and her grief and tears came uncontrolled.[8] After great difficulty she was permitted at last to take him home, but it was many months before she could bring him back to himself again.[9]

In the same town of Wisbech there were two boys of poor parents who were allowed into the prison to act as servants to the prisoners. In the course of a few months they learnt so much about the Catholic faith that they began slowly to shake themselves free of heresy which they had sucked in with their mother's milk and to hanker after Catholic teaching. Then they stopped going to church. And the keeper, too, observed that several times when they were ordered to go, they stayed away. So he got hold of them both on a certain festival day, and binding their feet firmly together, he had them put in the whipping stocks in the market place just out-side the prison, for all the people to see.[10] Later, when they were taken out, one of them escaped to Belgium and became a scholar at Douai. There he made great progress in his studies, gained a fine name for himself, and became a priest. Now he is busy harvesting souls in England.[11]

The other was recaptured and put in prison at Ely. There he lacked everything he needed, and suffered most severely for many months.[12] Eventually, with his fellow-prisoners, he was brought before the Assizes, where he was charged with being a Catholic. When his turn came, he went up and stood before the Bench.

' You are the boy who wants to become a Catholic,' said one of them. ' You have never attended Mass. How can you know what it is all about? Who put this mad idea into your head? '

Then all of them began to make fun of him. They saw

what a small boy he was. They jeered and called him a worthless little creature.

'You are right,' he said, 'I haven't seen much, or heard much about the Catholic faith. You can see, too, I am only a boy still. I haven't had much instruction or experience. But I do know this: it is the only true faith that leads men to salvation. It is centuries older than your new upstart religion.'

'Are you pronouncing about antiquity?' said they. 'What do you know? You were born only yesterday, you fool.'

'It's not me,' he retorted, 'but you and your historians. Yes, a man of your own persuasion, one of your own people, Holinshed. He says it plainly in his chronicle.'

They all denied that there was anything of the kind to be found in the book.

'There is,' he said. 'I am not lying. I know what I am saying.' And at the same time he produced from his pocket a large sheet which had been torn from a copy of Holinshed's chronicle.

'Look at the writer's name, first,' he said, ' then if you wish, you can read what's on this page. It is loose.'

They read the page in public, and felt embarrassed and abashed. Here was a description of the arrival of St. Augustine, the Apostle of England, with cross, litanies, and with every appurtenance of Catholic liturgy and ceremonial. It had been torn from a very large volume by a Catholic prisoner in Wisbech, who told the boy to keep it carefully in case he was called to answer for his faith. He would then have no need to say anything or argue. All he had to do was to show them this loose page.[13] Indeed, when the occasion came, that is what he did, and with such effect that he confused them completely and left them casting about for an answer. For the author was one of their most worthy writers and was shown to be an irreproachable witness to the extreme antiquity of the faith.[14]

The public Assizes in the Isle of Ely were held twice in the year, and at these times the Justices set up their court in our prison. At one of these Assizes two men and a woman were brought to trial for some offence or other and were condemned to death. Within a few days the sentence was to be carried out. Some of us, taking this opportunity to meet the criminals, were able, in the very short time available, to persuade them to become Catholics and expiate their sins by confession. It was a question merely of explaining the truth of the Catholic faith and the supreme need they had of it, if they wished to escape eternal punishment and enter into the happiness of heaven. It was more difficult, however, to get access to the woman. But here the two men were of great assistance. Their cell adjoined hers and, through a grating in the dividing wall, they were able to make her understand all that was essential to the faith and, in particular, the need of absolution in sacramental confession. She listened very eagerly and understood in a most remarkable manner all that was told her. Then she looked about for some way of making her confession. Time was very short, but with God's help a means was devised. All co-operated and great ingenuity was shown, and she achieved her desire.

When the hour of execution struck, they were summoned out by the ministers. Some Catholic friends had given them linen shrouds so that their bodies could be wrapped up for burial after execution. Now, in order to proclaim to the crowd of spectators that they were Catholics and as Catholics intended to die, they placed these shrouds round their necks and brought them down in transverse folds over their breasts in the form of a cross. To make the gospel of the Cross more apparent still they had stitched a black strip of cloth down the full length of their burial robes.

As they emerged from the prison precincts, they gave signs of their devotion both in words and gestures, their tears and sighs revealing their extraordinary fervour of soul. A vast crowd had gathered. It was full of admiration for the way in which, again and again, they deplored bitterly the crimes of their past life, and bewailed and protested that it was so late that they had understood the true doctrine which alone saved mankind and brought them to eternal life. Three times or more before they mounted the gallows all of them knelt down together and prayed for a long time, their tears flowing in a greater profusion still. Some heretics were for stopping them—such an undisguised display of Papistry ought not, they thought, to be tolerated—but the rest, who were by far the more numerous, had no hesitation in defending and praising them, and saying that they themselves hoped to be granted such tears of repentance and sorrow. As they stood on the ladder underneath the scaffold, they reiterated all they had said, with the same earnestness and flow of tears. All who listened were amazed, and it was remarkable how nearly everyone present felt pity for them. Finally, when the rope was being placed round their necks and they ceased speaking, they took some blessed seeds given to them by Catholics for the gaining of the plenary indulgence and, putting them in their mouths, they swallowed them in front of all the people, thinking that in this way they would benefit to the full from the favours attached to them.[15] Then they were turned off, and, as all had hoped and prayed, exchanged this miserable life for one of blissful happiness.[16]

News of this incident spread widely and it was talked about

in many different places. Eventually the Queen's close circle came to hear of it, and a severe reprimand was sent to the keeper of the prison for allowing such an incident to occur in public.

Page 148

[1] In July and August 1578 the Queen made her progress of Suffolk and Norfolk. On 4 August she was entertained by Henry Drury at Lawshall Hall, and on the 10th by another Catholic, Edward Rookwood, at Euston. After kissing the Queen's hand at her departure, Rookwood was commanded by the Lord Chamberlain to stand aside and, charged with being a recusant, was ordered to follow in the royal retinue to Norwich, where he was committed to goal. At Braconash, the house of Thomas Townsend nine miles from Norwich, nine of the neighbouring Catholic gentry who came to pay their respect to their sovereign, were either sent to gaol with Rookwood or bound over under a bond of £200 each to keep within the city boundaries. Finally, a mile from Norwich another Catholic, Robert Downes, after presenting the Queen with a pair of gold spurs and reading verses in her honour, was similarly treated. All these men were still in confinement or in bond when John Gerard rode into the city on his pony the day after his landing on the Norfolk coast, just ten years later. A. Jessop, *One Generation of a Norfolk House* (ed. 1879), pp. 66–7.

Page 149

[2] This was Francis Wodehouse of Breccles in West Norfolk, a kinsman of the Wodehouses of Kimberley who were reconciled by John Gerard. At the beginning of Elizabeth's reign he had been one of the most considerable squires in East Anglia and had built a mansion at Breccles, one of the finest example of Elizabethan domestic architecture in the county. A. Jessop, *One Generation of a Norfolk House* (ed. 1879), pp. 198, 212.

Page 150

[3] The story of Francis Wodehouse, whose stomach became like a raging furnace, is a most interesting example of the way the 'unconscious conscience'—the super-ego of the Freudian schema—can produce severe bodily symptoms by way of self-punishment. In other words, it is a clear case of hysteria. *E.B.S.*

Page 151

[4] This was Bishop Freake of Norwich, who had formerly been an Augustinian monk of Waltham Abbey. Although himself inclined not to take severe measures against Catholics, his hand was forced by the Council, who were very disturbed at the increase of recusancy in Norfolk. *Vic. Co. Hist., Norfolk*, vol. ii, p. 270.

⁵ Francis Wodehouse suffered severely for his recusancy until the end of the reign. In 1599 he was forced to sell Breccles and settle a few miles away at Cawston. There he died in poverty in March 1605 (A. Jessop, *ib.*). His son and heir John died two years later. It was probably to receive spiritual comfort and advice that Francis Wodehouse visited W. W. at Wisbech.

⁶ This was Evan Floyd, a son of Eleanor Wodehouse by her first husband. Cf. A. Jessop, *ib.*; *C.R.S.*, vol. 18, p. 233.

⁷ W. W. abridges his story. Evan Floyd, on an instruction of the Council issued from Norwich on 22 August 1578, at the end of the Queen's progress, was committed to the charge of Dr. Thomas Ithell, a Protestant who, like Andrewes (cf. *sup.*, p. 135, n. 1), had a reputation of making converts from Catholicism. Ithell was ordered to place the boy ' in some house and to confer with him for his conformity '. Accordingly he was handed over to ' Mr. Payton and to Mr. Holmes ', one of whom presumably was the ' cruel tutor ' mentioned by W. W. On 29 October the boy was reported to be ' so far reclaimed that he is willing to come to service and sermons ', and was released on bonds. His conformity was only temporary, for before the end of 1579 he was again committed, this time to the custody of the sheriff, and lodged in Cambridge Castle. *Acts of the Privy Council*, vol. 10, pp. 313, 320, 359; vol. 11, pp. 378-9.

Page 152

⁸ This was in January 1580, when the boy was ' so swollen in his limbs as he is in danger of his life '. Although, as the letter from the Council is careful to state, there was ' little cause to show favour to persons so obstinate, yet in respect of the recovery of his health, their Lordships have been contented, upon earnest suit made on his behalf, that he be removed to some gentleman's house in the county '. The boy's recovery was slow, for, twelve months after this instruction was given, a further three months' liberty was allowed him in order ' to repair unto the Baths for the recovery of his health '. *Acts of the Privy Council*, vol. 11, pp. 278-9; vol. 12, p. 51.

⁹ Evan Floyd recovered, married and remained an ' obstinate recusant '. His daughter Anne married Richard Carleton of Linton, Cambs., and had a large family. *C.R.S.*, vol. 18, p. 233; Harleian Society, vol. xli, *The Visitations of Cambridge, 1619*, p. 59.

¹⁰ This was the old market place, dating from the twelfth century, which was in view of the castle, not the new market place on the left bank of the river. Wisbech at this time was about half the size of Cam-

bridge, with some three hundred and ten householders. *Vict. Co. Hist., Cambridge*, vol. 4, p. 240.

[11] This was William Arton, who was ordained at Douai in 1603. ' He was led into the path of truth by the priests confined in Wisbech Castle, for he was born in that town and educated there.' In 1598 he had been a Catholic five years. The incident, therefore, occurred in 1592–3. *C.R.S.*, vol. 30, p. 50.

[12] The prison at Ely seems to have been used exclusively for the confinement of Catholic boys and the eldest sons of Catholic gentlemen, who ' some through age and others by infirmities and weakness of body ' were excused prison themselves and were forced to hand over their eldest sons as hostages to the Government. The boy prisoners suffered greatly from under-nourishment owing to the rising prices of bread and beer. In November 1596 the Council ordered the allowance for their diet to be increased. *Acts of the Privy Council*, vol. 26, pp. 327, 363.

Page 153

[13] In the 1586 edition of Holinshed the whole of Chapter xix, which describes the mission of St. Augustine and his landing in England, is contained on a single sheet (pp. 99 and 100). It is probable, therefore, that it was from a copy of this edition that the Wisbech priest tore the leaf which the boy gave to the Bench. In the first edition (1577) the chapter on St. Augustine extends over four pages.

Page 154

[14] According to the prison custom at the time, the priests at Wisbech were allowed to keep boys between the ages of thirteen and eighteen as their personal servants. The names of thirteen of them are given in a paper among the Harleian MSS. (no. 6998, f. 226), printed in Morris, *Two Missionaries*, p. 266. Many of them, like the boy in W. W.'s story, later became priests, and their career can be traced in the records of the seminaries abroad. Some were natives of Wisbech and the surrounding country; others claimed to be born locally, but were in fact sons of gentlemen from other counties and had been sent to Wisbech for their education. This is revealed by a comparison of the above list with the report of the examination to which the boys were subjected, when a strict regime was again enforced in the prison after W. W.'s departure to the Tower (*S.P.D., Eliz.*, vol. cclxxii, no. 107). Thus Thomas Everard, who had previously declared himself the son of a Yorkshire yeoman, admitted that he was the son of Sir Thomas Knyvett; and Nicholas Clayton turned out to be Nicholas Bagshaw of Chapel-le-Frith,

Derbyshire, a relative of Dr. Bagshaw. It is not surprising, then, that complaints, mentioned by W. W. later in his narrative (ch. 18, p. 167), were made to the Council that ' through the favour of the keeper, Gray, the prison was growing to be as dangerous as a seminary college, being in the heart and midst of England '. The interesting personal history of Thomas Dowlton, a ' poor lad ' from Wisbech, is given in Appendix C.

Page 155

[15] W. W. refers to a form of chaplet or rosary made of cereal seeds or at least of some material so perishable that no examples have survived.

[16] This is probably the incident mentioned by Fr. Garnet in a letter to Fr. Persons, on 8 October 1597. ' Two thieves were executed the last Assizes at Wisbech and were before reconciled by a priest in the same house, and went with great joy through the town, professing their faith, till they came to the gallows.' Stonyhurst MSS., *Collectanea P*, f. 548.

18

THE YEARS AT WISBECH

These events occurred as I have recorded them. And now came the day arranged for our journey to Wisbech. In all, there were about twelve of us, from different prisons, selected from the whole body of priests.[1]

The warders led us first to a public tavern and left us there. Then we were transferred to the keeping of the officials who were to supervise our transportation. With them was a fair-sized armed escort. As we took to the road a great crowd, men and women, stood watching us; and for a considerable distance beyond the city's boundaries, they followed us with their eyes until we disappeared from view. We must, indeed, have presented an unusual sight. All the way they treated us humanely enough; but at night they posted guards at the door of our rooms to stop all attempts at escape, and also to protect us from any violent assault by the heretics.

The day after our arrival at Wisbech the magistrates, who had been instructed by the Queen's Council to receive us, appeared.[2] They were to conduct us to the prison we were bound for. It was market day, and there was a large crowd—people gathered from nearly the whole of the district. As soon as we came out of the inn where we had spent the night, they formed dense lines on both sides of us and hedged the road all the way to the prison. Immediately we entered the castle we were segregated into cells, and shut in under bolt and lock day and night, except for the times of lunch and supper, and for half an hour before and after these meals when we were allowed to take a little air and get some exercise.

This was a general prison for thieves and criminals of every description. It lay within the ancient enclosure of the bishop of Ely's palace, and was surrounded by a massive wall. Beyond this lay a ditch which, if necessary, could be filled with water from the river. Inside it resembled a keep, built high on a lofty eminence, and encircled by an inner wall and moat. Everything, however, was in a state of ruin, in fact, almost collapsing, thanks principally to the avarice of the ʰeretical bishops. Without any concern for posterity, but with an eye merely to their own advantage, they had stripped it of its main materials—lead, roofs, beams, iron, glass— and sold them, allowing the rest to fall into ruin and decay.[3]

Here, besides other priests and laymen of quality I found Thomas Metham [4] and Thomas Pound.[5] The first was a priest, the second a gentleman of good family. Both had previously been received into the Society by Father Persons. For many years now they had suffered a great deal for the confession of their faith, but their courage had been outstanding and they had experienced many prisons, the Tower of London among them. Before their time the Bishop of Lincoln, Feckenham, the Abbot of Westminster, Doctor Wood, the confessor of Queen Mary, all of them men of distinction, had been confined in this prison—or, rather, sent here for internment, and here worn down by bitter suffering, by misfortune and by harsh and inhuman labour, had all died happily in the Lord.

This was our place also. And without any hope we entered

it as though we were stepping into our sepulchre. Debarred from the world outside, deprived of the sight of those dear to us, we were here enclosed for eleven whole years; some suffered a longer time, others a shorter, for, taken off by death they completed their term, not without great merit before God, gathered over many years.

The number of prisoners was not stable: new men were brought in later. The older ones, particularly the notable laymen, were occasionally released. Some died. But for the greater part of the time we were thirty, thirty-five or more, all, as I have said above, locked up in our cells day and night. We were let out only for lunch and supper, when we sat down together at a common table, with a warder always present. He took the head of the table while his wife sat at the other end; and both watched carefully lest any word passed between us which they did not catch. Then exactly half an hour after the end of the meal we were ordered back to our cells.[6]

We were supported at considerable expense by Catholics,[7] but hardly ever were we allowed to see anybody. If some person brought us money, then one or other of us, by himself, could meet him and receive the alms.[8] Night watchers were set inside the prison and out. Four justices, men of mark, were made responsible for the discipline of the prison and for everything that touched or in any way affected the prisoners. To assist them were ten or twelve aldermen, leading men of the town, in case any matter should arise that required more protracted attention. Then, hung in a public place, where all who wished could read it, was a large notice board on which a long series of regulations were written. These were imposed on the warder and on ourselves, and had to be observed. They concerned our food, the hours we had to keep, guests, books, trouble-making and other items too long to list here.[9]

Such was our way of life under these regulations for what must have been six years. There were also frequent examinations, searchings of cells,[10] wrangling and arguments with ministers and others,[11] besides formal discussions. But in the midst of all these causes of annoyance, we had this great source of comfort. Very frequently we were able to celebrate Holy Mass, for we soon learnt to arrange everything so cleverly that we were never short of vestments, chalices, and bread and wine for consecration.[12]

From the very beginning a great number of Puritans gathered here. Some came from the outlying parts of the town, some from the villages round about, eager and vast crowds of them flocking to perform their practices—sermons, communions and fasts. (The keeper of the prison, and his whole family, were Puritans, and the justices were sympathetic to them.) This was their ceremonial. In the first few hours there were three or four sermons, one after the other, and the remainder of their devotions. They then went to communion, which they would receive from their minister, not on their knees or standing up, but walking about, so that it could be called in a true sense a Passover. They also held a kind of tribunal, where the elders took cognizance of the misdoings of their brethren and castigated them at discretion. Each of them had his own Bible, and sedulously turned the pages and looked up the texts cited by the preachers, discussing the passages among themselves to see whether they had quoted them to the point, and accurately, and in harmony with their tenets. Also they would start arguing among themselves about the meaning of passages from the Scriptures —men, women, boys, girls, rustics, labourers and idiots—

Rebellion the effect of Monasteries

CONSPIRING PRIESTS

Figure 5.

What trusty Janizaries are Monks to *Rome*,
From their dark Cells the blackest Treasons come,
By the Popes License horrid Crimes they Act,
And Guild with piety each Treacherous Fact.
A seminary Priest, like Comets Blaze,
Doth always Blood-shed and Rebellion Raise;
   But still the fatal Gibbet's ready fixt
   For such, where Treason's with Religion mixt.

Babington with his Complices

Figure 10.

Here *Babington* and all his desperate Band,
Ready prepar'd for Royal Murder stand,
His Motto seems to glory in the Deed,
these my Companions are whom dangers lead.
Cowardly Traitors, so many Combine
To Cut off one poor Ladies vital Twine;
*In vain,—*Heaven's her Guard, and as for you;
Behold, the Hangman gives you all your due.

BABINGTON AND HIS
ASSOCIATES

A CALVINIST PRAYER MEETING OUTSIDE ANTWERP 14 June 1566
The Puritan meetings held within the precincts of Wisbech Castle (see page 164) were

and more often than not, it was said, it ended in violence and fisticuffs.

All this the Catholic prisoners, looking through the windows of their cells, were able to watch; for it did not take place in one of their temples or houses, but on a large level stretch of ground within the precincts of the prison. Here over a thousand of them sometimes assembled, their horses and pack animals burdened with a multitude of Bibles. It was a wretched and truly pitiful sight, but in some ways it was comic and laughable for the onlookers. When the gathering broke up after a long fast and an entire day spent in performances of this kind, they went off to a vast and elaborately set-out feast. And the affair concluded.

Later their first fervour slackened. Their chief supporters were removed from the scene, and they began to dwindle away and look for other places which they considered more suitable for the celebration of their sacrilegious gatherings.

Now, we had spent about six years in our solitary life.[13] And during this time we had innumerable annoyances and insults to endure. Not infrequently we suffered injury when pebbles and stones were hurled at us, sometimes in contempt, sometimes in sheer hatred. But thanks to the goodness of God we entered a better and freer life. After a long struggle and much argument with our keeper, we were granted unrestricted exit from our cells, only, of course, within the confines of the prison, also free passage for all our friends. No longer were we compelled to eat with the keeper at the common table; we could prepare our food as we pleased, provided each one of us paid twenty-four reals [14] for his cell. And when this fee was paid by thirty or more, occasionally even by forty of us, it was a substantial income for a shocking and sacrilegious service done by a man who deserved nothing at all. We had also our own dining-room, which was shared by all of us, and, separate from the keeper's lodging, our own kitchen, pantry, with other store places and working rooms. In fact, you might have imagined that we were almost living in our own free house. It was certainly an ample place for, as I said, it had been a bishop's residence, and there was more than sufficient space for everything. Nevertheless, the watch on our persons was maintained. The keeper saw to this, and he reserved to himself certain rights over us which he was reluctant to transfer to others, since it was his intention to grant or refuse them as changing times and circumstances suggested.

Now I must narrate an incident which certainly should not go unrecorded. It occurred during the period when we were locked in our cells from lunch time to supper.

One day, while Thomas Pound and the man who shared his room were sitting at lunch, the ceiling of their cell— beams, plaster, mortar and all—fell in. Nobody could have foreseen the danger that had been hanging over their heads. It was a dispensation of Providence that it occurred during the short interval for lunch; their lives would otherwise have been jeopardized; at least, they would not have escaped without serious bodily harm. Moreover, the part of the room where the priests offered their daily Mass was completely untouched. And this, we all remarked, was something more than a happy chance. It was here that the table stood which served as an altar. On the wall behind it were attached a number of pictures of the saints, to form a reredos. And the whole of this portion of the room—the exact length and width of the altar—was supported by a single narrow joist.

None of the pictures nor any part of the altar was so much as soiled by the falling dust and rubbish.

At the end of six years, therefore, I emerged from my dismal and narrow cell. And when again we began to enjoy the light, Catholics came daily to see us, and we were able to give them spiritual succour. We now set out to model our life on the pattern, as it were, of a college, arranging study classes and every other form of humanistic exercise. Days were fixed for cases of conscience, controversies, Hebrew and Greek classes, disputations and lectures. We also arranged for sermons, not so much for the benefit of outsiders, as to give useful practice to the priests.[15]

As soon as it became known to Catholics that we had been given freedom to see and speak with people outside, practically no day passed without some visitors.[16] There was an almost continuous stream of them—heretics as well as Catholics—to get our advice or dispute with us. I will do no more than mention here the visits of University professors and ministers with their hangers-on. Often they came with a numerous following to discuss religion with us. But, I must say, the throng of Catholics of every condition in life was so unending that it gravely alarmed the Queen and her Councillors.[17] They duly upbraided the keeper for allowing it.[18] However, the place was a long distance from the capital, the events did not take place under their eyes, and once a way had been broken through the barrier, it could be blocked by the keeper only with still greater trouble. They came from every part of the kingdom, some as to a holy place, undertaking a kind of pilgrimage;[19] others, as if they were celebrating a solemn feast, came for Communion, Mass and the sacraments so that the prison was scarcely ever empty, or we unoccupied in this work.[20] I say nothing about the problems and disputes which we settled, the regular letters we received from heretics and our answers to them, and to men, especially, who had not abandoned the faith, yet still maintained that the practice of going to heretical services was neither sinful nor forbidden.

And so, for the whole of the next five years, until I was removed and confined in the Tower of London, this was the manner of my prison life. If I am expected here to say something on my own account about our special way of life—mine, that is, Father Thomas Metham's and Thomas Pound's: after a few years we were joined by Ralph Bickley [21]—there is virtually nothing which I should note in addition to the common life of all, except this, that the usual hours for prayer, examination of conscience, exhortations and conferences, were carefully kept, unless there was some violent or urgent interruption.

Almost immediately after our new liberty had been granted to us—it was the year, I think, 1594—Father Thomas Metham reached the end of his life, and taking his farewell of us, passed peacefully to God. He was at least sixty years old, and had experienced many prisons, including the Tower of London for four years. There he had been seriously ill, and was later removed at the intercession of his friends. He was then transferred from one prison to another, and finally was taken to Wisbech. He was a man of learning, and before he became a priest had received a licentiate in Greek and Hebrew, and was remarkably well-read in many languages. Often, on very different occasions, when he was forced into discussions or debates with heretics, he won golden trophies for his distinguished defence of the faith. In the end he caught some slight infection and succumbed at once. After receiving the last sacraments, he fell asleep in God gently and contentedly, without anguish or struggle.[22]

I should not omit here the story of the conversion of the warder's remarkable daughter. It occurred after we had acquired this new freedom.[23]

With other natural gifts, uncommon in a girl of her years, she had an astonishingly acute mind. Ursula was her name, and she was married to a prominent Puritan. She herself had also a leading position in the sect, so much so that she was considered only a little less important than a prophetess. She would often listen to Catholics discussing religion with heretics, and would ponder carefully the arguments on both sides, contrasting sound Catholic reasoning with the flimsy and ineffectual positions taken up by the heretics. Sometimes, too, she would watch her husband, a most obstinate man, nonplussed for a reply and, more often, reduced to complete silence. True, at the beginning she herself was very ill-disposed towards us and most persistent, and there were times she entered the general discussion quite modestly with a word of her own. But, as the practice of disputations became more regular, the faith began to show and then broke in all its splendour on her mind. First she wavered. Next she was uncertain. Doubts formed in her mind, and she began to listen for the sake of instruction. Then, slowly, as step by step she drew towards the understanding of the truth, her father became suspicious. Eventually she reached the stage when she was convinced of the Catholic faith, and her attendance at their gatherings and conventicles became irregular and intermittent; this the father read as a clear sign of her alienation from their body, particularly when from time to time she spoke out on the Catholic side against the Puritans, and argued strongly against them, making use of the irrefutable proofs that had won her over.

It was then that he became fiercely incensed against her, and against Catholics in general, to the verge of insanity. He tried everything—arguments, enticements, threats—but he could not get the better of her. Nothing was left him, except to show openly his implacable anger and hatred and his solid alliance with the devil. He swore that he abominated the Catholic religion with such detestation that even if he knew for certain that he could only attain his salvation through it, and that there was no other way apart from it, still he would never embrace it. This blasphemy, which might have proceeded from the mouth of a damned man or from the devil himself, made a deep impression on the girl's mind and she became more than ever on fire for the faith, and cast about for some way by which she could effect her purpose without further offence to her father or hurt to herself.

At the time she was pregnant, and shortly expected the birth of her infant. It is hardly credible how much she had to endure from her wicked father and her unchaste Puritan husband (so the story went). They refused to allow a midwife or woman of any kind to assist her. They denied her everything that a woman at such a time most needs, unless she is to endanger her life. In fact, she would not have survived, had she not suffered a miscarriage.

God, however, assisted her, and she overcame everything. She recovered her health, and left the house where she had been in confinement—it was her father's house outside the prison—and returned home. Daily she had fights with her father, with her mother, who nevertheless loved her with a particular love, with her husband and others of their sect. But nothing altered her determination. She felt the truth

drawing her on, a spur of conscience she could not escape.
Through fear of God she could not retrace her steps. Her
father's command, however, and his mad rage held her back
from professing herself a Catholic and practising her religion.
When her father had begged or ordered her to go to church,
she had hesitated, found some excuse, or spurned his order
outright. But one day, on which custom made it obligatory,
the whole household, and both her parents, were on the point
of setting out for church and ordered her to join them. She,
pleading an engagement, excused herself. Finally she was not
only commanded to go, but physical pressure was brought to
bear on her. Still she resisted. The people watching the out-
rage were shocked. ' Base woman! ' shouted her father. ' How
dare you! ' Then, drawing out a dagger, he rushed at his
daughter. She fled. He pursued her, brandishing the naked
blade in a blind fury. ' Be off! ' he shouted. ' Out of my
house! ' She tried to dodge him and escape the danger,
taking good care all the time to retreat backwards with her
face towards him, imploring him to spare her life. But he—
possessed by the savagery of an untamed beast—pressed
after her like a madman to pin her with his dagger against the
door. However, she quickly seized the handle and got away,
a fugitive in exile from her father's house. Left alone in the
street she had nowhere to go and no one to whom she could
turn. All the neighbourhood feared her father. But an
honourable and wealthy woman having pity on her took her
in for the night. Then, with the help of the Catholics, it was
arranged for her to ride off on horseback as quickly as possible
to a certain Catholic house. So, finally, leaving her father and
the house where she was born and bred, her husband, her
children and all her kin, she lay hid henceforth with Catholics,
and spent with them the rest of her time. Whether she

had seen any of her family again, I do not know. Certainly for many years she did not, indeed she could not have done, for most of them had previously met a sudden death. Yet with a courage uncommon in her sex she endured the loss of all she possessed, with such spirit that her life had never been more happy or more in keeping with her desires. Indeed, this woman bore the cross of Christ manfully, even from the very beginning of her conversion, and went on bearing it for many years after it. God judged her worthy also of chains and imprisonment, as I have been told, on behalf of the faith.

NOTES

[1] There were exactly twelve priests in the party, in the charge of Thomas Gray, the keeper of Wisbech Castle, and two of the Queen's messengers, Robert Awfield and George Cobham. They set out on 21 January 1588, for Southwell in his letter of 22 January refers to their departure ' yesterday '.

[2] The names of these magistrates are given in an order of the Privy Council, dated 22 August 1587. They were appointed about six months before W. W.'s arrival at Wisbech. As ' overseers ' to Thomas Gray, the keeper, they were ' to give him their assistance as he may require and have need of it '. Before the end of September 1587 they had sent in a report to the Council which, on 9 October, endorsed the rules, mentioned later by W. W., ' for the bridling and reformation of the lewd demeanour of the prisoners in the castle of Wisbech '. The magistrates were again instructed ' to yield their assistance to Thomas Gray, the keeper, from time to time as occasion shall require '. This reorganisation was preparatory to the imprisonment there of W. W. and his priest companions. *Acts of Privy Council*, vol. 15, pp. 202, 257.

[3] Nothing remains to-day of Wisbech castle. The original fortress, built by William I, was destroyed in 1236, when an inundation of the sea demolished also a large part of the town. It was later restored, and again fell into ruin. At the end of the fifteenth century Bishop Morton built in brick yet another castle on the site and made it a palace for the bishops of Ely. During the long vacancy of the see (1580–99) it was used as a prison for selected Catholic prisoners, both priests and laymen.

[4] Thomas Metham, a Yorkshireman, the son of Sir Thomas Metham, the intimate friend of Thomas Percy, seventh Earl of Northumberland (executed 1572). He had been at work in England only one year (1574–5) before he was captured and imprisoned in the Tower. Foley, ii, pp. 608–13.

[5] Thomas Pound was born at Belmont, Hants., in 1539, ' the same year that Campion was '. His mother was the sister of the Earl of Southampton, who is said to have befriended him in various troubles. On Elizabeth's accession he became one of the favourite young men at her court, an eccentric, handsome and cultured youth, who wrote poetry and acted in masques which he himself composed. In 1570 he was reconciled to the Church, renouncing ' the favours of court [as] the very mermaid's allurements to perdition '. In 1574 as he was about to

leave England to join the Society of Jesus, he was arrested. For the next thirty years, apart from a few brief intervals, he lived in prison. He calculated that he had been transferred sixteen times to different places of confinement and had spent £4,000 of his fortune in fines. He had been admitted to the Society in 1578 but never became a priest. At this time he was described as ' of a full and handsome figure, a flowing beard, and a handsome countenance'. It was typical of him that throughout his long imprisonment he took great care of his dress, ' thinking thus to inspire ' his fellow Catholics. When finally he was set free in 1603 he lived quietly in London until his death in 1616 at the age of seventy-six. Cf. *The Rambler*, New Series, vol. viii (1857), pp. 24–38, 94–106; Evelyn Waugh, *Edmund Campion*, pp. 123–4.

Page 163

[6] ' Father William and his two companions ', wrote Fr. Garnet on 9 June 1588, ' are well, but as they are in very strict custody they write practically nothing to us. You will be learning about Ralph [Emerson] from his own letters. We were with him recently [in the Clink].' Arch. S.J., Rome, *Fondo Gesuitico*, 651.

[7] The collection of funds for the support of the Wisbech priests was organized by an old Marian priest, Alban Newton (or Doleman), living in London, ' a great friend to the whole company, [who] visits them two or three times a year, brings them the greater part of their maintenance and carries the common purse for them and is held in reverence by the whole of them. The most part of his money is in French crowns, and he commonly stays with them four or five days, making great cheer.' (Edward Hall, the porter of Wisbech, in a letter to Sir Edward Coke, *C.S.P., Dom. Eliz.* (1595–7), p. 186). One of W. W.'s extant letters is addressed to ' my very good friend Mr. Newton ' and was written sometime after November 1595. Westminster Archives, vol. 31, p. 105.

[8] Fr. de Peralta was assiduous in gathering information about W. W.'s life at Wisbech. From an English Catholic, W. W.'s fellow-prisoner for three years, he learned that his ' bed was on the ground, and he spent nearly the whole day and night in prayer '; and he had this confirmed indirectly by another prisoner who ' for five continuous years had never seen him [W. W.] in bed, though the two of them shared the same cell '. Fr. de Peralta, f. 220; cf. Appendix D for details of W. W.'s life at Wisbech.

Page 164

[9] At different times the orders for the government of the Wisbech prisoners were revised. In the Privy Council Register a revision of

November 1592 is given in full detail. The priests were permitted, for instance, to walk in the inner court or garden, but not beyond it, and there was to be 'no conference between themselves but at their ordinary meals and at that time there shall be no speech used of any matters that are in controversy for religion nor matters of state and government'. *Acts of Privy Council*, vol. 23, pp. 303–5.

10 A number of these searches were made on the orders of the Council, e.g., in October 1592, when the prisoners were herded into a secluded place while their rooms were ransacked for letters and papers which were to be sealed up and sent unread to the Council. *Acts of Privy Council*, vol. 23, p. 263.

11 Gray, the keeper, was a vigorous Puritan, and in the hope of making converts of his prisoners, introduced this custom of theological discussion several years before W. W.'s arrival at Wisbech. On 1 February 1584 he had written to Burghley suggesting that Dr. Andrewes, then making a great reputation as a preacher at Cambridge, should 'be appointed to preach, confer and dispute' with the priests at Wisbech (*C.S.P., Dom. Eliz.* (1581–90), p. 157). Later, in ch. 20, W. W. gives a most interesting account of one of these discussions.

12 At this time eighteen or more Masses were celebrated daily in Wisbech. *Apology for the English Seminary*, Arch. Eng. Coll. Valladolid, *Seville* 17b, 686, no. 1.

Page 165

13 W. W. was five and a half years in close confinement. (Cp. p. 196, n. 2).

14 The scale of charges was the same as that in the Fleet prison, a distinction being made between 'Doctors', such as Bagshaw and Norden, who were given the privileges granted to knights in the Fleet, and 'Gentlemen', who comprised all the non-doctors. Doctors paid 16s. a week for their commons, and 6s. 8d. for their lodgings, while the rest were charged at 10s. and 2s. 4d. W. W. gives the charge both for commons and lodgings for the gentlemen prisoners, and if the Spanish real is reckoned as roughly sixpence in English money, it tallies exactly with the rates prescribed by the Council. *Acts of Privy Council*, vol. 23, pp. 306–7.

Page 167

15 'They led a collegial and heavenly kind of life, both for inward virtue and external edification. Their prayer was frequent and earnest, their study was continual meditation of the holy scriptures and other

exercises appertaining to virtue. They lived in common both for their diet and distribution of alms that was sent unto them; they were present daily at public and private litanies and at some lesson or conference of controversies and cases of conscience for better instruction of their judgements. Their conversation was sweet both in words and countenance, their behaviour holy, and all this by the direction chiefly of . . . Father Edmund Weston.' R. Persons, *An Apologie in defence of Ecclesiastical Subordination in England*, pp. 64–5.

[16] Among W. W.'s first visitors was Fr. Garnet. Writing from London on 12 November 1593 Fr. Garnet said that he had just visited him. 'We were received,' he went on, 'most kindly by all and to do us honour they asked me to sing solemn High Mass. It is a college of venerable confessors of the faith and it will be a disaster if Fr. William is taken away, for the whole establishment will fall to pieces.' Arch. S.J., Rome, *Fondo Gesuitico*, 651.

[17] In its anxiety to put an end to the constant throng of visitors to Wisbech, the Council in May 1596 issued an open warrant to pursuivants for the capture of twenty-four persons who were known to be regular visitors—they were to be searched and sent to London for examination. On the list was Fr. Garnet, who is known to have visited W. W. on two occasions, and Mr. Hubert, who had shared W. W.'s first adventures on landing in England. *Acts of Privy Council*, vol. 25, pp. 418–9.

[18] On 12 October 1592 Gray, the keeper, was summoned to Whitehall to answer for the liberty allowed the Wisbech prisoners (*Acts of Privy Council*, vol. 23, p. 235). But it would seem that the regulations were not relaxed in any marked measure until the following year.

[19] 'Nowhere in England is there anything so magnificent as this college of priests or rather of martyrs, as St. Cyprian calls them. They number more than forty and the fine fragrance of their name is spread far and wide.' (Fr. John Curry to Fr. Persons, Stonyhurst MSS., Grene's *Collectanea M*, f. 193.) In December 1593, and again in April 1594, John Gerard's friend, Mrs. Jane Wiseman, visited Wisbech. She took with her the second time her two daughters, who were about to enter convents abroad, to be blessed by W. W.; she also made a 'rich vestment' for the priests, and 'did repent that she had not gone barefooted thither' in the manner of a pilgrim. *Two Missionaries*, p. 268.

Page 168

[20] Although W. W. does not, of course, even hint at it, there is no doubt his own reputation for holiness and spiritual discernment brought

a large number of visitors to Wisbech. 'Fr. Robert Persons told me several times,' writes Fr. de Peralta, ' that while he [W. W.] was in this prison he did more good than when he was free; that *he was the most esteemed and consulted man in England*; that a great number of Catholics came to receive the Sacraments from him, as well as heretics to consult him about their doubts and be reconciled to the Church; and that people of every class attended the spiritual conferences which he gave.' de Peralta, f. 220.

21 Fr. Ralph Bickley was admitted into the Society after Fr. Metham's death. Fr. Garnet, writing to Rome on 15 August 1597, asked leave to receive him: ' He is a very singular man. . . . He has sued [for admission] these twelve years. He is with Father Weston who greatly desireth it.' Fr. Bickley had been captured fifteen months before W. W., on 3 May 1585, and was exiled with him on the accession of James I. Later he returned to England and was again arrested in 1617, when he was accused by Abbot, the Archbishop of Canterbury, of ' distributing the bishoprics of this realm and dividing the kingdom to the Infanta, when you were at Wisbech '. In June 1618 he was exiled a second time after a year's imprisonment and died shortly afterwards at St. Omer. Stonyhurst MSS., *Collectanea P.*, f. 537; More, *Hist. Prov. Angl.*, Lib. viii, s. 22.

Page 169

22 Fr. Metham died, not in 1594 (as W. W. writes), but on 28 June 1592, after seventeen years of imprisonment. He was buried in the graveyard of St. Peter's and his death recorded in the parish register.

23 This was Ursula, daughter of Thomas Gray. The incident is referred to in a paper printed in Strype (*Annals*, vol. iv, p. 274) under the year 1594.

19

MIDSUMMER MADNESS

One of my fellow-priests in prison told me the following story. It happened while he was at the University of Oxford, and he witnessed it himself before his conversion to the faith; at the time he was still a Protestant minister.[1] Although the incident occurred long before this period—it was about the middle of Queen Elizabeth's reign—yet it was at this time, I mean the year 1595 or '96, that I first heard it; and it seems an appropriate tale to include in my narrative.

This is the story.

There was a certain youth from the county of Lancaster whose parents were Catholics. He himself had been brought up a Catholic, and after receiving a good grounding in the humanities at home, he was sent to the University of Oxford for his higher studies in logic and philosophy. Of the many halls for students there he went, by choice or accident, to Hart's Hall. (That is the English name, the Latin is *Aula Cervina*.)[2] Here, in heretical surroundings, he was unable to conceal his Catholicism, or dissemble the practice of his religion, for his fellow scholars and commoners noticed that he kept away from church and from college prayers.[3] His friends beseeched him to attend; his enemies menaced him; others, who professed to be impartial, advised him to go, and painted frightening pictures of the laws enacted against men in his case. In the end, unable to endure any longer this constant mortification, the poor boy (he was only seventeen or eighteen and had no one to whom he could turn for wiser counsel) agreed to hear a sermon by a certain Laurence Humphrey, an arch-heretic and dogmatising preacher.[4] Immediately it was over, a stab of conscience made him aware of the mistake he had made through ignorance and lack of guidance. For many days he went about dejected and distraught, his conscience stricken by the recollection of his sin. He told himself that God was his enemy now and was set to avenge Himself.

There was no way he knew to find a priest to reconcile him to the Church. So, agitated day and night by tormenting spirits, he fell almost into despair. In the midst of his distress there came a night, very wild and frightening, with thunder claps and lightning. He thought that the last hour of his life had come, when an account would have to be given to God of all his actions; and he imagined that this thunder had been sent by God as a forewarning of the harsh and terrible sentence that, at any moment now, would be pronounced against him. He trembled, perspired, and with arms outstretched to heaven he prayed with his whole strength, crying out and repeating every time more loudly and intensely, that phrase of the *Our Father*, ' And lead us not into temptation '. Nearly the whole of that night was taken up with these cries and moans; but shortly before dawn he saw what he imagined was a dove, its wings spread out, fluttering and beating itself repeatedly against the window of his room. This he interpreted as a good omen, as if this bird of innocence had been sent to him as a harbinger of peace.

Nevertheless, the sting of remorse remained firmly embedded. The following day he kept to his room, turning over in his mind endless despairing thoughts. What was he to do? The anguish he suffered made the thought of death in any form seem more bearable by comparison. And it was then that this incredible and fantastic scheme occurred to him, and it shows how his mind worked in his affliction. ' My sin,' he pondered and brooded, ' my sin has been grave. I can think of none graver. It is a sin against religion, and the scandal of it has been public. Satisfaction then must be made in a way that will undo the harm.' So he bided his time, and about Vespers, when they were all at supper, he took off every stitch of clothing to his bare skin. Then, leaving his room, he made his way furtively to the gate and out into the street. Taking small side lanes he ran as quickly as he could towards the market square in the centre of the city.

He had already covered a good distance and was hurrying on to the place when, by an unforeseen chance, he ran straight into the bursar of his own Hall. The man looked up, startled to see a figure, stark naked, racing down the middle of the street—it was a bright midsummer evening and the sun was still high—and as the figure came closer, the bursar recognised who it was.

' Mr. Marsh,' he addressed him, for that was his name,[5] ' what means this strange and unusual appearance? '

' Out of my way! ' was the answer. ' Let me pass. I am going to the market square, where I have business to do for my soul. I am going to summon the citizens, and protest and confess before them my sin against God and man. I am calling them to witness on my behalf in the Day of Judgment that I detest the deed I have done, and will never do the like again. So may I deserve to see God, if He pardons and shows me mercy.'

' Stop, you are mad,' the man answered. ' Come home

with me.' Then, covering up his nakedness with his gown,
he persuaded him to return. He put him to bed. But in no
time Mr. Marsh's exploit was known all over the house. They
raced one another up to his bedroom to see a man who (they
believed) was half demented, for they understood that he
had been driven to this by remorse of conscience at the
sermon he had heard against his religious convictions. Some
of them attacked him fiercely, anxious to talk him out of his
scruples and out of his religion all at once. But Marsh became
more and more incensed at them. He called them heretics,
damned, lost souls, enemies of God, evil men, and ordered
them out of his sight. But in the midst of all this railing and
wrangling he turned for odd moments to prayer, principally
to that phrase of the *Our Father*, ' And lead us not into temptation ', which he called out at the top of his voice.

For the best part of the night they went on arguing about
religion. They pressed and persisted, Marsh rebutting them
and rejoining with the same vehemence and vociferation.
But after a long time they saw the futility of it all and tired.
They had made no advance, and it was now far into the night
and past the time of rest. So off they went to bed. Marsh
was left alone in his room. With tears and sighs he continued
to beg God fervently to forgive him his sin. But his neighbour, the same man who told me this story, taking advantage
of this moment and the nearness of his room, came in to see
him. He told him to cheer himself, and take a little rest and
sleep that night. ' I am not the kind of man,' he said, ' you
perhaps imagine me to be. On religious questions I think like
yourself, no matter what pretence I make in my profession.'
(He was an Evangelical minister, well disposed to the Catholic
faith.) ' I know well how hard the goads of conscience can
strike at a tender mind. But rest assured now. I have a friend,

a physician, who knows how to cure men afflicted with your sickness. He will be willing to do it. Tomorrow,' he went on, ' the first thing in the morning get yourself ready and I will take you to the place where this man lives, and you will be able to discuss the state of your conscience with him,'— he was thinking of a Catholic priest whom he knew to be hiding close by the city.

It is not difficult to understand how heartened Marsh felt at these words. He came to himself at once, and his thoughts and longings were turned towards the daybreak which would bring the happiness he craved. But the devil enters the man who lies awake; and he dissipated entirely his good intent. The report of the affair could not be kept in bounds. It was round practically the whole town at once, and before the pair were able to leave the house early in the morning, they were forestalled by a crowd of visitors. It included some of the principal theologians, and among others a certain John Reynolds, their eminent Doctor of Theology, a cathedral canon and famous writer.[6] He approached Marsh, and tried hard but in vain with prolix arguments lasting many hours to impugn his faith and shake his determination. Marsh defended vigorously, falling back for support on the teaching and authority of the Catholic Church.

' But the whole lot of you Papists,' said Reynolds, '—are you not egregious idolators? Don't you venerate creatures instead of God? Thomas Aquinas, your finest doctor and theologian—you all defer to him—states as much in the plainest words. He says that the cross, a created object, mind you, is to be honoured with *latria* [7]—the honour, that is, which belongs to God immortal and which ought not to be given to any but the true God.' [8]

' I am no theologian,' answered Marsh, ' and I don't know

what St. Thomas says. But I am willing to vouch for it that no Catholic, however badly instructed, much less an outstanding doctor, ever said that the worship due to God alone should be given to his creatures. And you cannot show me any place where St. Thomas says it.'

' I will,' said Reynolds, ' and if you like I will put the passage under your nose, so that you can read it yourself.'

' Then stop arguing,' said Marsh, ' and do what you say.'

Reynolds then left. He did not return in person, but some hours later sent in the book with a passage marked. His orders to the minister were to allow Marsh to read nothing except that one place only.

When Marsh had read it and wanted to go on, the man put his hand on the book, and covered the rest of the passage.

' There is no need to go any further,' he said, ' you've seen enough. The cross is a creature and still it is to be worshipped with *latria*. What more do you want? '

' I want to read the rest,' said Marsh. ' I want to see the sense of the passage.'

A struggle started and there was violence on both sides, Marsh trying to pull the hand away, the other man struggling to keep it there.

' To hell with you, you heretic,' cried Marsh, ' yes, you and the whole lot of you. You think unholy things of God. Get out, you cursed crew. You're no better than Cain or Judas. You loathe the truth. You fight against religion, and are lost to God. Leave me alone.'

With these and other words he turned on them every now and again; and often too in the middle of the disputations he interjected a prayer, saying with vehement affection and spirit, his eyes and hands lifted aloft to God in heaven, ' And

lead us not into temptation '—that more than any other
petition.

The whole of that day and the next there was a continuous
coming and going of heretics. They riled and teased
the lad without shame, in all they said and did. They tied
him up in a bundle like a madman; then—it was the height
of summer—they pressed him down between two feather beds
and all but suffocated him. Within two days, either they
killed him (I do not say they did) with their merciless pressure
and bullying, or he wasted away in sheer agony of mind.
Possibly it was both. Anyhow, deprived of all human assistance, but not, I am certain, of God's—for all his horrible
torment derived from a single sin—he breathed his last.

A certain Catholic once told me this reply which he made
to the pseudo-bishop of Winchester and his assessors when he
was summoned with several other Catholics to appear before
them.[9] They all came up in order. One after the other they
gave intransigent answers to questions about their faith,
and were sent away. Then came his turn.

'Now, my good fellow,' they said, 'and what have you
to say?' Had you seen him you might have thought that
he was a simpleton. Indeed, he was a poor man, a tailor
who tried to make a modest livelihood with needle and
scissors.

'Are you,' they went on, 'still stuck in your ignorance?
It's certainly gross enough. But perhaps it is not so surprising
in a person like yourself; you are so shockingly simple-
minded. Of course, you have been deceived and led astray.
But you must surely be able to understand this. It's not all
that difficult, and it doesn't require much intelligence. You
know that wood and stones must not be made into gods and

worshipped. That is what you Papists do. It is all nonsense. Believe the truth. You can see those things are not gods; they're idols, false and silly things, images of the true God.'

' We know no God,' he said, ' and we adore none save the creator of each and all and the Redeemer of this world. And we know well the difference between a likeness of Christ and Christ in person reigning in heaven, between Peter and Paul and their presentation in pictures.'

' On the contrary,' they said, ' how can you say you don't stretch out your hands to images, to wood and stones, kneel to them, burn incense and prostrate yourselves before them, pour out your prayers to them? What more could you do to God Himself? What greater reverence could you show Him?'

'I beseech you, my lords, to favour me,' he answered, ' you who are learned men, and allow a simple and unlettered fellow to say just one word. If any one of you or any servant of yours were out with the hounds and entered a hall or some other place decorated with hangings and tapestries which had pictures of stags or hares or other animals woven on them, do you imagine the hounds would be so senseless and stupid to chase after the pictures as if they were real beasts and try to catch them? So, I beg you, allow us human beings as much sense and intelligence as you allow brutes and dogs. You ought to realise that even the most unlearned of us are sufficiently instructed by the Church to know the difference between God, Christ, the saints, and statues of them or their painted pictures. We certainly do not honour images in the place of God and the saints, but we turn our thoughts to them and contemplate them by the assistance of their representations.'

The heretics were dumbfounded as they listened to this

reply—such an extremely simple one, brought home with a true and wisely chosen illustration. And as there was no further retort they could make they committed him to prison.[10]

NOTES

[1] Probably Thomas Bramstone, a fellow of St. John's College, who was ordained priest at Douai in 1586. Cf. J. Foster, *Alumni Oxonienses*, vol. 1, p. 171.

[2] Throughout Elizabeth's reign Hart's Hall was a refuge for Catholics. Until the new regulations concerning attendance at services were promulgated in 1580, the year of this incident (cf. *inf.*, p. 188, n. 5), it was easy for Catholic members of Hart's Hall to avoid attendance at Protestant service, for the Hall had no chapel. Perhaps for this reason it flourished as did no other College in this reign. Its members more than doubled during the long tenure of office by the Principal, Philip Rondell (d. 1599), who, as Antony Wood observes, was 'in his heart a Papist, but durst not show it'. Among its Catholic members were Alexander Briant, Francis Throckmorton and John Donne. Richard Holtby, who later became a most distinguished Jesuit, and Thomas Neal, the Professor of Hebrew, who had been ejected from Exeter College for refusing to attend service, were for a time its most influential tutors. Cf. G. S. Hamilton, *Hertford College*.

[3] In 1580 Convocation ordered regular sermons, 'forcing the youth not only to be present at them, but to give an account to their tutor of them'. It was in the following year that Edmund Campion, on the occasion of a University sermon, had over four hundred copies of his *Decem Rationes* distributed in St. Mary's Church. In the following November (1581) a decree was passed making it compulsory for all students to subscribe to the Thirty-Nine Articles, the Book of Common Prayer and the Act of Supremacy. A. Wood, *History and Antiquities of the University of Oxford*, vol. 2 (ed. 1796), p. 199.

[4] Laurence Humphrey (d. 1590), the most learned preacher in Elizabethan Oxford. Tobie Mathew said of him that he 'had read more Fathers than Campion the Jesuit ever saw, devoured more than he ever tasted, and that he had taught more in the university than he had ever learnt or heard'. His extreme Calvinism stood in the way of his appointment as bishop. As Regius Professor of Divinity, President of Magdalen and Vice-Chancellor he probably did more than any other divine to rid the University of Catholicism. Not only did he stock his own college 'with a generation of nonconformists, which could not be rooted out in many years after his decease, but sowed also in the divinity school such seeds of Calvinism, and laboured to create in the younger sort such

a strong hatred against the Papists, as if nothing but divine truths were
to be found in the one, and nothing but abominations were to be seen in
the other.' A. Wood, *Athenae Oxonienses*, i, pp. 557–60; *D.N.B.*,
vol. xxviii, p. 245.

Page 180

⁵ Francis Marsh matriculated from Hart's Hall at the age of seventeen,
on 20 May 1580. His burial on 7 July the same year is recorded in
the Register of St. Peter's-in-the-East. A. Clark, *Register of the University of Oxford*, vol. 2, Part 2, p. 93; A. Wood, *City of Oxford*, vol. 3,
p. 255.

Page 182

⁶ John Reynolds, a brother of Fr. William Reynolds, the Catholic
controversialist and professor of Cardinal Allen's seminary at Douai.
In 1572 William, then a commoner of Hart's Hall, was 'earnest for reformation, while John his brother of Corpus Christi College, stood affected
to the Roman Catholic religion. . . . This difference of judgment proved
a fire ball of contention between them, and engaged them in a strong
duel and set disputes, whereupon both being strengthened by each
other's arguments, William turned a zealous Catholic and John a strong
Puritan.' John was one of the principal translators of the Authorised
Version as his brother William was of the Douai. In 1586 John was
appointed to a temporary lectureship, founded by Francis Walsingham,
for the confutation of Catholic doctrine, and in this capacity lectured
three times a week in full term to large audiences. In 1596 he published
De Romanae Ecclesiae Idolatria—the subject which he had debated with
Francis Marsh sixteen years earlier. Anthony Wood says that he excelled
in memory 'not only for S. Augustine's works, but for all classic
authors', and had 'turned over all writers, profane, ecclesiastical and
divine, all the councils, fathers and histories of the Church'. A. Wood,
Athenae Oxonienses, vol. i, pp. 613–15.

⁷ *Latria* [worship] is the theological term for the 'devotion' which
man should give to God alone.

⁸ The reference is to the *Summa Theologica*, ii 2ae, quaestio xciv,
articulus 1. In the *Summa* St. Thomas lists the objections to the doctrine
he is exposing at the head of each article. Reynolds's chaplain manifestly placed his hand over the expository part of the text, allowing
Marsh to read only the objections.

Page 184

[9] Thomas Cooper, Bishop of Winchester 1584–94. In order to ' extirpate ' Catholics, he offered (May 1586) to give the Council two hundred ' most able and strongest-bodied [of the] common and inferior sort [of Papists] to serve as pioneers or labourers in the Army [in Flanders], besides the numbers of that kind already there '. Such forced labour may have been the fate of the Papist in W. W.'s story. *Acts of Privy Council*, vol. 14, p. 125.

Page 186

[10] It is difficult to believe that Elizabethan bishops and ministers did, in fact, think that Catholics worshipped images and statues, but the evidence strongly bears out their ignorance of the traditional Christian teaching. The silly charge of idolatry made in countless books by Protestant ministers persisted into the early part of this century. Among many other contemporary instances that of Fr. Boast shows that priests were considered as superstitious as the rustic in W. W.'s story.

' One pleasant thing I heard reported generally, that a minister entering with him [Mr. Boast] into some argument about images, and alleging out of Deuteronomy xxvii, *Maledictus homo qui facit sculptile*, as he interpreted, " Cursed is the man that maketh any image ", Mr. Boast answered merrily, " Then," said he, " cursed is he that maketh the knave of clubs " (for by that term was the minister termed, when he was student in Oxford, for his deserts), and so was he dashed.' J. Morris, *Troubles*, Series 3, p. 195.

20

A PRIEST FROM PATMOS

A Greek, from the island of Patmos, relying on letters of recommendation which the English ambassador to Turkey had given him in Constantinople, came to England to collect alms for the release of certain captives. These letters he handed over to the Queen's Council when he explained his business, and received from them permission to beg. He visited many towns and cities, and in the course of his planned itinerary called at Wisbech. Here, on a certain festival day, his good cause was announced from the pulpits, and he collected a very generous donation from the people. News of his arrival reached us, and we asked to see the man and speak with him. This was granted. He wore ordinary, rather threadbare, clothes; and he knew just sufficient Latin and Italian to explain his meaning and understand others in the same languages. The place where we had gathered to watch and listen to the proceedings was filled with a mass of people who had crowded in, and among them was the evangelical minister,[1] with some of the principal townsfolk.

We asked him many questions, particularly about the reason for his journey to this distant and remote part of the world, and about the way he had come. And while he was talking he produced his letters patent from the two Patriarchs of Constantinople and Alexandria. They were written on parchment in most clear and elegant Greek characters, and both were duly endorsed by the pendant seals of the two bishops. The seal of Constantinople was slightly larger. It was of white wax and carried the effigy of the Blessed Virgin. That of Alexandria was black, and bore the likeness of St. Mark. As he unfolded these letters, we asked to have them read and explained in English to all present. Apart from stating the main purpose of his mission, they touched on a number of points bearing on religious questions controverted by the heretics, chiefly the mystery of the Unbloody Sacrifice. This gave occasion for something to be said on religion in the presence of the minister and the people. We asked him, therefore, more detailed questions. What did his religion and the Greek Church say about images? For example, those he carried about in public? Or the impressions of the two seals? What use should be made of these images? What about their adoration? And the real presence of the Body and Blood of Christ? And Mass? Purgatory? The cult of saints? The need of good works for salvation? To all these questions he gave answers very much in harmony with Catholic truth. And the heretics who were present and heard him saw that, with the exception of his peculiar errors which had little common ground with their own doctrines, the Greek and Latin Churches thought and felt very much alike as against present-day heretics. Consequently the whole crowd stood speechless, noticeably the minister, who was reckoned a great preacher by his flock, and an uncommonly learned man. They had no idea what to do with themselves. Every subterfuge had been forestalled. There was nothing whatever they could answer, for, on other occasions—and this is what embarrassed them most—they had boldly claimed that the Greeks were similar to their own sect and patronised them.

Now up to this point of my story I have proceeded in order. And I have narrated with care everything that happened while I was in prison at Wisbech, and all that I saw or gathered from trustworthy sources. But I have not thought it necessary to recount every detail, but merely what seemed to me better established or of greater significance and historical moment or importance. Now the last chapter remains. It deals with my transference to the Tower of London, and the reasons for it, so far as I have been able to discover them.

For almost eleven years I was confined in this prison. During the first six, or about six (my memory may not be good) I was bolted and barred in. For the remaining five I was allowed a good deal more freedom, along with the other prisoners. This was after our first keeper was removed from the scene by a most ghastly death,[2] and in his place we had another man who was anxious to be considered a gentleman. He claimed to have served for a time in the household of the Treasurer, William Cecil, and to have received through his favour and patronage some kind of civil preferment: he had been a magistrate or keeper of the public peace. This man, as I said, acquired also the rights of our custody—it was an office that carried with it large annual revenues and emoluments with a minimum of work. Now both in his capacity as our keeper and in virtue of the authority which he was used to exercise over layfolk, he felt confident and qualified to deal both with ourselves and with any discord that arose amongst us.[3] Moreover, he had on his side—it should never have been allowed to occur—men who favoured, yes, even encouraged, his pretensions, who asserted that all business touching priests and all their quarrels—I mean everything apart from questions of religious belief—should be judged and determined according to the laws of the realm and the decrees of the Queen's Council, so that it would appear altogether unexceptionable if our keeper, who had been a magistrate and a justice, heard and decided controversies of this kind. This opinion of theirs appeared to most of us, and to me among them, more than unworthy and unjust, no matter whether it was conceived with the object of getting themselves into favour or from genuine conviction.[4] And to me, chief of all, it caused further estrangement from the keeper and led to complaints being made against me to the Queen and her Councillors.[5] It was said in addition—let the men who fabricated the story look to the justice of it—that I received a secret despatch from Cardinal Cajetan,[6] which, among other things, was supposed to broach a plot for the murder of the Queen and of another person, who was far from being a prince or even of princely origin. Perhaps the fabricator of the lie fancied that the only way he could give this other man distinction was to associate his name with that of the Queen and make them partners in a joint threat of assassination.[7] Thus he might make of him some sort of second father and protector of the country's weal. This man I will not name, although he has been named in this connection in a book printed and published in England.[8]

Now the pursuivants, who conducted me and some others from Wisbech to London (I shall speak of this later) told me in confidence the reason for my removal: namely that I had meddled in Spanish politics and favoured the Spanish party. At the same time they mentioned by name the authors of this accusation. Later, the Commissioners assigned to adjudicate cases concerning Catholics brought against me other charges, apart from this, when I stood my examination before them. I will speak about this in the proper place, as soon as I come to that point in my narrative.[9] Indeed, I think it was the persistent complaints of these malicious men which had me cast into the Tower. They felt certain that unless I was put out of the way and had my mouth stopped, they would never be able to come to a decision on the matters which they had set in motion.[10]

Let that suffice for the affairs of Wisbech.[11]

In my next letter your Reverence can expect an account of the preparations for my journey to the Tower of London, and the way it was made. Then, at long last, I shall be able to conclude my narrative and thus satisfy the command of your Reverence and our Superior. Any other things which happened at Wisbech or in the Tower, which I judge better not to insert here, I am only too happy to omit altogether or at least leave over to be told by others.

Towards the end of the year 1599 (I think it was) the Queen's Council gave an order for me and three others to be transferred to London.[12] They effected this by sending letters of mandate to the Justice whose business it was to make visitations of our prison when occasion arose. As usual they gave no warning of the day and time of their arrival, but took us by surprise when we were unprepared and expecting nothing of the kind. They came at lunch time. We were all in the refectory, and had just got seated at table. The meal was not even begun, when the Justice was announced at the door. He had a large retinue with him. He did not actually enter the room, but stood just inside the doorway and remained there. First he called for me, ordering me from the room. Outside he handed me over to two or three men of his party to prevent me having a word with anyone or doing anything. Then he summoned two other priests, Christopher Southworth and Giles Archer, and that noble gentleman, Thomas

Pound; these likewise he handed over to a guard, and gave orders for them to be watched with the same care.

Then immediately they went round all the cells, and searched them with great thoroughness. Nothing went unexamined— books, letters and manuscripts, no matter what they were, and every single thing they found in the way of relics or pictures, sacred or secular, it made no difference to them. However, they did not come upon any of our sacred vestments or chalices, for we were always very concerned about them and took care not to leavě them in places where they might be seen. In fact, every day after they had served their use they were hidden away in some secret place. Daily experience had made us familiar with their tricks, and we had acquired a fair measure of caution.[13]

When their zest for searching was satisfied, they announced that we were to leave for London. We were to be ready to start the journey the next day. But the whole of that day and the following night we were kept separately, each in his own cell with his own guards. The men deputed to watch me let me understand in a friendly manner that, immediately on my arrival in London, I would be clapped into the Tower, so that I should reflect and see whether there was anything I wanted to settle first. In fact, they treated me with great kindness, and they allowed anyone who wished to come and speak with me in secret.

NOTES

[1] This was Mathew Champion, who was presented by the Queen in 1586 and remained Vicar of Wisbech until 1613. Cf. List of Vicars in Wisbech Church.

[2] Thomas Gray, the first keeper, died after October 1592. The relaxations to which W. W. refers were introduced in the course of the next year, after five and a half years of close confinement. Cf. J. H. Pollen, ' The Stirs of Wisbech ' in *The Month*, July 1912,

[3] In a letter of 3 November 1598, William Medley, the keeper, wrote to Robert Cecil, begging his favour on the ground that he ' was bred up under Lord Burghley, being thereto preferred by Lady Burghley, whereby, as well during his daily attendance, as in his other late dependency, he has received divers favours '. *Hat. Cal.*, vol. viii, p. 421.

[4] Invariably in any form of prison life the most intense and bitter quarrels are caused by a section of prisoners playing up to their captors. Here at Wisbech it destroyed all sense of camaraderie and made social relations extremely difficult among the priests who had such a good cause in common. W. W. is most moderate in his criticism of the factious priests, who took up the pretence that they were loyal servants of the Crown who had a duty to co-operate with the keeper in the enforcement of prison regulations.

[5] Later the keeper seems to have formed a most high opinion of W. W., for Fr. Henry More tells this story which, he says, he had on the authority of Thomas Garnet. ' The magistrate, who was Weston's keeper at Wisbech, happened one day to be reading a copy of Watson's *Quodlibeta*. Coming on a certain passage which disparaged Weston and spoke contemptuously of him, he instantly hurled the book away in great indignation, and swore an oath that everything said against Weston was a lie: the priest had led a holy and innocent life at Wisbech, and he personally set such store by the man's sanctity that he earnestly hoped that he would have a place in his prayers.' Henry More, *Hist. Prov. Angl.*, lib. iv, s. 25.

[6] This charge was based on a lying deposition of the factious priest, Thomas Bluet, to Brewster, the assistant keeper at Wisbech. ' With tears in his eyes he [Bluet] told me . . . he feared there might [be] letters from a Cardinal that was Governor of the English College at Rome

[viz., Henry, Cardinal Cajetan] to Edmunds [W. W.] and his Jesuitical faction to swear all the priests to the obedience of the Infanta of Spain.' Petyt MSS., Inner Temple, 38, f. 399. Cf. Persons's *A Brief Apologie*, ch. 10.

[7] W. W. is here referring to the Squire Plot, a supposed attempt to poison the Queen by spreading a lotion on the pommel of her horse's saddle. The other person, the partner in the ' joint threat ', was the Earl of Essex, who was to be despatched by the same poison applied to his chair while he was at sea. Squire was condemned and executed on the evidence of John Stanley's confession and letters, documents which the Government itself admitted were faked (*Hat. Cal.*, vol. viii, p. 396). The best exposure of the whole fiction is Nicholas Fitzherbert's *Apologie in Defence of Himself* (1602) to which W. W. refers; but it has still to be established to what extent the plot was fabricated or at least used by the Government as a pretext for the removal of Bagshaw from Wisbech so that, after a short screening imprisonment in the Tower, he could be employed for the disruption of the Catholic body. It is significant that Bagshaw was sent for from Wisbech, on a faked charge of complicity in the plot, on 7 October, some weeks before Squire actually implicated him in his confession. *Hat. Cal.*, vol. VIII, p. 384.

[8] This is Nicholas Fitzherbert's *Apologie in Defence of Himself and other Catholics, falsely charged with a feigned conspiracy against Her Majesty's person*, etc. (1602). In the very first page the author links Essex's name with the Queen's, and goes on to expose what Augustus Jessopp has called the ' monstrous fiction ' of the Squire Plot.

[9] Cf. *inf.*, ch. 21, p. 204.

Page 194

[10] There is no doubt (I think) that Fr. de Peralta is right in saying that the reason for W. W.'s transference to the Tower was the Council's alarm at ' the great work that he [W. W.] was doing even in prison and the trust that everybody had in him, as well as the great authority in which he was held by all alike, heretics as well as Catholics' (f. 221). It is a reason, of course, that W. W. would not have believed, even if he had been told. But now that the Government was employing the factious group of priests, both at Wisbech and outside, to drive a wedge into the Catholic body, it was imperative that W. W. whose word counted for more than that of any other priest in England at that time, should be cut off from all intercourse with Catholics, as indeed he was for the next three and a half years. The other two priests who were taken with him Giles Archer and Christopher Southworth, as well as

the layman, Thomas Pound, probably knew too much about Bagshaw and Bluet to enjoy safely the comparative freedom of Wisbech.

[11] The only accurate account of the troubles at Wisbech is that given by Fr. Persons in *A Briefe Apologie*, ch. vi, pp. 62–83. It is more reliable both in fact and judgment and based on fuller documentation than Fr. Pollen's article on the same subject in *The Month*, July 1912.

[12] W. W. was committed to the Tower on 19 December 1598 (not, as he says, 1599), the day of his arrival in London (cf. p. 209, n. 9). As he took ' three days ' over the journey, he would have left Wisbech on 16 December.

Page 195

[13] As appears from W. W.'s letter to Newton, all the requisites for Mass were hidden in the ' old ruinous chapel ' of the castle. W. W. may have been responsible for the choice of place ; at least he defended it, although he was charged by the factious priest of being ' sacrilegious, excommunicated, irregular [and] scandalous ' on this account. Westminster Arch., vol. 31, p. 105.

21

THE ROAD TO THE TOWER

So the morning dawned when once again we were made a spectacle to men and to the world. A countless crowd of people gathered to watch us, both within and beyond the castle enclosure. And while they stood by, the horses were saddled and nine, perhaps ten, guards assembled who were to escort us the whole length of the journey and take us to court. It was also their business to prevent us conferring privately with one another or having any word at all save in the presence of a witness. Then after much fussing and hustling we mounted our horses in full view of the spectators, and set out with a large guard of soldiers. Scarcely had we gone a mile and a half, when a fast rider was posted after us. In as short a time as possible he had caught up with us, and at once stripped us of the packbags in which we carried our cassocks, shirts and those few other things we needed, as men do who are bidden off to prison. They suspected we had secretly taken away certain things, and by coming on us unexpectedly they had hoped to discover our deceit.

We then continued on our way. The man, however, returned with the packs as fast as he had first come. Only our breviaries had been stolen. Apart from them, there was nothing that took their fancy or was worth snatching.

A little further along, two of those men they call pursuivants met us on the high road. They had been sent on the authority of the Council for the very task that had just been completed: to arrange, that is, for our transference to London, and to carry out a close search of all our cells and common rooms, examining the walls and ceilings for our secret hiding places. As they had been forestalled in their work, they spared themselves the rest of the journey and attached themselves to our party. Hereafter I was handed over to these two guards, who clung to my side incessantly and did not leave my room even at night.

It was winter, and very wet and cold. The roads were muddy, and when we came to an inn we warmed ourselves and dried our clothes. My companions, also, had their own rooms with their own guards assigned to each. I took great pains to show consideration to my keepers. I told them to light a blazing fire, and to lie down while supper was got ready, or ordered a glass of wine or other refreshment for them, and said that I would pay. The whole day we had gone without a meal and had toiled, practically fasting, on a tedious journey. So while they were busy looking after the horses, I took their cloaks and laid them out before the fire, and with these and other attentions I gained the good-will of them both.

'Beware of my companion,' one of them said. 'He is a great rascal. Don't confide in him the slightest thing that could be used against you.' And the other man told me the same about his mate, each giving reasons why I should do well to suspect the other of special knavery. But actually there was no need for this. Their loathsome occupation as pursuivants of Catholics told me enough about them, and I knew how little trust I could place in either. Without scruple or risk of rash judgment one might well have presumed they were more than ordinarily wicked men.

These men told me the reason why I had been summoned:

namely, that I was deeply attached to the Spanish party, and had defended their claim to the English succession, both privately and in company, even in open debate; [1] and they added that the priests in Wisbech were split into factions in support of conflicting princes. Some were for the Spanish side, others the Scottish. Hence the discord among them.

Now these accusations were very serious. (No greater calumny against me could have been fabricated.) And it was easy, therefore, to understand the alarm of the Queen's Council and their sending for me. Furthermore they named the chief people who had accused me, [2] and mentioned many other things that certainly could never have reached the ears of the heretics unless certain persons had manifestly betrayed me. [3]

So a great part of the journey I spent talking to them on these subjects. And because I was well in their favour, they allowed me to have private conversations with other persons, and once actually kept watch at the door while I heard a man's confession—saying, as they did it, ' We don't want to pay large fines in money for letting one of those rogues find you in secret conference.' They said this, I am certain, to make much of the small kindness they had done. Nevertheless, I knew that on this present journey they were behaving abominably to the men who, against their wishes, had joined the escort. They had hoped for greater profit, and would have got it, if the transportation had been in their undivided charge. [4]

In three days we reached London. From our inn we were taken to the Queen's court. [5] Spattered all over with mud and grime from the road we must have presented a sorry sight to the courtiers. For two whole hours, at very least, we were kept waiting on their decision. Then, after a long deliberation, without even seeing us, they sent us back to the inn. But I must mention an incident that occurred there. One of my companions getting cold with the long waiting and becoming rather restive, interrupted the protracted sitting by taking an occasional brief walk up and down. I tried to do the same. But some seedy-looking courtier or other, who had been sitting with his arms crossed, charged at me heartily and squarely, with the whole weight of his body, as I was walking between two guards. I saw him coming, stepped aside, and made way for him. A large number of people were watching. On my return, he came at me again. Again I side-stepped. Then, yielding place to him, I sat down. Possibly he thought that here were priests—and Jesuits at that (they were despised more than the dregs of the rabble and loathed by men of every class)—giving themselves airs at court. No doubt he thought that this was no place for such men to presume to walk up and down, or even raise their eyes and look another man in the face.[6]

So we were dismissed and returned to the inn with our full accompaniment of guards.

Back at the inn, we had supper. It was time now we retired to rest. We were weary from the day's business. But two messengers from court came to hustle us off to prison immediately. One of them entered my room. He had a large number of attendants with him.

' In the Queen's name,' he said, bringing down his arm on me, ' I arrest you.'

' There's no need for that,' I said. ' I have been the Queen's prisoner many years already.'

' I am obliged to put you through a thorough examination,' he said, ' to see whether you are carrying any arms or letters on your person, or in your baggage.'

This he did. He delved into every pocket and corner of my clothes and baggage. Then he fastened my arm with a rope. ' Get along with you,' he ordered, ' you're to go to the Tower of London.' The priest Giles Archer received the same treatment. But my other two companions were taken off separately to different prisons.[7]

So the two of us were led away. I went first. He followed with his own escort. We were dragged through a long city street [8] till at last we reached the Tower, and were brought before the Lieutenant.[9] He asked us many questions, principally concerning Father Gerard, who a few months earlier had made good his escape. He said he would give a vast sum to recapture him.[10] Then two warders were summoned and assigned us each to our cells; but before being led off we embraced and took leave of each other as for the last time. How he fared, I do not know.[11] But it was my lot to fall into the hands of another brutal plunderer. As soon as the door was shut on me the fellow appeared. ' You are Edmunds,' he said, ' and you are a Jesuit. I belong to the Queen's service, and it's my job to deal with you and the likes of you in the way you deserve. First, hand over your crucifix. You always go about with crucifixes, rosaries and medals.' Then he put both hands on my chest and with one tug ripped my gown from the neck to my ankles. 'Where's that crucifix?' he said, and searched the rest of my person and clothing all over. ' If I don't find your crucifix,' he continued, ' I will unstitch every garment you have on.' At last he hit upon it. Delighted with the prize, he gave me no more trouble.

I wondered now what new accusation they would find to bring against me and what witnesses they would produce to support it. But they gave me a very long respite, and during several weeks of concern and anxiety as to my ultimate fate, nothing further was said or done.[12] Eventually they did summon me and brought me before the commissioners.[13] First they asked me the usual preliminary questions. What was my name? my country? birthplace? place of education, and ordination to the diaconate and priesthood? Then they sought to put me under oath to give direct and truthful answers to the rest of their questions. I told them they could ask whatever they wished. In what was lawful for me to mention, I would satisfy them without being bound by an oath. If they asked anything unlawful, no oath would make me answer. 'It's not our present business,' they said, ' to deal with religious questions: for instance, the fact that you are a Jesuit and a priest, and have entered the realm against the established laws and will of the Sovereign. Nor do we intend to enquire about the Masses you have said since your entry; the houses where you have stayed; the people you have drawn from the Queen's allegiance and reconciled to the Pope. We release you from anxiety on all these counts. You have nothing to fear there. You are charged with graver things, matters of life and death for you.' Then, in sequence, they brought out the four principal heads of accusation against me. I had in my possession seditious books treating perniciously of the state of the realm, principally one, ascribed to Father Persons, which discussed the rights of various claims to the succession.[14] Then, that the priests at Wisbech had fostered parties and factions among themselves, and had held public discussions on these claims and made them subjects of daily conversation; and while some favoured one successor, and others another, I was the chief protagonist of the Spanish faction.[15] Moreover, I had known of the approach of the vast Armada of the Spaniards against England, and had not given information about it; and, in addition,

through couriers and correspondence, I had previous knowledge of two of their warlike expeditions, the first against
England, the second against Ireland, and I had held my
tongue.[16]

There were other similar items in the indictment, but my
recollection is not sufficiently accurate to recall them now.
They gave me, however, a long account of the turmoils at
Wisbech, specifying incidents and personalities which I
would so much rather had been kept within the prison walls,
not published to the heretics with so much scorn and infamy.[17]
Finally, after they had failed to get the information they
wanted, they covered me pretty well with insults and jibes,
and sent me back to prison.[18] Even considering the range and
number of their questions, they had shown themselves fair
adepts at abuse; but still, with that strange inner hatred they
nursed, they gave signs of regretting that they had not said
everything they might have done. I do not refer to all.
Some, indeed, if not from moderation, then out of respect
for their own persons and position, wished to appear more
balanced than the rest. But even one of these men threatened
to squeeze blood from my nails and finger tips—a sufficiently
ill-concealed threat of the horrors of the rack and torture to
fill me with fear.[19]

Shut again in my cell, I lay there hourly and daily expecting
sentence of death. The time and place were well suited to
prayer, and, had not my eyes failed me, to reading and study
also. But the sight of one eye was completely gone, and a
film forming over the other made it more than half blind,
so that I very nearly suffered complete loss of sight. Moreover, owing to a chronic headache, sleep had become all but
impossible. I had, in fact, practically none; and for the
space of eight, nine, ten or more days I scarcely had two or

three hours' sleep—and that only with the aid of sleeping draughts.[20] So all the time I suffered severely from a most grievous inflammation of the eyes and head. Indeed these troubles caused me much greater suffering and depression than the tedium of prison life, my close confinement, or the excessive solitude due to my total segregation from the world outside.[21]

Once, right under my eyes, a Catholic was carried out for burial in most mean style. Unless I am mistaken, he had endured eleven whole years in this vile prison for the sake of his religion, yet his spirit remained undaunted. Humberstone was his name. My warder told me that an unsparingly cruel man had been deputed to look after him. Apart from his habitual brutalities, he would inflict savage blows and lashes on Humberstone until, in the end, under these and all the other countless sufferings of his imprisonment—the squalor, the confinement, the solitude, the underfeeding, the scourges and cudgelling—he lost the balance of his mind.[22] Drained utterly of bodily strength he became helpless for nearly three years before his death, and was confined to bed: without help—and it was very rarely given him—he could not even turn over and lie on his other side. The same warder told me this also about Humberstone. His father, a heretic who had obtained the favour of the Queen, had been granted permission to remove his son from prison and bring him home. He begged his son to come. He implored him insistently again and again, but he could not get him to yield to his entreaties. In the midst of all his tribulations the son preferred to remain gloriously in prison for his faith, with a most assured hope of salvation, rather than pass his days with a heretic, even his own father. Indeed, he knew for certain that with him he could never escape the deceits, blandishments, persuasions and other wiles of heretical company.[23]

Not unlike this was the case of another gentleman, a pattern of singular probity. He was my prison neighbour, though we were separated by massive walls and heavily barred and bolted doors. Formerly he had held high rank in the Catholic army fighting the heretics in Flanders. But after striving bravely in the line for several years, some matter of business brought him back to England. Here he fell into the hands of the heretics. On interrogation he replied that he was a Catholic—forthrightly, as became a soldier. He was clapped into the Tower, and there I found him on my arrival, bravely completing his fifth year of imprisonment, worn down by many infirmities and wants. His mother was anxious to take him out, and a short time before I left the fortress she went to great expense and effort, and employed intercessors with the Queen to this end. At length she obtained permission. But he would not avail himself of it for fear of admitting that he had ever offended the Queen and broken the law by going out of the kingdom without a licence—an admission that was made a condition of his release. It was for reasons of religion and conscience that he had gone abroad. He saw no crime in it and refused to regret his action and proclaim himself sorry. So he stood firmly by his resolution. And though his mother, sisters and friends came every day beseeching him and striving to move him with tears, he remained steadfast in his conviction.[24]

NOTES

Page 201

¹ This charge, though lacking any substance, is interesting in view of Cecil's negotiations in the following year. From the middle of 1599, if not from an earlier date, Cecil interested himself in the claims of the Infanta, and from then until the execution of Essex favoured her succession rather than that of James (cf. p. 229, n. 6). With great secrecy he arranged to have two portraits of the Infanta specially painted and brought over to England (*Hat. Cal.*, vol. ix, pp. 345, 391, 440) and was 'constantly and excessively commending her excellencies' (*Correspondence of James VI with Robert Cecil*, p. 83). There is also evidence that Cecil sent letters in cipher to Persons, who at this time was also in close touch with Thomas Sackville, the son of the Treasurer, Lord Buckhurst, a friend of his from Oxford days.

² W. W.'s chief accusers were Dr. Bagshaw and Thomas Bluet. On 13 October Bagshaw had been transferred from Wisbech to the Tower on the pretence that he was to be confined more closely, but in reality to consult with William Wade. 'Many Catholics waited anxiously news of his fate. Then it became known that he was being treated with great favour and in almost daily converse and conference with Wade, the Secretary of the Council. Next, by his and Bluet's management the four prisoners whom he had held in greatest loathing at Wisbech were transferred to very strict custody ... in London. This last assertion can be confirmed and verified by the plain statement of witnesses. For while Fr. Edmund [W. W.] and the other priests were on their way to London, one of the Queen's servants, a pursuivant as they are commonly called, told this Father [W. W.] that he and his companions had been betrayed by their fellows.' Then after stating how Edmund Calverly, formerly Bagshaw's intimate and confidante at Wisbech, threw this accusation in his teeth when Bagshaw later visited Wisbech, the writer goes on to explain that Bagshaw had suborned Brewster, the Assistant Keeper of Wisbech, to co-operate with him in this plot; and that Brewster himself testified to this, adding bitterly that he had not received the payment Bagshaw had promised him for this service; in fact, he was out of pocket owing to the expense of his journey to London and stay there in an attempt to secure the money. English College Arch., Rome, *Scritture, Ext. III, iB De Bagshao.*

³ The circumstantial detail of these accusations so far from proving W. W.'s guilt shows that inside information provided by the factious priests had been used by the Government to spice the false charges

brought against him. The extraordinary confession of William Watson (April 1599) shows that it was Dr. Bagshaw, W. W.'s principal accuser, who was responsible not only for talk, but for intrigue about the succession among the Wisbech prisoners. T. Graves Law, *The Archpriest Controversy*, vol. 1, p. 210 sq.

⁴ This party, seven in number, did in fact receive fifteen pounds between them for conveying the Wisbech prisoners to London (*Acts of the Privy Council*, vol. 29, p. 381). The second escort, under William Ball, were paid twenty pounds. P.R.O., *Treasury Chamber Accounts* (1598), f. 340.

⁵ At Whitehall.

Page 202

⁶ Cf. Robert Southwell, who describes the Catholic subjects of the Queen as ' common steels for every merciless and flint hearted man to strike out upon them the sparkles of his fury '. *Humble Supplication*, p. 16.

Page 203

⁷ Fr. Christopher Southworth was taken to the Gatehouse (*C.R.S.*, vol. 2, p. 287), Thomas Pound to the Wood Street Counter for six weeks and then to the Tower. *The Rambler*, new series, vol. viii (July 1587), p. 28.

⁸ The Strand and then Thames Street.

⁹ 19 December 1598 is the date of the mandate issued by the Privy Council to the Lieutenant of the Tower, instructing him to ' receive into his charge Giles Archer and William Edmunds, two Jesuits . . . from Wisbech . . . and to see them kept close prisoners '. From W. W.'s account the mandate would appear to have been carried out the same or the following day. *Acts of Privy Council*, vol. 29, p. 273.

¹⁰ Gerard had escaped not ' a few months earlier ', but in October 1597, just fourteen months before this interview. However, this is still later evidence of the anxiety of the Lieutenant, Sir John Peyton, to get Gerard back into his hands. In July the following year (1599) John Lillie, who had organised Gerard's escape, was captured, and Peyton recommended that he ' should be put to the manacles for the discovery of Gerard's places of resort and abode (*Hat. Cal.*, vol. ix, p. 237). The treatment Lillie received is described in *John Gerard* (p. 156). W. W. was at that time so completely dependent for his

information on what he saw or was told by his warder that he seems to have been unaware that Lillie, his fellow Jesuit, was confined in another part of the Tower.

[11] Fr. Archer remained in the Tower until he was removed to Framlingham Castle in the summer of 1601. ' To Framlingham ', wrote Fr. Garnet on 7 July 1601, ' went out of the Tower Wright, Archer, Pound, Alabaster.' Stonyhurst MSS., *Collectanea P*, f. 539.

Page 204

[12] The political situation at this moment was so tense, prior to Essex's departure for Ireland, that the politicians had no time to trouble themselves with W. W. despite their pretence that he was an important prisoner.

[13] The date of W. W.'s examination is unknown, but on 24 December 1598 William Wade had been instructed by the Council to use extraordinary care in examining W. W. and the four other prisoners recently transferred from Wisbech. The matter for the examination was to be provided by Wade, who was to report his findings ' that thereupon we [the Council] may give you such further direction as shall be thought meet in what sort they shall be further dealt with '. *Acts of Privy Council* , vol. 29, p. 401.

[14] This was *A Conference about the Next Succession*, the joint work of a number of English exiles, printed at Antwerp in 1594. The first part is an historical and legal argument showing the people's right to alter the direct line of succession for just causes. The second part is a genealogical discussion of the claims of various contenders for the throne. The book caused a great stir in England and it was made high treason for any person to have a copy in his possession.

[15] Cp. Fr. Archer's testimony (Appendix D). ' He disliked talking about the latest news or happenings in the world outside, and usually led us to converse on spiritual topics or on subjects connected with our studies.' This, like all the accusations brought against W. W. at the time, illustrates Garnet's comment, ' It was Fr. Weston's observation always that the factions, when they committed any fault, would . . . presently exclaim of the other for the like, though without any ground at all.' Garnet to Persons, 14 July 1601. Stonyhurst MSS., Grene, *Collectanea P.*, f. 537.

Page 205

[16] In the autumn of 1597 an Armada of 136 ships and 9,000 men which put out from Ferrol was forced by storms to return to Spain.

Likewise, both in 1596 and 1597 other Spanish expeditions had set sail against Ireland and had been dispersed at sea.

[17] The reference is principally to Bagshaw's *True Relation of Wisbech* and Bluet's *Important Considerations which ought to move all true and sound Catholics, who are not wholly Jesuited,* and Watson's *Quodlibeta,* all published with Government support in 1601.

[18] No reports of this examination seem to have survived. Doubtless it was known that W. W. was completely innocent, and the official accounts of the examinations were therefore reckoned of no importance.

[19] W. W., like Southwell and other brave priests, shuddered at the prospect of the rack. On the eve of his departure for England Southwell wrote to John Deckers, ' Pray now about my body's death, that I may usefully escape it or manfully endure '.

Page 206

[20] See ch. 23, n. 1 for Fr. de Peralta's very detailed account of W. W.'s suffering in the Tower. Sometime between 25 March and 24 June 1600 he saw a physician for the first time, and thereafter regularly. Cf. Tower Bills, in *C.R.S.,* vol. 4, pp. 235–6.

[21] By some means Fr. Garnet was able to get information about W. W.'s condition, and tried to obtain his release. ' I am in hand to get out our cousin William ', he wrote to Persons on 14 January 1600. ' If it be done it will cost well . . . his eyes are not well yet and one, he thinketh, he shall never use ' (Stonyhurst MSS., *Collectanea P.,* f. 546). W. W.'s account of his isolation is confirmed by Fr. de Peralta: ' There he was for a little over five years without going to confession or speaking to anyone or receiving any written message from any person . . . [Nor] could his friends succeed in bribing the keeper to take him any gift or letter, even though they offered him a great deal for this service.' de Peralta, f. 227.

[22] For a period, at least, this man seems to have had charge of W. W. ' His keeper,' says Fr. de Peralta, ' was a cruel and inhuman heretic, who never spoke a kind word to him . . . but sometimes even assaulted him, giving him blows and beating him with a stave ' (de Peralta, f. 221). No redress, of course, was possible against the brutality of prison warders, hence, as Southwell points out, ' every warder, porter and gaoler ' was ' an unresisted Lord with absolute discretion over his Catholic prisoners '. *Humble Supplication,* p. 34.

Page 207

[23] This was Robert Humberstone. The Tower Bills (*C.R.S.,* vol. 4, p. 223 sq.) confirm W. W.'s statement that he was given occasional

attention in his last days of suffering, being allowed ' physic, surgery and a woman that kept him in his sickness '. This expense is charged against him in the last quarter (viz., Midsummer, 1599) in which his name appears. He would have died, therefore, sometime between 25 March and 25 June 1599. Like W. W., Humberstone had been arrested at the time of the Babington Plot (*C.R.S.*, vol. 2, p. 257), and was then described as a Lincolnshire man and ' a most obstinate conveyor and concealer of priests and their superstitious trumperies ' (*ib.*, p. 276). There seems to have been no other charge made against him. He had been transferred to the Tower from the Gatehouse on 25 July 1590. *C.R.S.*, vol. 21, p. 346.

[24] This was Edward Lingham, who, for reasons of conscience, had left England as a young man and had served as a free-lance soldier in the wars of the Netherlands. In the autumn of 1593, when he was an officer in Sir William Stanley's regiment, he fell in with Fr. Henry Walpole who was then at St. Omer, waiting to cross to England. On 20 November 1593 he sailed with Walpole from Dunkirk and after an adventurous voyage was put ashore with him at Bridlington, Yorks, on 4 December. One of Walsingham's spies who had been tracking them in another vessel landed shortly before them and they were immediately hunted down and captured on 7 December. Topcliffe was sent up from London to examine them in York Castle and recommended that Walpole and Lingham should be sent to the Tower and examined under torture. Walpole was hung up fourteen times, but there is no record of Lingham's torture. A. Jessopp, *One Generation of a Norfolk House*, pp. 187, 190, 236; *C.R.S.*, vol. 4, p. 223 sq.

22

A TRIPLE ESCAPE

I am now going to tell a story that has its amusing side, at the risk of my narrative going a little off its course. The authority for the tale is the teller, and I shall tell it as it was told to me.

After two years in this prison, I had another warder who used to visit me and bring me things I needed. 'The nights,' I said to him, ' are long and dark, particularly in solitude and in winter time. Bring me what's needed to light a lamp, some steel and tinder. When I asked this favour of my former warder, Trench—that was his name—I was surprised that he refused me the kindness.' ' *I* am not surprised,' he said. 'He had good reason. Not many months back one of our prisoners made use of these very things to effect his escape.' Then he began to tell me the following story. The man was a Catholic, but his Catholicism was not the reason for his imprisonment here. He had been detained a long, almost interminable, time, and though his case had been heard and examined, it appeared that justice had fallen asleep. There was no sentence.[1] He seemed, so to speak, to lie buried in the darkness of the tomb, having passed out of the recollection of his fellow-men.[2] Then he started to consider by what means he could make his escape. So, being a skilled artisan, he made a file from a scrap of wrought iron. With this he began slowly to saw through the iron bars and eventually,

by working at them every day, he made a way out for himself.
He then scaled the wall, swam across the moat, and got away.
The next day, on entering the cell, the warder saw it was
empty, its inmate flown. The news was cried by heralds
throughout the whole city, and a hunt was started for his
recapture. Meanwhile, by walking hard, he put six miles
between himself and the city; but on the road he stopped at a
glover's shop to buy a pair of gloves, and here a traveller,
who had left London that same morning, looking the man
up and down, noticed that his clothes were soaked.

'The heralds were crying for a man all over the city,' he
said, 'a prisoner who escaped from the Tower. He could
have got out only by scaling the walls and swimming the moat.
Look at this fellow. All his clothes are wet! See! He may
be the very man!' They had him arrested and brought back.
When the matter was gone into, he was identified and once
again locked in, heavily loaded with irons, and fastened by
a long chain to a wooden pillar in the middle of his cell.

With patience laboriously come by, he put a good face
on the discomforts he suffered.[3] But afterwards, when it
was thought that he had been sufficiently punished for his
escape, his fetters were undone, and once again he was given
the freedom of his cell. The incident was forgotten, and he
was treated the same as before. Nevertheless, this did not
satisfy him, and he now began to think out some fresh plan.
By the same means as last time—the secret of his file had not
been detected—he found a way of escape. But as the wall he
had to descend was higher this time, he procured a rope
(where he got it, I do not know) and slid down it. But it
was too short, and left him dangling a good distance above the
water. So, releasing his hold, he dropped into the moat.
There was a heavy splash, and in the silence of the night the

guards pacing the other side heard the noise. At once they guessed that a prisoner had escaped from the Tower, and began running about in every direction. But the man watched for his moment carefully, emerged from the water, and took to flight. Feeling his pursuers upon him, he began to shout, 'There, there he goes!' The runner hardest on his heels dashed forward, hoping to win commendation for recapturing the fugitive. He came level with him, then brought his hand down on his shoulder, to hold him back a second until he could overtake him. But he felt the wet clothes. 'You're the fellow,' he cried. 'Stop!'

So he was re-arrested. They took him back again and this time locked him up and guarded him with still greater care. But after the lapse of some time a new plan occurred to him. He was most ingenious at devising fresh stratagems.

First of all he made a habit of never greeting the warder when he came into his cell, and never speaking to him when he left. He did not even look at him. Pretending to be busily occupied, he sat facing the window with his back turned to him. Meanwhile he had manufactured a number of things which he fancied would be a help in his new project of escape.

The day came which he had fixed for his flight. Previously he had completed a dummy of himself in a long gown of the kind he usually wore. Then covering its head with a hat or cap, he placed it in position facing the window, hoping that when the warder entered and saw the model he would notice nothing unusual, but simply take it for the same person he always found sitting silently in that place with his back turned on him. Meanwhile he had transformed himself into the perfect blacksmith, made up and dressed in every detail, tools in his hand and slung from his belt. At the usual time the warder entered the cell. He briskly put down the things he was carrying in the place he always did. But the prisoner, who had been hiding behind the door, quickly gave him the slip and hurried downstairs, leaving the warder completely unaware of the trick that had been played upon him.

A woman, however, happened to be passing and noticed the man. It was at a time of the day and in a place where no one was allowed to be about without a warder.

' Good fellow,' she said, ' who are you? Where do you come from? '

He answered that he had just done a blacksmith's job upstairs.

' But you can't go visiting prisoners' cells,' she said, ' unless a warder is with you. Stop! Let's check and see who you are.'

While this conversation was going on, the warder returned on his round.

' Do you know this fellow? ' asked the woman. ' Just a minute ago he came down from where you were.'

The warder looked him up and down, and only after some while did he succeed in recognising him, so completely transformed were his appearance and his clothes.

' Will you never stop trying your tricks? ' he said. ' Now, get back with me.'

Again he locked him up in his cell. But one or two years later, after his own warder had given security that he would behave as a loyal subject—for he was under suspicion of some treason or machination against the Queen—he was released on no initiative of his own.[4]

NOTES

[1] This was Edmund Nevill. He had been held a prisoner in the Tower since 1584 for his supposed connection with the Parry Plot. Although he had been examined twice, he had never been tried.

Edmund Nevill was the son of Richard, grandson of John Nevill, third Lord Latimer and of Barbara Arden, of Parkhall, Warwickshire. After serving in the Spanish army in the Netherlands he returned to England at the beginning of 1584 to establish his claim to the Latimer Barony. About the same time there returned also William Parry, a Government spy who had been working as an *agent provocateur* among Catholics on the Continent. Parry, enjoying the special favour of the Queen as the reward of his discoveries, was made M.P. for the new royal borough of Queensborough; then, thinking to do a service to Burghley, whose son Thomas had married the daughter and heiress of the last Lord Latimer and was enjoying the Latimer inheritance, he endeavoured to entangle Edmund Nevill in a bogus plot involving the assassination of the Queen. Although there is no evidence that Burghley had knowledge of this intrigue, Parry was right (as W. W.'s story shows) in thinking that he would be glad to have Nevill out of the way. Nevill, however, who was infinitely resourceful, forestalled Parry and delated him to the Government before Parry had time to develop his plot. From his confessions (*S.P.D.*, *Eliz.*, vol. clxxvi, nos. 47, 48) there is no doubt that Nevill behaved with cunning, correctness and loyalty: indeed he reported that Parry was amazed that he was ' so scrupulous, seeing how greatly she (the Queen) sought his ruin '. The Government, faced with the dilemma of deciding whether to act on Parry's word or Nevill's, chose to hang Parry. Although, of course, it would have been convenient for Burghley to remove the man who claimed property that was in the hands of his family, it was even more convenient to destroy Parry, and thus stop Leicester in the Netherlands running his own bogus conspiracy against Mary, Queen of Scots by means of Parry and Poley at a moment when he and Walsingham were ready to open what later became the Babington Plot. Cf. *Hat. Cal.*, vol. iii, p. 101; Leo Hicks, ' The Strange Case of Dr. William Parry ' in *Studies*, September 1948; *D.N.B.*, vol. xl, p. 247.

[2] In a letter to Leicester, dated June 1588, he asked that his wife might visit him, and concluded: ' From my purgatory, or rather earthly hell, where tormented with ten thousand melancholies, I humbly kiss your hands.' Strype, *Annals*, vol. 3, Part i (1828 ed.), pp. 458–61.

Page 214

[3] In another letter, dated 25 September 1585, Nevill wrote: ' Except the secret judgements of God do punish me for my offences committed against His divine Majesty, I cannot conjecture why so many calamities should fall on me.' *S.P.D., Eliz.*, vol. clxxxii, no. 36.

Page 216

[4] On 3 January 1598, Nevill was removed from the Tower to the Fleet prison, and was probably released from there some time after Burghley's death on 4 August the same year.

After gaining his freedom, Nevill appears to have gone to Flanders, thus observing his promise to the Queen ' to behave as a loyal subject '. (In 1584 he had told Parry that if he failed in his case he ' would prefer to live simply abroad than . . . thus discontent at home '. *S.P.D., Eliz.*, vol. clxxvi, no. 48.) On the death of his cousin, Charles Nevill, sixth Earl of Westmorland, on 16 November 1607, he would have been entitled to that Earldom if it had not been forfeited. He was not able, however, to obtain the repeal of its attainder. He died in Brussels in 1640, and there is a monument to him in East Ham church. *Complete Peerage*, vol. 7, p. 486.

23

ENVOI

So here I remained until the Queen's decease. I was much weakened by failing sight and sleeplessness. My days seemed to hold no contentment, my nights no respite. Mind and senses were worn by constant preoccupation and wakefulness, and death appeared to me as something more desirable than life.[1] During the whole five years the Lieutenant visited me but twice, and then not for my own sake but because other business brought him to this part of the Tower. He gave me leave to mount the roof of my cell occasionally to breathe a little fresh air. The permission was given on condition that I pledged my word I would not attempt to escape. But this, surely, was superfluous. The place itself was sufficient security, without any undertaking of this kind. A man could only throw himself down. There was no way he could escape unhurt.

Though this concession did me some good, it was no pleasure, so numerous were the discomforts. For while I was on the roof, more often than not I would be shut out from my cell far into the night, with no shelter from the cold, wind, rain, and even snow. There was nothing to protect me from the elements except a small awning full of holes. And I will mention only the frequent showers of stones, thrown at me from above by heretics; the hissings and other expressions of hatred and contempt I came in for, as soon as they saw me pacing up and down. Some man, however, watching me from high up (I don't know what motive inspired him), threw me a few pieces of silver. As they fell to the ground I heard them jingling close to me, but I took no notice of them. I let them lie without turning to look. ' Sir,' he said, ' will you not accept them? ' Then I realised they came as a gift from some kindly soul who wished me well, so I thanked him and gathered some of them up.[2]

About this time the tragedy of the Earl of Essex occurred. The affair was quickly quashed and killed: and the Earl, too, at the same time. But I will mention only one or two things which I saw with my own eyes from my prison window.[3]

One day while I was sitting alone in a listless mood in the other part of my cell, I heard an unusual commotion—men running here, there and everywhere, the clanging of arms, and above the din, men's voices. Pikes were being brought out, mail-jackets and muskets. Crossing to the window, I saw a strange sight. Just below was the path leading to the main armoury for weapons of every type, and I watched a crowd of men, coming and going, carrying every conceivable kind of arms. They brandished them about with great show, hurrying as fast as they could. And intermittently I heard threats—threats of death, too, if this thing or that was not done quickly. It was an unexpected and startling scene. What was the sudden reason for it all? An attempt against the Queen? The city? The citadel itself? What could be the cause of all this desperate haste, this dragging out of munitions and brass cannon?

When supper time came and my warder brought me my meal as usual, he was wearing helmet and breastplate; in one hand was a halberd, in the other a tray. And this amazed me even more. ' What's all this flurry and commotion for? ' I asked. ' All this clashing of steel and muster of men-at-arms? '

' We're done for,' he said, ' we are betrayed. All of us—every man jack of us. The Earl of Essex, and nearly all the nobles of the kingdom, have taken up arms against the Queen. It's a dastardly thing.'

He blurted out these few words. Then he put down my supper, and rushed away.

Now, in an internal rising like this—presuming I had been told the truth—what could be expected save an immediate siege, perhaps the seizure of the Tower? But in a matter of a very few hours it had subsided. All was over. The Earl was surrounded in his house, and captured there the next day around midnight. With part of his noble following, he was put in the Tower and a few days later, not very far out of sight of my window, he was beheaded. A large scaffold had been erected and he was led to the place with two or perhaps three evangelical Ministers. The whole of the previous night they had exhorted him to make a good death. First he gave a long speech—about the Queen's mercy to him, the ingratitude he had shown her by this treasonable plot—then he laid his head beneath the axe, and paid the just penalty for his ill-spent youth.[4] Such was the Earl's unhappy end.[5] A few of his associates in the conspiracy were executed in other places, but most of them bought back their lives at a ransom.[6]

So the time passed. The Queen now was well advanced in years. Her bodily vigour and the vices of her younger days had languished alike with her increasing age. And, as I heard, her grief at the Earl's death left her so cast down in spirit that she had not strength enough to recover from her extreme distress; and there was no choice for her but to surrender to death.[7] I have no need to tell your Reverence

what happened or the details of her dying.[8] Nor, had I the
wish, is there much that I could say, so completely was I cut
off from converse with men and from news of those events.
There was nothing I could learn apart from what my warder
chose to tell me. But this I did witness. During those few
days in which she lay dying beyond all hope of recovery, a
strange silence descended on the whole city, as if it were
under interdict and divine worship suspended. Not a bell
rang out. Not a bugle sounded—though ordinarily they
were often heard. About midnight on the Vigil of the
Annunciation of the Blessed Virgin she breathed her last.[9]

The next day about eight or nine o'clock the new King,
James of Scotland, was proclaimed in the main street of London
—with such precision and thoroughness had the Council
calculated every detail.[10] Then they came to the Tower,
crying out and publishing the proclamation with great pomp.
It was all done within view of my window, and I watched
the style and order of the proceedings. Meanwhile couriers
were despatched to Scotland. There was no delay. King
James had determined not to tarry. In a short time he had
settled with great expedition the affairs both of his kingdom
and court, and was hastening to London.[11]

The Tower, this fortress of ours, was made ready for him,
as the most ancient of the royal seats and palaces. To honour
the occasion the prison gates were flung open to numerous
captives, principally those whose cases were known or had,
as it were, become obsolete with the lapse of time. Mine,
with many others, fell into this class. Accordingly, one of
the royal household came to me and in the King's name
proclaimed that it was the Sovereign's pleasure that I should
be released. At the same time he instructed the warder to
allow my friends to visit me until the preparations for my

departure were complete. But the man replied that he had
received me into custody on a written warrant and had been
ordered to keep me in strict confinement till the Lords of
the Council made known their wishes regarding me. Therefore, without another such warrant he could not set me at
liberty or even allow me greater freedom. So here I stayed
on for a whole month or more until the funeral of the dead
Queen, which was celebrated with great magnificence as
befitted an august ruler.

One day five of us were released. The others had been
detained for different reasons; I was the only priest among
them. But with the rest my warder invited me to dinner,
and did me the honour of seating me at his own table. He
treated me affably, making up to some extent for the injustice
he had done by detaining me after the King had given his
mandate for my release. He handed me eighty reals, and
also obtained a room for me outside the prison walls, where
my friends could come and see me.[12]

So, after five years in the Tower, and seventeen years
altogether in prison, I came out of confinement. The hour
was after dinner. A large company followed me. However,
I was not yet a free person, for a triple guard was to escort us
as far as Calais.[13]

Meanwhile a boat had been equipped and was waiting for
us on the river Thames, which flows beneath the walls of the
Tower. A vast crowd of people had collected to see the
sight. And as I was led out of prison, some Catholics, who
mingled with that great gathering, fell on their knees and
begged my blessing. Then, with very many Catholics
following on my way, I was taken to a house close by till
the hour for sailing came. On entering I found this place,
too, crowded with another throng of people who had come

to watch us. Many were Catholics and had assembled to greet and congratulate me after so many years of solitude and confinement. Others sent messengers with money. One pressed a purse into my hand, so full that it could hardly be shut; and I think it must have contained, so to speak, his entire substance. But while I admired his lavish generosity, I suspected that the man was poor, and declined his gift. There is no need to say more of the spontaneous gestures of these men. It required almost violence not to accept the gifts they offered, for I took only what seemed necessary to cover the expenses of the journey.

Two hours later we said farewell to our friends and embarked.[14] They returned to their homes, while we made our way to Dover, partly by water, and partly by more direct route overland.[15] Canterbury was one of the towns we passed through. Here we stayed at a public inn, and one of the townspeople, whom I knew, came to visit me. While we were having a talk together in private, the hostess joined us but at first stood a little way off. Then, waiting her moment, she came closer.

' Sir,' she said to me, ' may I ask you, have you a wife? '

' Yes, I have,' I answered, ' and a large family, too.'

She was quiet, suddenly. I, also, said nothing for a little while. Then I added:

'Not the kind of family you think. I am a priest, and priests are not allowed to touch a woman. As for the children I mentioned, they are spiritual children—sprung from the seed of orthodox faith and sound doctrine.'

And I developed this a little. My words moved her; and she seemed to relish and draw pleasure from them, and, in our English way, she took my hand.

' I call you a truly blessed people, who do these things.

As for our ministers, they dedicate their lives to all that is the contrary. I would almost say they were knaves. Nothing will content them. They clothe and feast their wives finely as if they were ladies of the land. Their daughters they bring up altogether above their station, and so fastidiously that, unsatisfied with ordinary husbands, they have no shame in seeking a spouse of noble blood.' [16]

So she said. I don't know whether on any previous occasion in her life she had seen a priest or spoken to a Catholic. But I record the encounter and what she said to show how attractive even to the ears of heretics (excluding, of course, the badly corrupted) is the teaching and practice of the Catholic faith, if only it is made known; and how close is our people to accepting the faith, if it were possible to preach it freely among them.[17]

Going on from here we reached Dover the same day. The following day we crossed to Calais in France. All the time we were accompanied by three guards, one pursuivant, that is, and two household servants of the King. Their task done, the guards returned to England, while I with two other priests set out on our journey to St. Omer.

Now a short time before I was liberated from the Tower, a prisoner had been brought in who had served in the late Queen's bedchamber. Immediately after the Queen's death, this man had discussed her successor, King James, with a friend and associate who had drawn him into conversation. What a happy time they would all have now, he had said, for the King was a very great zealot for the Gospel. He would take sharp vengeance on all Catholics and persecute them.

' Shut your mouth,' said the other man, ' you don't know yet what James will do. And you cannot be certain what stand he will take on matters of religion.'

These words the other man reported to the Council. No time was wasted. At once they sent to arrest him, and on laying hold of him they opened a box of his at the same time and found a certain book of Father Persons, called *The Directory*, but in the version corrupted by a heretic.[18] Straightway the man was dragged off to the Tower of London and lodged immediately below my cell.[19] It was a pestilential place. One day when his warder was with him and he heard me walking up and down over his head, he asked who was above him.

' He is a Jesuit,' said the warder.

' I can well believe that,' he answered, ' for nobody but a good man ever sees this place.' And he added, ' I have never set eyes on a priest in my life. However, as soon as I get out of here, the first thing I shall do will be to search out one of them and speak with him.'

And at the same time he asked the warder to greet me on his behalf and he sent me a small present of some wax candles.[20]

FINIS

NOTES

¹ Fr. de Peralta, after remarking that W. W. was very reluctant to mention his experiences in the Tower, continues: ' When I pressed him to speak, Fr. Weston told me something of what he suffered in his great isolation. . . . [How] after a few months had passed, he endured fierce assaults from demons, of the kind that the ancient Fathers of the desert experienced: and he observed that there was no greater torment than a solitary confinement extending over a long period of time.' De Peralta goes on to narrate what W. W. had told an English priest. ' He confided to him in strict secrecy that in these conflicts, both visible and invisible, the onslaught was unremitting both day and night, and now that the devils had him by himself they threatened to swallow him up and have done with him: they boasted that they would persuade him to hang himself and brought him ropes and knives so that he could do it. And they buffeted him night and day, preventing him from sleeping and taking any rest. To such an extent did he suffer from insomnia that in the course of fifty days he did not get as much as ten hours' sleep.

' To combat this solitude and the assaults of the demon he armed himself with prayer, vigils and penance and with constant reading of the Bible, the only book he was permitted. Ordinarily each day he prayed for six hours, more on special days. . . . And in his first year or two in the Tower he dipped all his food in water, in order to destroy its savour and mortify himself. Then one day he observed that this practice was harming his health and he gave it up. Usually he slept on the floor. But once the Lieutenant of the Tower, entering his cell on a visit, was moved by compassion—for it was a very cold and damp place—and ordered a bed to be brought in. That night he slept in it, but when he opened the Bible the next morning the first sentence he read was from Proverbs, chapter 26. *Sicut ostium vertitur in cardine suo, ita piger in lectulo suo*—as the door turns on the hinge so the slothful man turns on his couch. And then the very same day when the servant brought him his food he ordered him to remove the bed.

' What with his continual lack of sleep he was unable to give his attention to anything, and, besides, at this time he had almost entirely lost his sight and hearing. Distraught by his sufferings he wished to die, for living was an unending death, and, in any human reckoning, he could live but little longer. One day in this state of extreme distress— he told the incident to a Father of the Society (who himself was undergoing great torment and persecution from devils and felt abandoned by

God) getting him to promise that he would not say a word about it in his lifetime—one day, I say, while he was at prayer calling attention of God to his afflictions, incapable, it seemed, of enduring them further, he saw with his physical sight a thread descending like a ray of light from the sky, and at the same time heard a voice, " With this thread you are attached to my good keeping. I am with you and shall not abandon you." And this consoled him greatly and reconciled him to his sufferings, giving him such peace of mind and sense of oneness with God that his soul was suffused with contentment and nothing henceforth troubled him.' de Peralta, f. 221–3.

Page 220

2 Fr. de Peralta [f. 222] tells the same story, prefacing it with a remarkable incident. ' The Earl of Essex, who came to Cadiz as Captain-General, entered the Tower one day with some gentlemen and, walking round the walls and towers, happened to see Father William . . . rapt in prayer, his hands raised up and his eyes fixed on heaven. He and his company were more than a quarter of an hour watching him, while he [W. W.] did not move an eyelid or stir in the smallest way. When they came to leave, the Father was in the same posture in which they found him, so that the Earl commented to his friends, " This man does not appear to be such a great rogue as they make him out." On a different occasion another man saw him in the same posture and threw him some coins. When the Father did not pick them up, he came back again and threw him more, saying, " Sir, why will you not accept this money? " ' Fr. de Peralta finally remarks that W. W. had ' many raptures and ecstasies ' in prison, and ' many visits from Our Lord '.

3 W. W. goes on to describe the rush to the armoury in the White Tower on the day of the Essex rising and the Earl's execution on the scaffold erected on Tower Green. As W. W. witnessed the first incident, and all but had a view of the second, it is clear that he was imprisoned in the Beauchamp Tower in the centre of the inner fortifications on the west side. There are three storeys in this tower, the second level with the rampart on to which it formerly opened. There is a walk the whole length of the rampart between the Devereux Tower at the north end and the Bell Tower at the south. It would have been here that W. W. took his exercise: stones could have been thrown at him from the roof of any of the three towers along this side.

Page 221

4 Garnet, discussing the rebellion of Essex, who ' had made his nest in the pinnacle of all worldly glory and happiness ', remarks that ' the

Puritans were anxious by every means to impute these tumults to the Catholics ', and adds, both with disgust and relief, that ' the Earl, before he died, made this notable profession: " I thank God that I am not an atheist, for I believe that there is a God; neither am I a Papist, for I do not look to be saved by my own merits." And certainly he was speaking the truth, for he had neither the true faith nor any saving merit whatever.' Garnet to Aquaviva, 11 March 1601. Arch. S. J., Rome, *Angl.*, vol. 31, f. 172.

[5] W. W., who got only such news as his gaoler gave him, is probably reporting the general gossip about Essex. Though he was spoiled and in some ways irresponsible, Essex was capable and more brave and generous than his political opponents.

[6] The Essex rising began on Sunday, 8 February. On the 19th the Earl was tried, then executed on the 25th. The reasons for the rising are still very obscure. The Earl himself justified it as a measure of self-protection against the threat of murder by his opponents. Most historians have brushed this statement aside, saying that Essex merely used the threat as a device to rally his supporters. However, there can be no doubt that it precipitated his action, which played so perfectly into the hands of Cecil and was perhaps designed by him to do so (*C.S.P., Dom. Eliz.* (1598–1601), p. 597). The following considerations bear out Essex's contention. Before the rising James VI had decided to send Mar on an embassy to Elizabeth. In view of Cecil's previous support of the Infanta's claims to the English throne (cf. *sup.*, p. 208, n. 1), such an embassy would have placed Cecil in an extremely critical position. James's previous ambassador, Hamilton, who had been recalled in February 1600 had, as Cecil knew, already accused him to the Scottish king of favouring the Infanta (*C.Sc.P.*, vol. lxvi, no. 78). Only the removal of Essex could make a complete *volte-face* possible for Cecil. It is significant, therefore, that all references to James were either ignored or glossed over by the prosecution at Essex's trial, and that within a month of the execution Cecil was using Lord Henry Howard, a strong supporter of Essex, though in fact probably Cecil's spy, to open secret negotiations with James for his succession. Thus when Mar actually arrived in March 1601 Cecil was able to pass off the charge that he had been in favour of the Infanta with a bland statement that it was the duty of the Queen's Minister to examine all claims to the crown. He protested his ' innocency of being Spanishly infected ' (*Hat. Cal.*, vol. x, pp. 155–6) and at once entered into negotiations with Mar, which were kept secret from the Queen, for James's succession. *C.Sc.P.*, vol. lxvii, no. 16.

[7] Among other authorities, Scaramelli, the Venetian Secretary in London, confirms this statement of W. W. about the Queen's distress at the death of Essex. Writing on 27 March (N.S.), he says in the course of a very well-informed despatch: ' The Queen's grief reached such a pitch that she passed three days and three nights without sleep and with scarcely any food. . . . She fell to considering that the Earl of Essex who used to be her intimate might have been quite innocent after all. . . . So deeply does her Majesty feel this that on the first day of Lent this year she recalled the anniversary of so piteous a spectacle and burst into tears and dolorous lamentations, as though for some deadly sin she had committed, and then fell ill of a sickness which the doctors instantly judged to be mortal.' *C.S.P.*, *Venetian*, vol. ix (1592–1603), no. 1162.

Page 222

[8] In the last six days of her life the Queen became ' quite silly and indeed idiotic ', but shortly before dying she returned to the full possession of her senses and it was clear from her prayers that she hoped that ' God would not reckon against her in the next life the blood of priests shed by her '. *C.S.P.*, *Venetian*, vol. ix (1592–1603), no. 1166.

[9] W. W. is speaking from what was generally known. Other contemporary accounts also suggest that the Queen died of melancholia. ' Her Majesty hath been by fits troubled with melancholy these three or four months, but for this fortnight extreme oppressed with it, insomuch that she refuseth to eat anything, to receive any physic or admit any rest in bed within these two or three days . . . She would not hear the Archbishop speak of hope of her longer life, but when he prayed or spoke of heaven, she would hug his hand. It seems she might have lived if she would have used means; but she would not be persuaded. Her physicians say she hath a body of a firm and perfect constitution, likely to have lived many years.' Massingham's *Diary* (23 March 1603), p. 145.

[10] Scaramelli is more detailed. ' No sooner was the Queen's death known, which was the very hour it took place, at 2 o'clock on the morning of the third of this month [April, N.S.] than the Council in view of the great doubts and anxieties manifest among the nobility and people lest some rising should happen, gave orders for the solemn proclamation of the new king. This took place on the fourth. . . . The ceremony, though carried out with all pomp, fell so flat that there was evidently neither sorrow for the death of the Queen nor joy for the succession of the King.' *C.S.P.*, *Venetian*, vol. ix (1592–1603), no. 1169.

[11] James set out from Edinburgh on 5 April [O.S.].

Page 223

[12] This was probably W. W.'s second warder, for Fr. John Copley, who was in the Tower at the same time, testifies to the esteem this man had for W. W. ' He spent so much of his time in constant prayer, in tears and fasting, that his warder, who also had charge of me, declared that in all the time he had been at the post he had never come across a holier man than the Jesuit Weston.' Vatican MSS., *Barberini* xxxi, 75, f. 142.

[13] In charge of the party was John King. On 19 May the Council gave instructions that he was to be paid for his services in ' providing and furnishing a ship for conveying the Jesuits and seminary priests out of the realm '. P.R.O., *Treasury Chamber Accounts* (1603), f. 96.

Page 224

[14] The date of W. W.'s departure is given in a letter of Fr. Garnet: ' 14 May 1603. Yesterday went from London Father Weston, a man beloved and admired of his enemies. He hath almost lost his eyes.' Then, after naming the priests who went with him, he adds: ' All broke away but poor Father Weston.' Stonyhurst MSS., *Collectanea P*, f. 547.

[15] The party went down the river by barge as far as Gravesend, and thence overland through Canterbury to Dover.

Page 225

[16] The historian Clarendon noted as a symptom of the social and moral chaos following the Civil War that the daughters of distinguished houses married divines or made other ' low and unequal matches '. By contrast with the Elizabethan clergy, the great majority of Catholic priests were well-born. When the Proclamation of 1591 stigmatised Catholic priests as ' unnatural subjects . . . very base of birth ', Southwell was able to retort: ' how many of them are knights ' and esquires' sons and otherwise allied both to worshipful and noble houses and heirs to fair fortunes, let their own friends and parents dispersed throughout the whole realm bear witness! This only we may say in answer to our objected baseness that in the small number of Catholic priests of our nation (which reacheth not to a tenth of the Protestant ministry) there are very near as many, yea happily more gentlemen, than in all the other clergy of the whole realm.' *Humble Supplication*, p. 7.

[17] This was also Fr. Garnet's view. After eighteen years on the English mission he declared that if toleration were granted, England would be largely Catholic again within twenty years. Earlier, in a letter

of 10 May 1587, W. W. had written more fully: ' We feel—and our enemies are of the same opinion—that when persecution threatens the Church does but increase and expand from day to day, and that when persecution ceases (at God's bidding) then at once an immense harvest will be gathered and they will all come pressing in through the crowded gates of the Sacred City in serried columns. I have no doubt of this. I do not mean to say that there are not still an infinite number of most obstinate heretics, but simply this, that if we are given the freedom to treat of religion, I am certain we shall conquer and draw them to us.' Arch. S.J., Rome, *Fondo Gesuitico,* 651.

Page 226

[18] Fr. Persons's *First Book of the Christian Exercise,* later known as *The Christian Directory,* first published in Rouen in 1582, was issued two years later in London by Edmund Bunny, a Calvinist divine, who perverted the text and added an appendix, urging with a specious moderation conformity to the Anglican worship. Before Persons' death in 1610 the *Directory* had been printed at least fifteen times in its Protestant version. Leo Hicks, *Letters and Memorials of Fr. Persons, C.R.S.,* vol. 39, p. xlv.

[19] This was Philip May, servant to the Lord Chamberlain, Hunsdon. He was arrested just four weeks before W. W.'s release on the information of Robert Prickett and was examined under torture ' on his assertions as to the King favouring Catholics '. His four examinations are in the State papers. *C.S.P., Dom. James I* (1603–1610), pp. 4–6.

[20] ' He went first to the seminary of St. Omers in Flanders, and he was so worn out by the ill-treatment he had received—what with his head-aches and loss of sight and hearing, that nobody thought, naturally speaking, that he would live more than six months. However, he recovered a little in Flanders and then, by order of Fr. General, went to Rome, and after some months there came on to Valladolid, where he spent a few more months, and then to Seville in the year 1605.' de Peralta, f. 223.

APPENDIX A

FR. HEYWOOD'S JOURNEY INTO EXILE

See page 17

The following account of Fr. Jasper Heywood's journey into exile is given by Fr. Edward Rishton, a Douai priest, in his supplement to Nicolas Sander's *Anglican Schism* (ed. 1877, pp. 327–32). Rishton had been Heywood's fellow-prisoner in the Tower, and was one of the same party of exiles. The account suggests that W. W.'s conversation with Heywood in the Tower (cf. p. 10) took place in the presence of a warder; it also explains W. W.'s reluctance to accept the offer of friends who tried to secure his own release from prison on condition that he went into exile (cf. p. 118).

'At that time both the old and the new prisons were filled with the confessors, and in one prison, the Marshalsea—that is the name of one of the prisons of London—there were about thirty priests beside laymen. Some also of those who with Father Campion, or soon after, had been condemned to death, were kept in the Tower, and in other prisons of the city, waiting these three years for the headsman. These, but not all of them, though under the same sentence, nor yet the only ones, were chosen for banishment, and with them certain others taken out of nearly every prison in London. Others then were shut up in the many prisons throughout the land, but of these not one was released.

'When the authorities had determined the day on which these prisoners were to embark, they sent to the keeper of every prison the names of those who were to be sent out of the country, with orders to inform the prisoners of the day on which they must depart, in order that they might make provision for their journey and their sustenance afterwards, for they were to be maintained at the public expense—expected by many—only so long as they were on board the vessel that carried them. But as they in the meantime were kept in prison, and allowed to speak to no one except in the presence of their jailers, they could not obtain much help for their journey, or for the endurance of the banishment to which they were driven. In this light alone, that banishment must have been regarded as most calamitous by men deprived of their all. When they were told of the queen's resolution, they laboured every one of them to the utmost of their power, to obtain from their friends some provision for their needs, in the way of clothes and money.

' The day came at last, though often changed, but for what purpose I do not know; and those persons who had been charged to see us transported, went from prison to prison demanding of the keepers thereof those who had been singled out for transportation. We were all brought to the ship moored in the Thames, near the gate of the Tower, and ordered to go on board. Thereupon some of us, especially the reverend Father Jasper Heywood, made a public complaint in the name of all, that we ought not to be driven out of our country without cause, having committed no crime, without a legal trial and clearly not convicted. He also said that we would go no farther, and with our own consent would never forsake our country and the Catholic people who dwell therein, but would rather die there in their presence as a testimony to the faith which we and they held in common. Our country and their salvation were to us infinitely more precious than our own life.

' Then, when nothing was to be gained in this way, we asked to be shown at least the letters and orders of the queen by which we are condemned to be banished for life. But nothing was shown; the vessel sailed, and we went to sea after many a farewell and with the pity of our friends.

' When we had been two days at sea, and had gone far away from land, the reverend Father Jasper Heywood and others once more pressed the queen's servants with great earnestness to allow them to see and read the sentence of our banishment. The men were persuaded, and showed the warrant, in which was read as follows: " The aforesaid persons, by the confession of themselves and others, found guilty of sedition and of plotting against her majesty and the state, all of them either legally convicted of those same offences, or for the like offences kept in prison, though deserving the last penalties of the law, are, under this warrant, ordered by her majesty, who in her goodness wills to deal more gently with them for this once, to be transported beyond the limits of the realm."

' When they read this they all cried out in one mournful protestation, that a most false accusation had been brought against them, and that they were most grievously wronged, seeing that not one of them, or of their fellow-Catholics, had ever uttered one word that could be construed into a confession of rebellion or conspiracy against the queen or the country, and that one certainly of those whom they were taking away at the time, had been publicly acquitted, after a trial, of that most false charge. Father Heywood then spoke much to the same purpose, again and again imploring those who were in charge to take them back to England that they might be put on their trial publicly, or at least that they might be put to death for Christ, and in defence of their innocence, rather than be sent to a strange land accused of offences which they had certainly never committed. To this the answer was, that it was not within their power to do that which was asked of them, and that they must obey the orders of the queen.

' We went on, consoling one another as well as we could, and rejoicing that we could bear patiently this reproach for the name of Jesus. At last, by the help of God, we landed at Boulogne, and having said farewell to those who brought us thither, we departed for different towns in France, each one according to his means.

At last we all came to Rheims, finding our brethren or our superiors
in great distress about us in every place to which we came. They
had heard the lying stories which the heretics, or those who
wished us ill, had spread abroad, namely, that frightened by the
dangers that were around us in England, we had of our own accord
taken measures to bring about our banishment, that we had abandoned our work, or—and that was still worse—had come to some
agreement with the heretics in matters of religion. But they rejoiced
in our Lord when they heard the story fully related, and when
many of us moreover declared their readiness to return, whenever
our superiors bade us, without counting the cost. But our enemies
everywhere without any restraint speak of us whom they did not
put to death, but banished, as instances and evidences of the
queen's kindness. They persist in this, and urge it with so much
shamelessness, that they will have it that the more they banish,
the more must the great kindness of the queen be remarked, and
the more it must commend itself to foreign nations. The same
fraud and cruelty were lately practised upon two-and-twenty
prisoners taken out of the jails of York and Hull, and carried over
to France; all except one being priests, and even he was a deacon.
These, for the most part, were worn out not only by bonds and
imprisonment, but by old age. Some of them were sixty, others
seventy years old, others were still older, and one of them was
eighty years of age.

'Some of these, though they were very old men, had spent a
great part of their life in prison; and there were those among them
who for six-and-twenty years had most patiently and bravely borne
all those miseries which the wickedness of so many years, and of
such heretics, is wont to inflict upon prisoners.

'Soon afterwards, on the 24th of September, thirty priests and
two laymen, brought together out of different prisons, were with
the same intention driven out of the country. This is the way
they think they can obtain a reputation for humanity and mercy.
But it is very foolish, and nothing else but the kindness of thieves,

who are wont to boast that they have given their lives to those from whom they have not taken it. It is more probable that they act thus for the purpose of burdening the seminaries, which they know to be poor, for the maintenance of so many priests. But there is no counsel against God: " The earth is our Lord's and the fulness thereof." '

APPENDIX B

EDWARD GRATELY AND THE BETRAYAL OF THE EARL OF ARUNDEL

See page 20

In his admirably edited volume on Philip Howard (*C.R.S.*, vol. 21) Fr. Pollen does not make sufficient allowance for the possibility of the Earl's betrayal by an *agent provocateur*, namely, by ' the man ' in W. W.'s narrative, who, previously unknown to the Earl, came forward ' by sheer chance and undertook to arrange the details of the escape and carry it through faithfully '. The evidence that this was Edward Grately (later an open apostate) is, I think, conclusive. In the first place there is the assertion of Cardinal Sega in 1597, in the course of a report on the state of the English College in Rome, that Grately ' was credited by most Catholics with the betrayal of the Earl of Arundel ' (Foley, vi, p. 17). Sega's statement is supported both by Anthony Tyrrell, who claimed (*C.Sc.P.*, vol. viii, p. 670) that Grately himself told him ' how he had won the Earl to forsake his country upon information made to him ', viz., Allen's supposed message; and secondly, by the best authority for the Earl's career, viz., the *Life*, written by the Countess's chaplain, whose information is always most accurate. As Pollen himself admits (*C.R.S.*, vol. 21, p. 67) this writer ' took it as obvious that Grately must have been the miscreant responsible for the Earl's arrest '.

There can be no doubt that immediately after the Earl's arrest, Grately was responsible for a gross act of treachery. Against the express instructions of the Earl, he made public a letter which he had written to the Queen and entrusted to his keeping for use *only if* the escape was successful. If this was not treachery, then it was a supreme act of folly by a man who had lost his head in a moment of great excitement; an improbable explanation since Grately always showed himself a most level-headed intriguer, and at no moment more than at this crisis.

Pollen curiously dismisses the accusation made by the author of the *Life* by arguing that if the Earl had suspected Grately's treachery, he would have mentioned it in his defence (*C.R.S.*, vol. 21, p. 67). But, in the first place, there is no complete or trustworthy report of what the Earl actually said at his trial (1589), and, secondly, it is most unlikely that he ever suspected Grately. Cut off in the Tower from all the sources of information available to the Countess, the Earl had no reason for believing that Grately, who had insinuated himself into his confidence and become his chaplain, played him false. Indeed the Government was most careful that the traitor should not be discovered, for his discovery would have destroyed the case for the prosecution by showing that the Earl had taken to flight at the provocation of its own agents. Moreover, in order to save its case and enhance the reputation that Grately had enjoyed among English Catholics at the time of the Earl's reception, the Government fostered the report that it was he, not W. W., who had reconciled the Earl to the Church—a story which W. W. could not confute, for at the time (1589) he was a close prisoner at Wisbech.

The Earl, as the Government knew well, was in fact reconciled while Grately was still on the Continent. He had arrived at Rheims from England on 25 September 1584—in the arraignment the date given by the Government for the Earl's reconciliation is 30 September—and appears to have crossed back to England at the end of October, for Dr. Barret noted in the College diary on 8 November that Grately had returned to England, instead of going, as he had announced, to Pont-à-Mousson, where

William Gifford, his intimate, was to receive a doctorate (T. F. Knox, *Douai Diaries*, p. 203). On reaching London he got an introduction to the Earl as the bearer of a bogus message from Allen, although he had not so much as seen Allen since leaving Rheims on 27 September (before the Earl's reconciliation) and thus insinuated himself as his chaplain at Arundel House (*Life*, p. 58). This message is the 'letter' to which W. W. refers. W. W. does not say that he saw the letter—it was evidently non-existent: no such letter was produced at the trial, nor is there any reason why Allen should have taken the risk of writing, if he was hoping shortly to see the Earl in person and converse with him. From this moment Grately, as appears from W. W.'s narrative, under-took all the arrangements for the Earl's escape; at the same time, in collusion with the Government, he made the arrangements also for his arrest.

After making public the Earl's letter to the Queen, Grately escaped, probably with the connivance of the Government, via Newcastle. On 14 June (N.S.) the Diarist at Rheims notes that he left again, supposedly for England (*Douai Diaries*, pp. 206, 263). Apparently while at Rheims he was completely incommunicative about the Earl's capture. Allen was at the College then. Had Grately nothing to conceal, he certainly would have given first-hand information, particularly if he had been what he claimed seven months earlier to be, viz., Allen's special messenger to the Earl; indeed it can be taken as certain that he said nothing, for had he told of his alleged co-operation in the Earl's escape, it is incredible that Allen would have permitted him to commit the supreme folly of returning to England—for he would have been the most sought-after priest in the country as the man most closely involved in the Earl's crime. After giving out, then, that he was going back to England, he turns up at Rouen in August, where he was equally secretive with Nicholas Berden. In September he is in Paris and in secret communication with Walsingham. Grately's movements and conduct, therefore, in the ten months (November

1584 to September 1585) can be explained, it would seem, only on the supposition that Cardinal Sega, Anthony Tyrrell and the author of the Earl's *Life* are correct in charging him with the Earl's betrayal. Cf. J. H. Pollen, *Philip Howard, Earl of Arundel, C.R.S.*, vol. 21; T. F. Knox, *Douai Diaries*; J. H. Pollen, 'Dr. William Gifford in 1586' in *The Month*, April 1904.

APPENDIX C
THE WISBECH BOY, THOMAS DOWLTON
See page 160

'My examination and usage first before the Mayor of Rye in the beginning of June 1595 and afterwards at Lambeth before the Bishop of Canterbury and the rest of the Commissioners, and my answers to them as follows. The Mayor of Rye caused me to be searched so they found xxxs. sewed in my doublet, which the Mayor took from me. Within two days the principal women of the town did intreat for me to him that he would set me at liberty, but he would not in any wise grant it, except I would go to church, and then he said I should have my money again and he would give me some more to make me recompense for the two days he had kept me in prison. And then I said unto him that if he had more right to it than I, much good may it do him, for to their church I would not go. Within three weeks after, the Mayor riding up to London caused two footmen to bring me after. Then was I brought to Lambeth before the bishop and the rest of the Commissioners, which, hearing that I was a boy of Wisbech, three or four of them at once were very earnest at me why I would not go to church; and I told them I could not answer so many at once, and therefore I desired the Bishop of Canterbury and the rest of the Commissioners to let me go back again and tomorrow I would give them my answer in writing, for I would not answer to anything by word of mouth. Whereupon they sent me back to the Gatehouse, from whence I was brought to see them again the next day, to whom then I delivered in writing this answer following which before my coming from Wisbech I had learned by heart to have it always in readiness in any such time of need.

My answer why I will not go to church.

First because I think it not good and godly to go to it. Secondly if you could prove it good and godly to go to it, then you would and ought to go to Wisbech Castle and consult the priests there, but if any few come out there they so confound them that they dare not come there any more. Thirdly if it were good and godly to go to it, I am sure the Catholics in Wisbech Castle and in other prisons would not leave their lands and lie in prison for flying from it as they do. Fourthly if I should go to your church I should sin against God and the peace and unity of the whole Catholic church, exclude myself from all holy sacraments and be in danger to die in my sins like a heathen. But although I am but a poor lad I am not so far to obey you, having a soul to save as well as any other Catholic. Fifthly I hear say that England hath been a Catholic Christian country a thousand years before this Queen's reign and her father's. If that were the old high way to heaven then why should I forsake it? I have no goods to leave, I pray you give me leave to save my soul. My soul doth hunger after my maker, God made man, under the form of bread, whom none but the priests can give me; while you do keep both them and me from the old mass, I dare not go to your new communion.

This my answer was read from man to man throughout the bench but in secret, only to themselves, whereupon I was presently sent away with a pursuivant to Doctor Stanhope to be committed by him, as I was, to Bridewell where they kept me eight months in the hemp house, where every day's task is to bunch five and twenty pounds of hemp or else to have no meat. And then I was chained nine weeks to a block and a month besides with it and five months without it in Little Ease and one of the turrets which is as bad, and five weeks I went in the mill and ten days I stood with both my hands stretched above my head against the wall in the standing stocks, whereof one day, because I would not work on the Assumption of our Blessed Lady, they said I should fast as well as play,

and would let me have no food at all. And last of all for my freedom
and release from the hemp house work and such like, I had twenty
lashes of the whip upon the trosse, since which time I have been
ever since Ash Wednesday, being the xxv of February, in commons
with the Catholic laymen, eight of us together at the charge of
ten groats a man the week, with very slender commons through
the dearth there of things, and oppressions withal upon us, but
yet by God and good men other ways so comforted that I would
not have missed my time there spent for a great deal more misery.
And at last God so wrought that we took our leave of that place
the third of November 1596.' *Hist. MSS. Commission,* 12th
Report, Appendix, Pt. iv, pp. 334–6.

APPENDIX D

THE CONDUCT OF FR. WESTON AT WISBECH

See page 174

The following testimony to W. W.'s unimpeachable conduct at Wisbech was given by the secular priest, Fr. Giles Archer, who at the instigation of Dr. Bagshaw was transferred to the Tower in December 1598 in company with W. W., Fr. Southworth and Mr. Thomas Pound. It was written in 1602 as a refutation of Bagshaw's slanderous pamphlet, *A True Relation of the Faction begun at Wisbech by Fa. Edmunds, alias Weston, 1595 and continued since by Fa. Walley, alias Garnet, the Provincial of the Jesuits in England,* etc.

'I shall now say something about the virtues which I and others of his companions and brethren in religion noted and admired in Father Weston. We were with him for ten years and were eye-witnesses of all I state, living in a close daily intercourse from which we drew strength and consolation. It was common knowledge that for seven years he never would lie down for a rest during the day however exhausted he might be through work and study. Throughout the whole year he kept to a strict time-table. At four in the morning he got up from the ground on which he lay and never reclined again until eleven at night. He found his recreation in instructive conversation with others. He disliked talking about the latest news or happenings in the world outside and usually led us to converse on spiritual topics or on subjects connected with our studies. Throughout these seven years his only exercise was a little walk up and down once a day. He was most abstemious, never tasted wine (apart from his Mass) or spirits or even strong beer if small beer was available. So carefully did he measure his words in conversation that none of his critics ever found it possible to tax him with any frivolous utterance, yet he was invariably affable and courteous, especially to those who opposed and disliked him.

' If one of his penitents fell foul of anybody he took it very much to heart and spared no pains to bring about a reconciliation. In many cases he insisted on their making a personal apology to those they had hurt. He was above all anxious to preserve peace and harmony amongst us. If all else failed he would fall on his knees before the offenders pleading that they should at once forgive one another, even though both of them were his own personal enemies. However gravely insulted he might be, he never would utter one word in self defence.

' In all our devotional exercises he was the moving spirit. He introduced the practice of reciting litanies daily after dinner for the conversion of England and several times arranged for the Quarant' Ore before the Blessed Sacrament for the same intention. He often preached to us to our own great consolation. When the reading at table became rather irregular, he put himself on for a time as the reader of the Scriptures in spite of his wretched eyesight. To this we must add his daily lectures on Theology, Greek and Hebrew and his presiding at our theological " disputations ".

' He turned the tables on those who had given him good reason for being displeased with them by showing them special favour. Thus, on the death of the venerated Mr. Metham he gave a larger share of his books and clothing to Dr. Bagshaw and Mr. Bluet than to any of the others. His own clothing was wretched and worn and utterly insufficient to shield him from the cold. He did not even possess a waistcoat.

' His grief when a letter was written to Dr. Bagshaw denouncing him for his thefts can hardly be imagined: he bitterly reproached and blamed the writer though he was one of his own closest friends. He once gave away the big sum of 480 crowns (scudi)

keeping no more than 8 in his purse for current expenses. There
was no obligation whatever to make such a gift. He did it in the
hope of bringing the feud between this person and another Catholic
to an end. . . .

' In this shameless and lying account we are told that Father
Weston did not equitably apportion the money that was received
for the support of the prisoners but showed undue favour to certain
persons. I state—" coram Deo et in verbo sacerdotis "—
pledging my priestly word that there was nothing he hated more
than being dragged into this kind of business or having any charge
of money. Any sums he received were at once passed by him
to those whose office it was to keep the money. On the death of
Mr. Metham, who had long held the post of bursar, he at once
arranged for Mr. Bluet to succeed him so that he might keep free
from this kind of work.

' Though I was one who enjoyed his close friendship I
received little if any financial help from him, while others—
whom he could never expect to win over—were very generously
treated.

' He is accused of " pride ". Yet he never allowed anyone to
do him personal service, whereas if any fell ill he was foremost in
helping to make their beds, dry the blankets and warm their under-
clothing and nightshirts before the fire. Again when we had the
Quarant' Ore, he swept the place out, arranged the altar and polished
the candlesticks as if he were a paid servant.

' He had square tables made for us to sit at during meals in order
to avoid precedence, since it was impossible to express honourable
distinctions under this arrangement.

' Finally—what by itself is proof of Father Weston's high
virtue, is the fact that, once he was taken away from us, all the
devotional practices together just lapsed; the number of prisoners
increased but the gifts of charity dwindled. At length all the
prisoners were removed to another prison with disastrous con-
sequences.'

The following are not the exact words of the above-mentioned Mr. Archer but correctly convey his meaning.

'It is high time to say something about the quality of Dr. Bagshaw—on the principle that the contrast of extremes cannot fail to catch the eye. He was a sworn enemy of the Society and of Father Weston. He was regarded as the prime mischief-maker. He had been expelled from the English College in Rome. . . . Later on he had gained his Doctorate in Theology at Padua. . . . On his arrival at Wisbech, Father Weston gave him a shirt and other things. . . . When a quarrel with much exchange of insults broke out between Dr. Bagshaw and Mr. Bluet (himself a priest at Wisbech and very hostile to Father Weston) the good Father fell on his knees before them. Regardless of anything save the glory of God and the maintenance of peace in all hearts, he implored them both to forgive and forget with such earnestness that he vowed he would remain on his knees until they made friends again. Much to our joy his intervention proved irresistible.' (*Translated from the Italian.*) English College, Rome, *Angl. 38*, *II*, f. 187–90.

APPENDIX E

THE LETTERS OF FR. WESTON

The letters of Fr. Weston cited or quoted in the notes have been found in various archives since Fr. Morris first edited the incomplete Stonyhurst copy of the *Autobiography* in 1875. It is probable that others will come to light: indeed W. W. complained in the only extant letter written while he was at liberty in England (cf. *inf.*, no. 2) that several letters of his to Fr. Persons had gone astray. Apart from a few fragmentary paragraphs from letters written in his last years in Spain, the following is a list, in chronological order, of all the complete letters which are at present known to exist.

1. To Fr. General Aquaviva, dated Paris, 12 June 1584 (Arch. S.J., Rome, *Gall. Ep.*, xiv, f. 43). W. W. states that he received Fr. Aquaviva's instruction to go to Paris two days before Christmas, 1583, but was unable to leave Seville before the end of Easter week 1584 owing to the wintry conditions in Spain. In Paris he met Fr. Persons and learnt from him what he already suspected, that he was to be sent to England. He speaks of his great happiness at his assignment and asks Fr. Aquaviva's blessing on his work. It is from this letter that the signature on the front cover of this book is taken.

2. To Fr. Robert Persons, an undated letter from England, signed E(dmund) H(unt) (Stonyhurst MSS., *Anglia* i, no. 28). It was written after April 1586, for it refers to the arrest and execution of Fr. Robert Anderton and Fr. William Marsden on 25 April that year. As it contains no mention of Fr. Garnet or Fr. Southwell, who arrived in the following July, it was probably sent in May or June. It has been used extensively in the notes.

3. To Fr. General Aquaviva, dated 10 May 1587, and written in the Clink (Arch. S.J., Rome, *Fondo Gesuitico*, 651). This letter is a report on the conditions of Catholics in England with special reference to their sufferings in the months following the 'discovery' of the Babington Plot. Apart from the passages quoted in the notes it contains some general reflections on the state of religion in England: 'This people,' he says, 'suffer from two principal evils . . . heresy and an immoderate pursuit of good living.'

4. To Mr. Newton, viz. Fr. Alban Doleman, an old Marian priest, sent from Wisbech sometime after November 1595 (Westminster Archives, vol. 31, p. 105). This is a short letter used in the notes on the chapters dealing with Wisbech.

5. To Fr. General Aquaviva, dated Wisbech, 27 March 1598 (Arch. S.J., Rome, *Fondo Gesuitico*, 651). A very long letter written to order and containing a most important and full statement of the Wisbech 'stirs'. As far as I have been able to find out, it has been used by no writer on the subject, apart from Fr. Persons who had it in front of him when he wrote his chapter on Wisbech in his *Briefe Apologie* (1602).

6. To Fr. Oliver Manareus, Provincial of Belgium, dated, as no. 5, Wisbech, 27 March 1598 (Stonyhurst MSS., *Anglia* ii, no. 34). It covers the same ground as no. 5, and reveals, in addition, W. W.'s great affection for Fr. Garnet. Answering the charge that he was constantly at odds with his Superior (sixteen heads of difference had been listed by his detractors), W. W. writes with intense feeling: ' There was never a man to whom I was more closely united in bonds of peace and friendship. . . . I will say nothing of our noviceship together, when in the same city, at the same time, in the same house of Sant' Andrea, under the same teacher the two of us were formed to the ideals which we share in common. Then, when he joined this mission two years after me in company with that most holy martyr, Fr. Robert Southwell, no one could have been more welcome than he or received with greater love. We spent several days worshipping God together

and praying and discussing our common business.   Then we
shared out our work and strengthened by each other's company
we went off to our own tasks.   It was only a few days afterwards
that I was arrested and taken off to prison.   Then time and again
he sent me letters full of affection and messengers to give me news
and to comfort me in my straits.   Sometimes he visited me himself.
All these offices of a very dear father he did me in London.   Then
I was transferred to Wisbech, and here again he visited me, although
it involved a long journey for him, which he undertook, I must
add, with great apprehension on my part and with considerable
risk to his person.   Here too he showed me all the tokens of his
immense love as he had done before, sending me letters and
messages.   And I say nothing of the gifts he gave me, little things
which have such force in fostering and enhancing mutual affection.
This is the man they say I have no love for.'

7. To Fr. General Aquaviva, dated Wisbech, 19 May 1598
(Arch. S.J., Rome, *Fondo Gesuitico*, 651).   This is a short letter
of thanks to Fr. Aquaviva for permitting him to take his final
vows as a Jesuit.   The interest of this letter is the evidence it
contains that the General of the Jesuits gave no credence to the
calumnies against Fr. Weston.

APPENDIX F

CHRONOLOGY OF FR. WESTON'S CAREER

1550   Born at Maidstone, Kent. Nathaniel Southwell, *Catalogus Primorum Patrum*. Stonyhurst MSS.

1564   Student of Christ Church, Oxford. J. Foster, *Alumni Oxonienses*, vol. iv, p. 1605.

1569   February 17th. Matriculated.

1570   Student at Lincoln's Inn. *C.R.S.*, vol. 22, p. 102.

1571   At Paris. de Peralta, f. 217.

1572   At Douai. T. F. Knox, *Douai Diaries*, p. 5.

1575   Summer. Makes pilgrimage to Rome for Holy Year. T. F. Knox, *Douai Diaries*, p. 24.
       November 5th. Entered Jesuit novitiate at Sant' Andrea, Rome. *Two Missionaries*, p. 8.

1576–84   In Spain at Montilla, Cordova, Cadiz, San Lucar and Seville. de Peralta, f. 217–8.

1579   Ordained priest. *Two Missionaries*, p. 10.

1584   Easter Saturday. Leaves Seville for Paris. Arch. S.J., Rome, *Gall. Ep.*, xiv, f. 43.
       August 26th. Leaves Paris for England. p. 7, n. 1.
       September 10th. Lands on the Norfolk coast. *ib.*
       Late September or early October. Reconciles Philip, Earl of Arundel to the Church.

1585   April. Attends conference of Catholic laymen and priests at Hoxton. p. 28, n. 3.
       Summer [?]. Visits Somerset.

1586 {
July 13th. Meets Fr. Garnet and Fr. Southwell in London. p. 75, n. 3.
July 15th-23rd. At Harlesford for the 'glorious octave'. p. 77, n. 10.
August 3rd. Arrested and imprisoned in private house. p. 79, n. 20.
September. Transferred to the Clink.

1588 January 21st. Sets out for Wisbech. Cf. p. 173, n. 1.

1598 December 19th. Begins solitary confinement in the Tower. p. 209, n. 9.

1603 May 13th. Leaves the Tower for exile on the Continent. p. 231, n. 14.

1603–5 At St. Omer, Rome, Valladolid. *Two Missionaries,* p. 280.

1605–14 At Seville. *ib.*

1614 June. Appointed Rector of the English seminary at Valladolid. *ib.*

1615 April 9th, at 2 a.m. Dies at Valladolid. de Peralta, f. 226.

INDEX

255